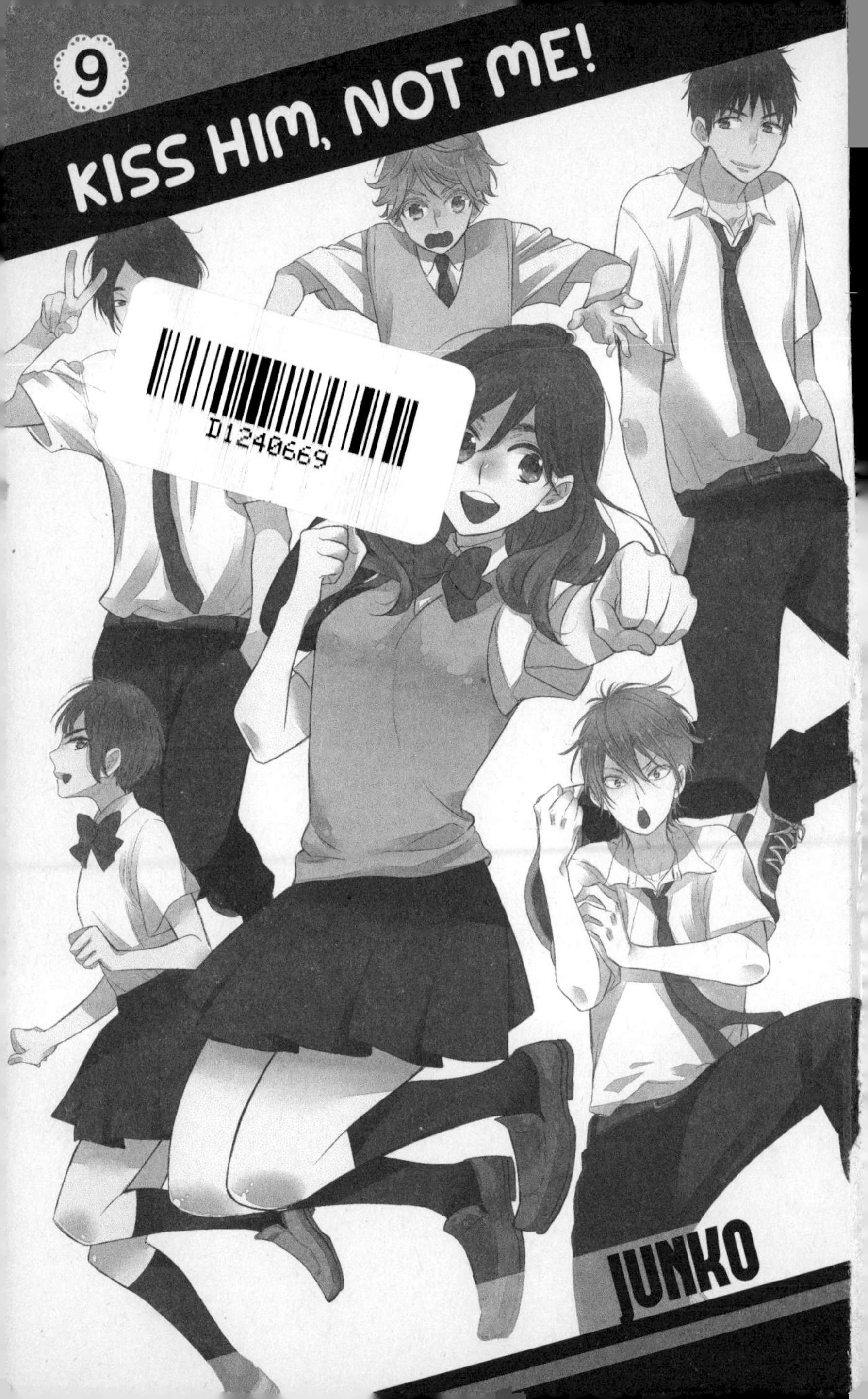
9
KISS HIM, NOT ME!
JUNKO

CONTENTS

STORY

SHINOMIYA'S GRANDMOTHER, WHO LIVES IN NORWAY, HAS BEEN HOSPITALIZED!! HIS PARENTS DISCUSS MOVING TO NORWAY AS A FAMILY, BUT **SHINOMIYA**, UNWILLING TO LEAVE ALL HIS FRIENDS, **RUNS AWAY** FROM HOME. AT **KAE'S** HOUSE, **SHINOMIYA** TELLS EVERYONE HIS SITUATION, WHEN HIS DEAR FRIEND **THOR** CLIMBS OUT OF HIS BACKPACK. SURPRISED BY THE SUDDEN APPEARANCE, **KAE** REJECTS **THOR**! A STUNNED **SHINOMIYA** DECIDES TO GIVE UP ON **KAE** AND MOVE WITH HIS FAMILY. DURING THIS TIME, **THOR RUNS AWAY!! KAE** FINDS **THOR** DROWNING IN THE RIVER, AND JUMPS IN TO RESCUE HER! **SHINOMIYA**, WHO IS NOW CONFIDENT THAT **THOR** LIKES **KAE**, DECIDES TO STAY BEHIND IN JAPAN. MEANWHILE, A **SUSPICIOUS FIGURE** WATCHES HIM IN THE SHADOWS...!!

I ♥ BL

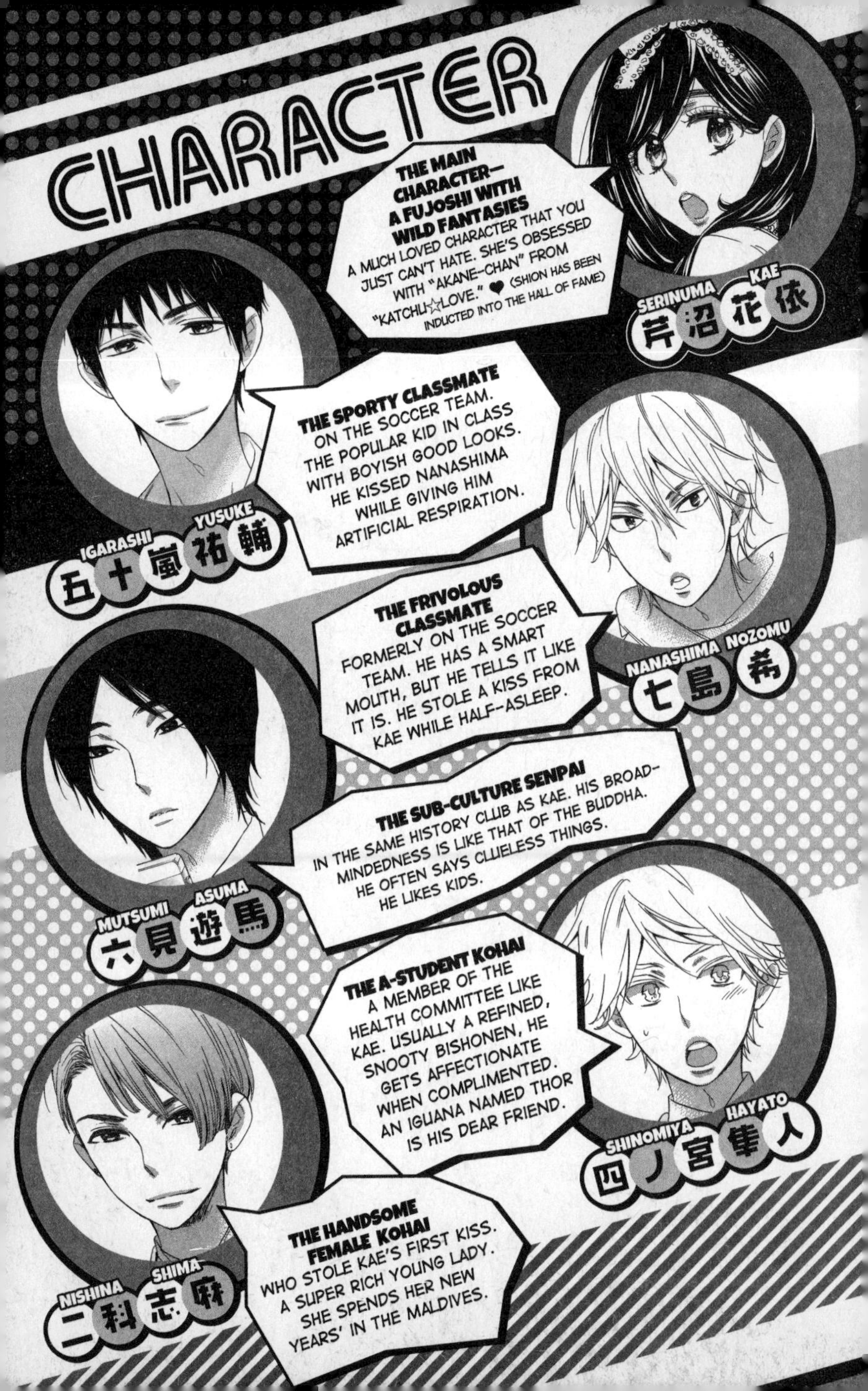
CHARACTER
THE MAIN CHARACTER—A FUJOSHI WITH WILD FANTASIES
A MUCH LOVED CHARACTER THAT YOU JUST CAN'T HATE. SHE'S OBSESSED WITH "AKANE-CHAN" FROM "KATCHU☆LOVE." ❤ (SHION HAS BEEN INDUCTED INTO THE HALL OF FAME)
SERINUMA KAE 芹沼花依
THE SPORTY CLASSMATE
ON THE SOCCER TEAM. THE POPULAR KID IN CLASS WITH BOYISH GOOD LOOKS. HE KISSED NANASHIMA WHILE GIVING HIM ARTIFICIAL RESPIRATION.
IGARASHI YUSUKE 五十嵐祐輔
THE FRIVOLOUS CLASSMATE
FORMERLY ON THE SOCCER TEAM. HE HAS A SMART MOUTH, BUT HE TELLS IT LIKE IT IS. HE STOLE A KISS FROM KAE WHILE HALF-ASLEEP.
NANASHIMA NOZOMU 七島希
THE SUB-CULTURE SENPAI
IN THE SAME HISTORY CLUB AS KAE. HIS BROAD-MINDEDNESS IS LIKE THAT OF THE BUDDHA. HE OFTEN SAYS CLUELESS THINGS. HE LIKES KIDS.
MUTSUMI ASUMA 六見遊馬
THE A-STUDENT KOHAI
A MEMBER OF THE HEALTH COMMITTEE LIKE KAE. USUALLY A REFINED, SNOOTY BISHONEN, HE GETS AFFECTIONATE WHEN COMPLIMENTED. AN IGUANA NAMED THOR IS HIS DEAR FRIEND.
SHINOMIYA HAYATO 四ノ宮隼人
THE HANDSOME FEMALE KOHAI
WHO STOLE KAE'S FIRST KISS. A SUPER RICH YOUNG LADY. SHE SPENDS HER NEW YEARS' IN THE MALDIVES.
NISHINA SHIMA 二科志麻

KiSS HiM, NOT ME!

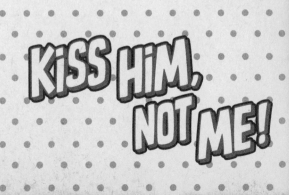

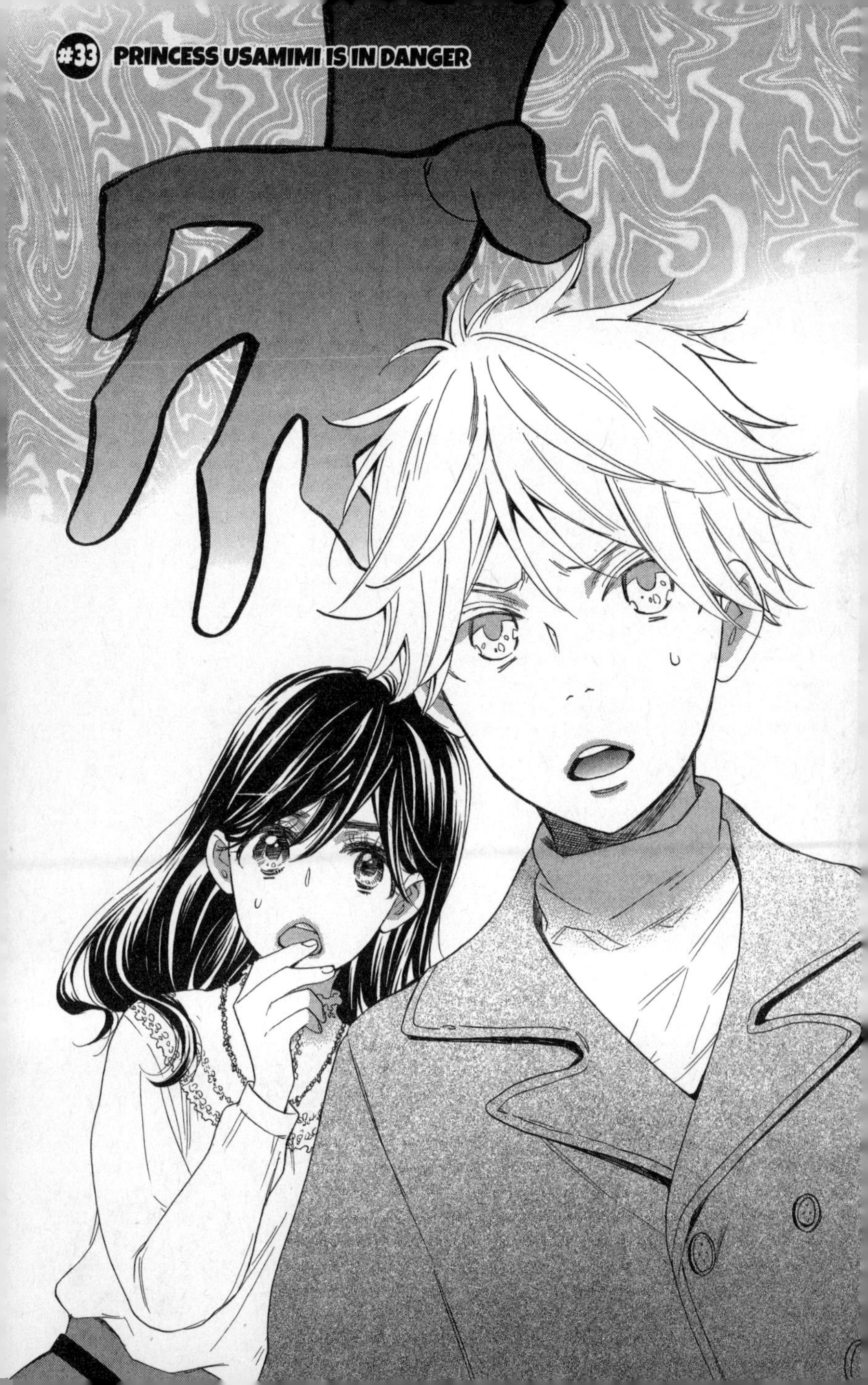
#33 PRINCESS USAMIMI IS IN DANGER

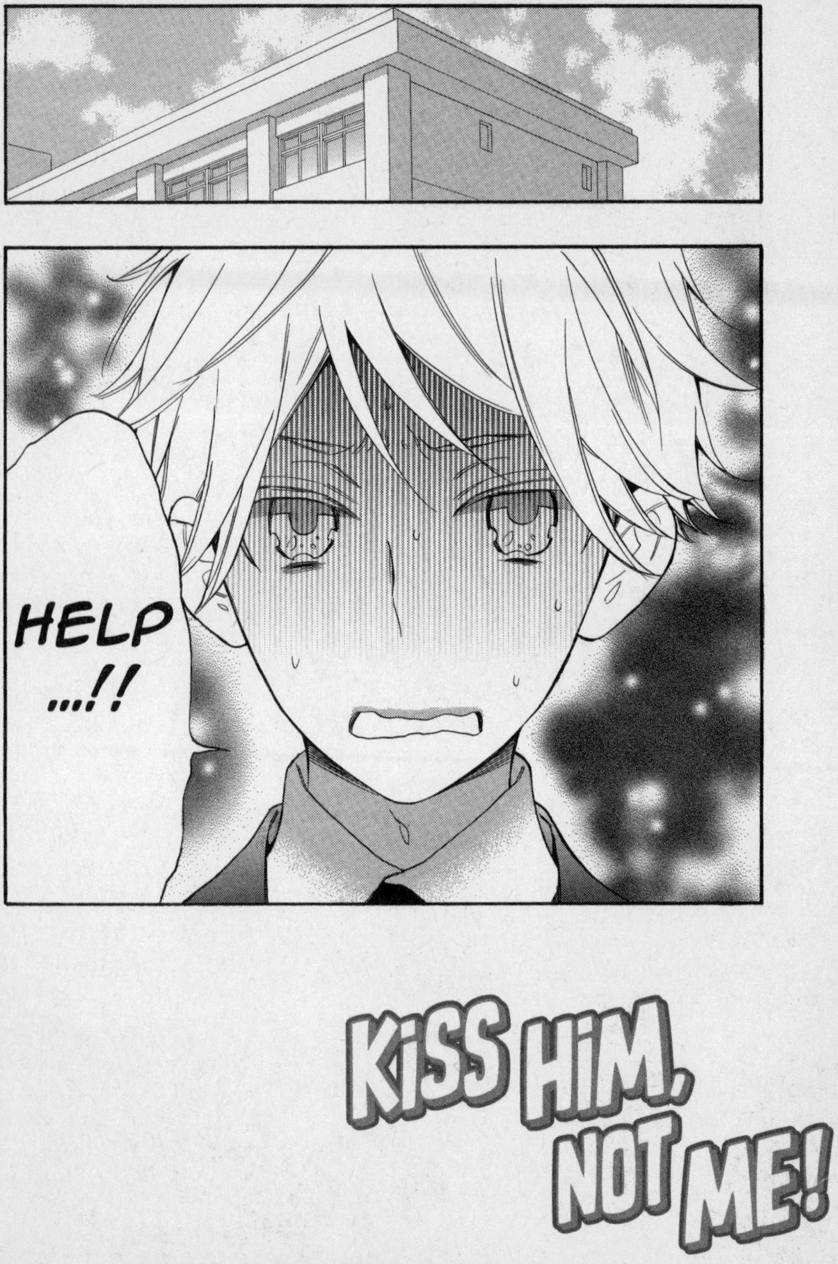
HELP ...!!

KiSS HiM, NOT ME!

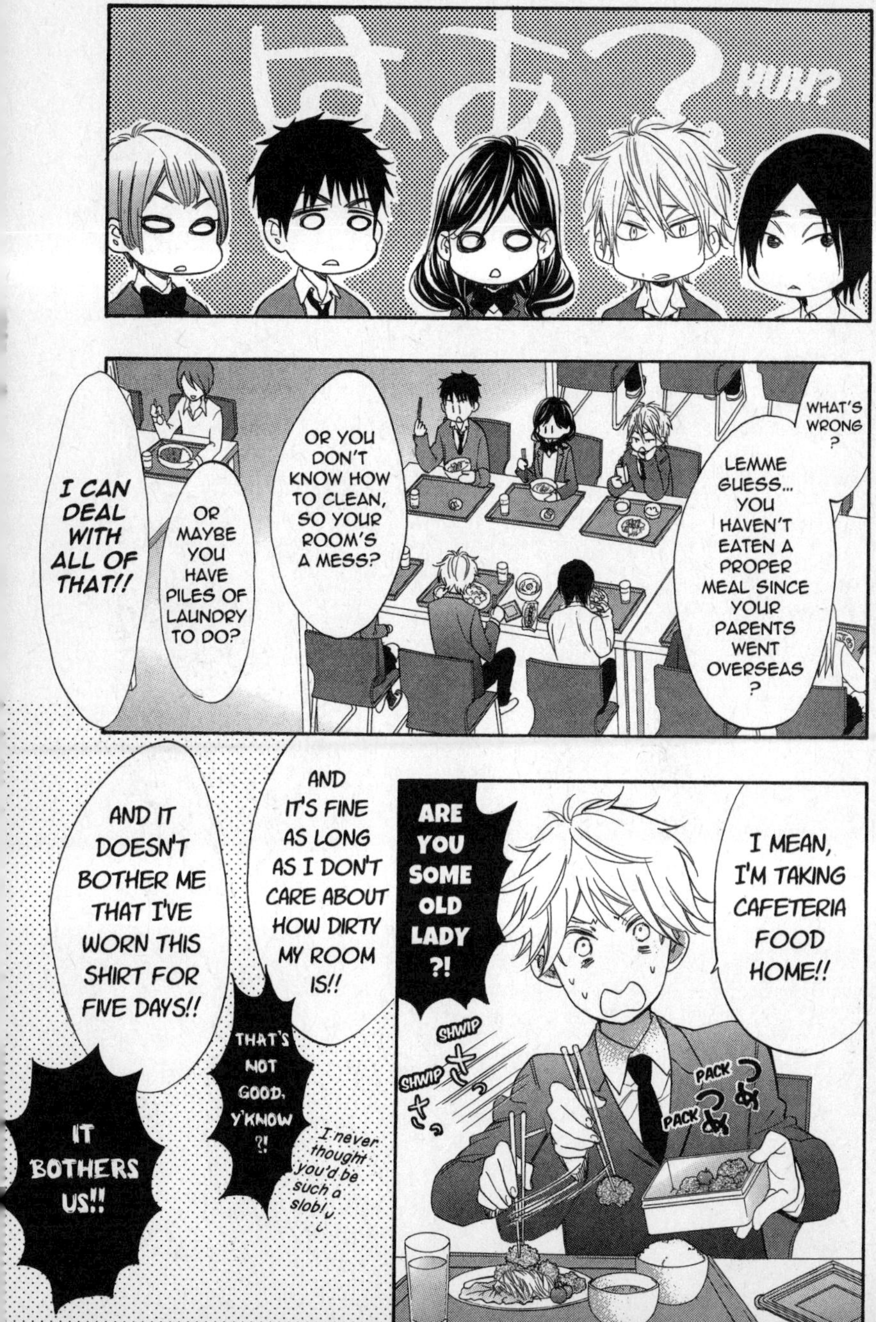
はあっ
HUH?
WHAT'S WRONG?
LEMME GUESS... YOU HAVEN'T EATEN A PROPER MEAL SINCE YOUR PARENTS WENT OVERSEAS?
OR YOU DON'T KNOW HOW TO CLEAN, SO YOUR ROOM'S A MESS?
OR MAYBE YOU HAVE PILES OF LAUNDRY TO DO?
I CAN DEAL WITH ALL OF THAT!!
I MEAN, I'M TAKING CAFETERIA FOOD HOME!!
ARE YOU SOME OLD LADY?!
つめ PACK
つめ PACK
さっ SHWIP
さっ SHWIP
AND IT'S FINE AS LONG AS I DON'T CARE ABOUT HOW DIRTY MY ROOM IS!!
AND IT DOESN'T BOTHER ME THAT I'VE WORN THIS SHIRT FOR FIVE DAYS!!
THAT'S NOT GOOD, Y'KNOW?!
I never thought you'd be such a slob!
IT BOTHERS US!!

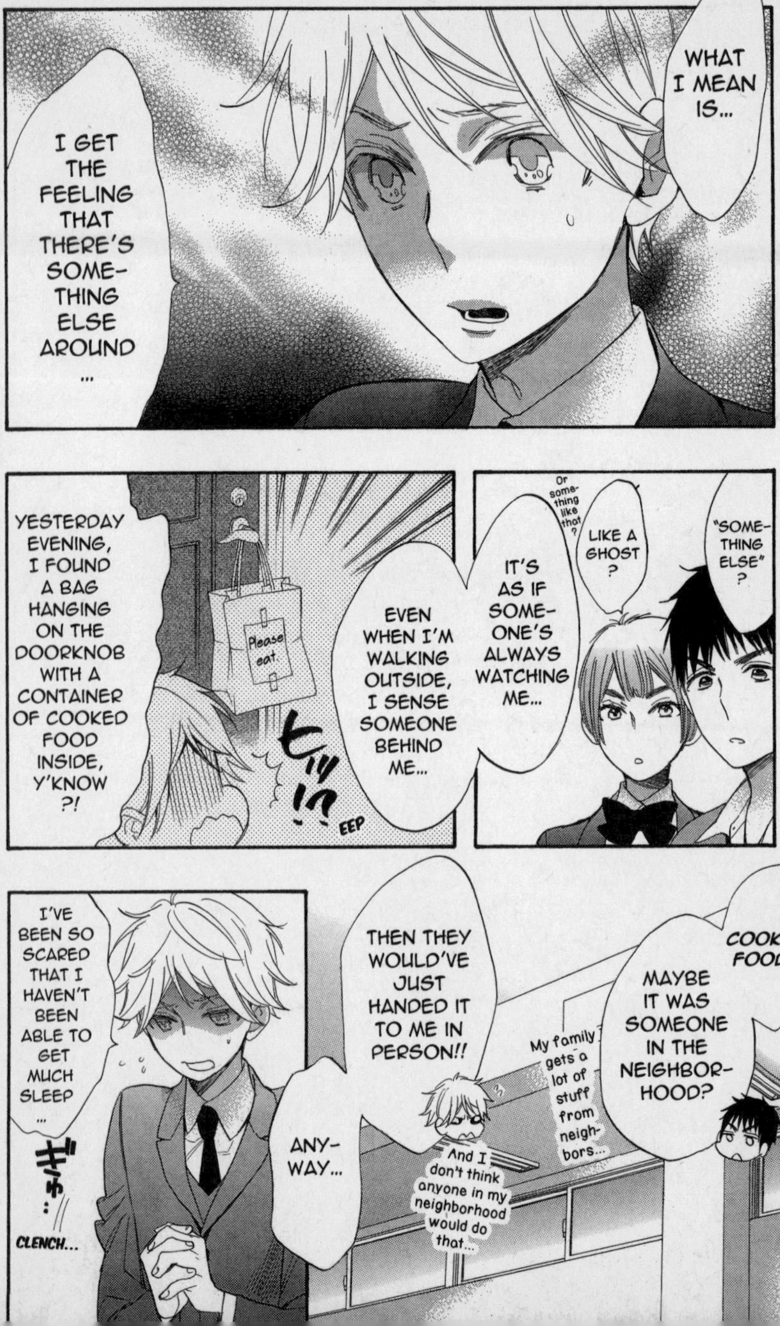
WHAT I MEAN IS...
I GET THE FEELING THAT THERE'S SOMETHING ELSE AROUND...
"SOMETHING ELSE"?
LIKE A GHOST?
Or something like that?
IT'S AS IF SOMEONE'S ALWAYS WATCHING ME...
EVEN WHEN I'M WALKING OUTSIDE, I SENSE SOMEONE BEHIND ME...
YESTERDAY EVENING, I FOUND A BAG HANGING ON THE DOORKNOB WITH A CONTAINER OF COOKED FOOD INSIDE, Y'KNOW?!
Please eat
EEP
COOKED FOOD?
MAYBE IT WAS SOMEONE IN THE NEIGHBORHOOD?
My family gets a lot of stuff from neighbors...
THEN THEY WOULD'VE JUST HANDED IT TO ME IN PERSON!!
And I don't think anyone in my neighborhood would do that...
ANYWAY...
I'VE BEEN SO SCARED THAT I HAVEN'T BEEN ABLE TO GET MUCH SLEEP...
CLENCH...

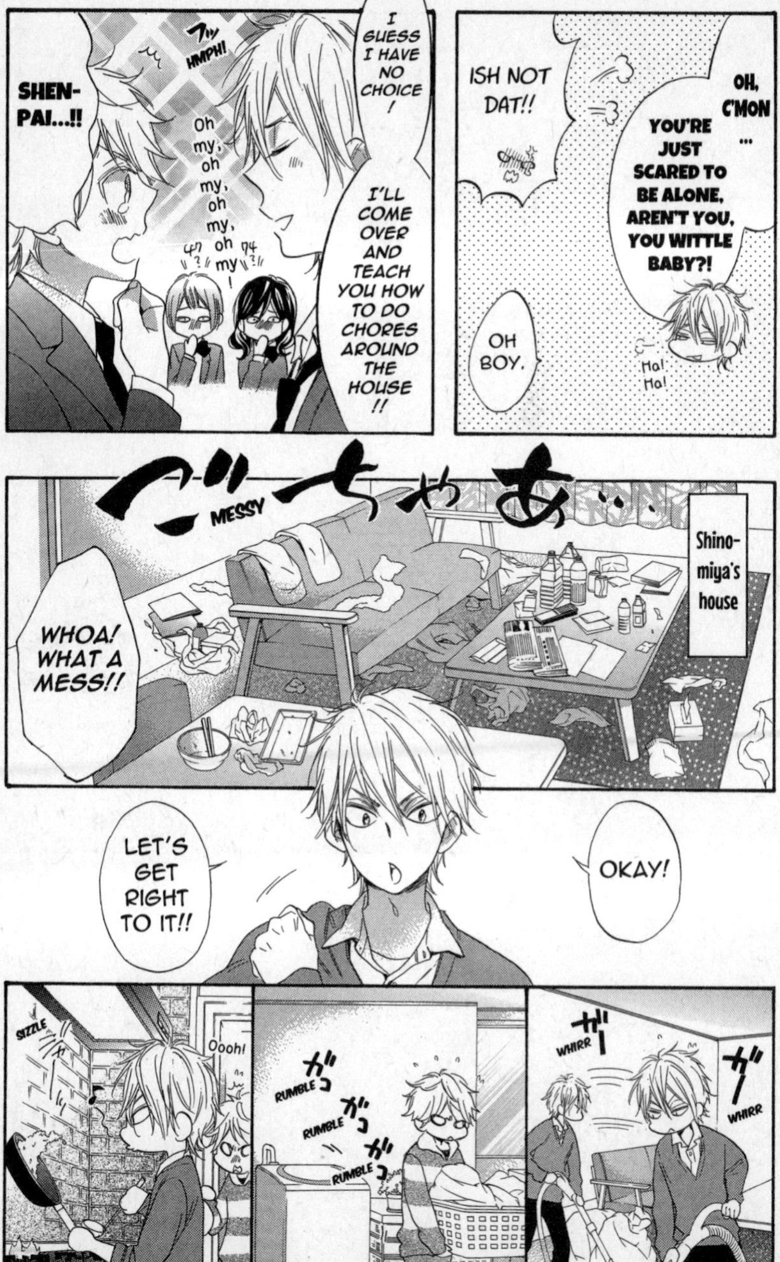
OH, C'MON ...
YOU'RE JUST SCARED TO BE ALONE, AREN'T YOU, YOU WITTLE BABY?!
ISH NOT DAT!!
Ha! Ha!
OH BOY.
I GUESS I HAVE NO CHOICE!
HMPH!
I'LL COME OVER AND TEACH YOU HOW TO DO CHORES AROUND THE HOUSE!!
SHEN-PAI...!!
Oh my, oh my, oh my, oh my!
Shino-miya's house
MESSY
WHOA! WHAT A MESS!!
OKAY!
LET'S GET RIGHT TO IT!!
WHIRR
WHIRR
RUMBLE
RUMBLE
RUMBLE
Oooh!
SIZZLE

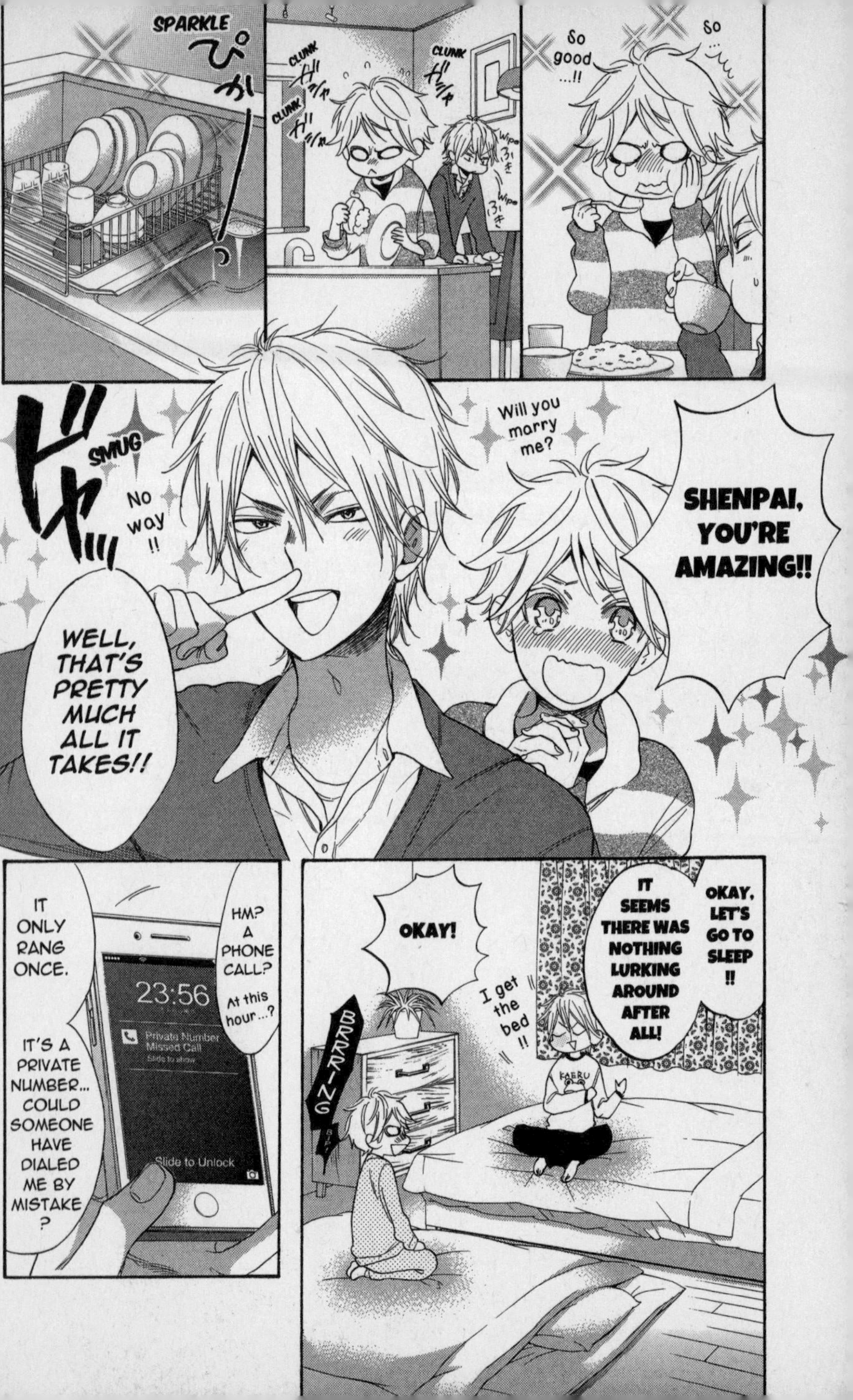
So ...
So good ...!!
CLUNK
CLUNK
CLUNK
Wipe
Wipe
SPARKLE
SHENPAI, YOU'RE AMAZING!!
Will you marry me?
No way !!
SMUG
WELL, THAT'S PRETTY MUCH ALL IT TAKES!!
OKAY, LET'S GO TO SLEEP !!
IT SEEMS THERE WAS NOTHING LURKING AROUND AFTER ALL!
OKAY!
I get the bed !!
BRRRING
HM? A PHONE CALL?
At this hour...?
IT ONLY RANG ONCE.
23:56
Private Number
Missed Call
Slide to show
Slide to Unlock
IT'S A PRIVATE NUMBER... COULD SOMEONE HAVE DIALED ME BY MISTAKE?

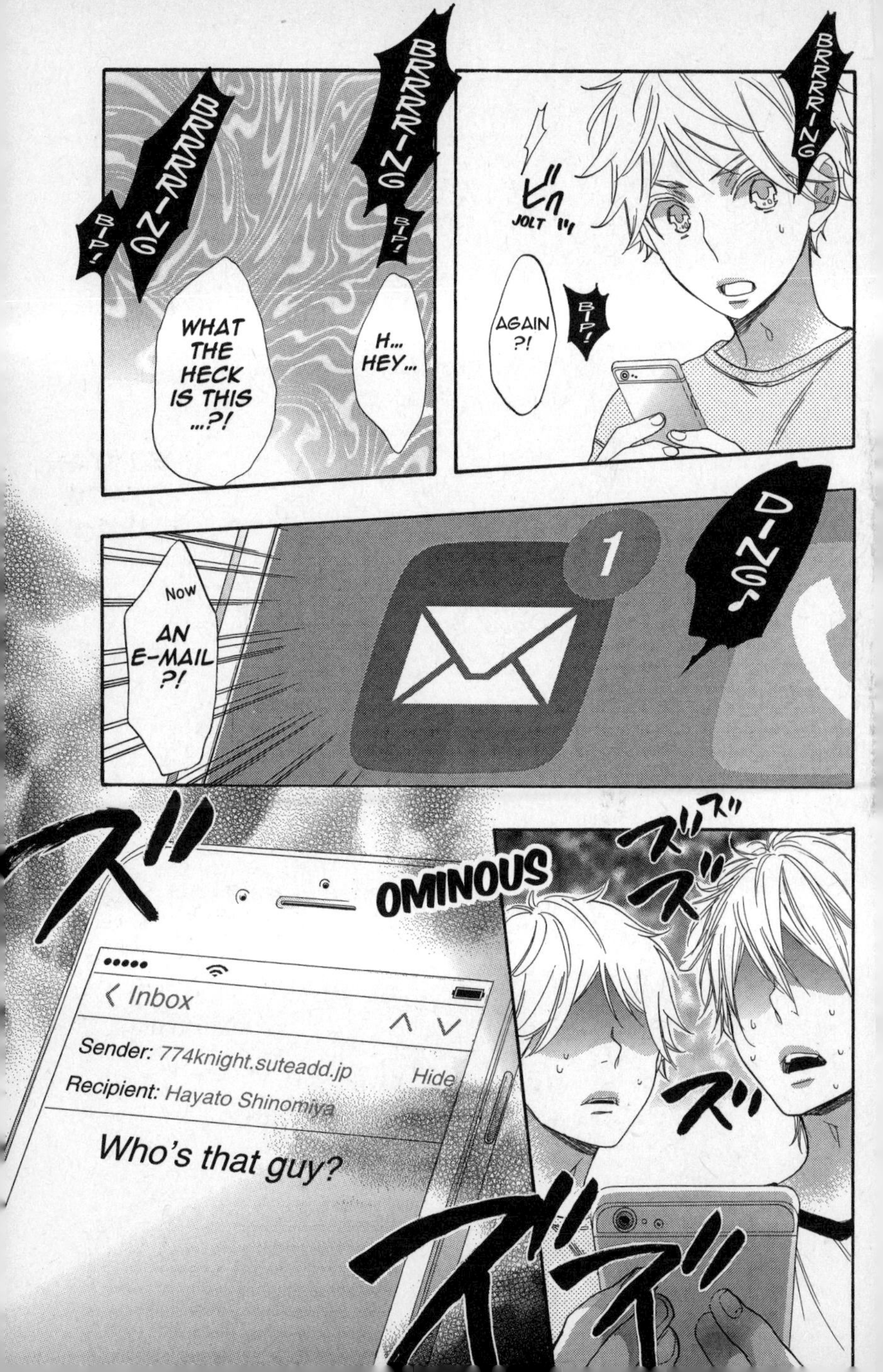

BRRRRING
JOLT
AGAIN?!
BIP!
BRRRRING
BIP!
H... HEY...
BRRRRING
BIP!
WHAT THE HECK IS THIS ...?!
DING♪
Now AN E-MAIL?!
OMINOUS
< Inbox
Sender: 774knight.suteadd.jp
Hide
Recipient: Hayato Shinomiya
Who's that guy?

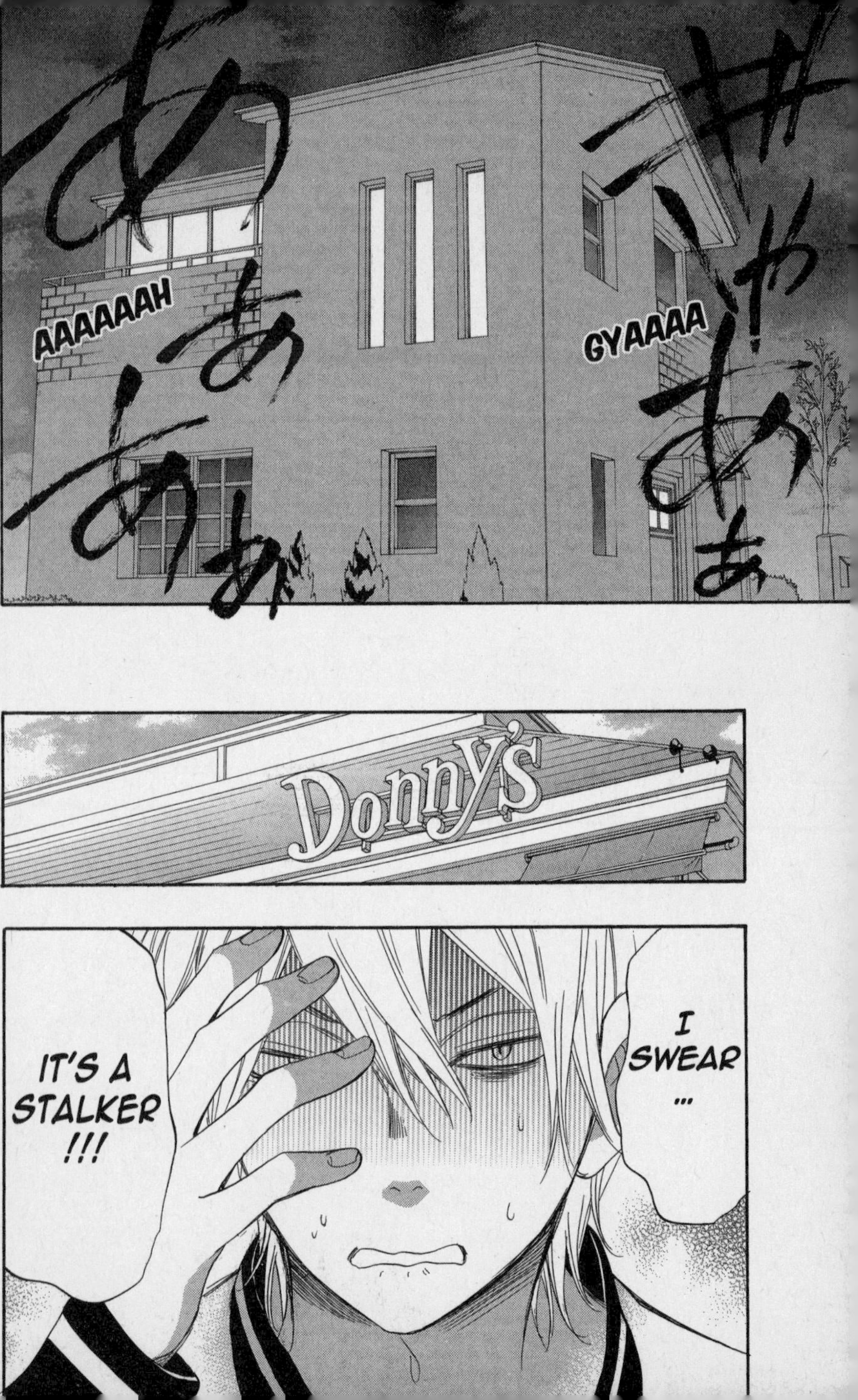
GYAAAA
AAAAAAH
Donny's
I SWEAR ...
IT'S A STALKER !!!

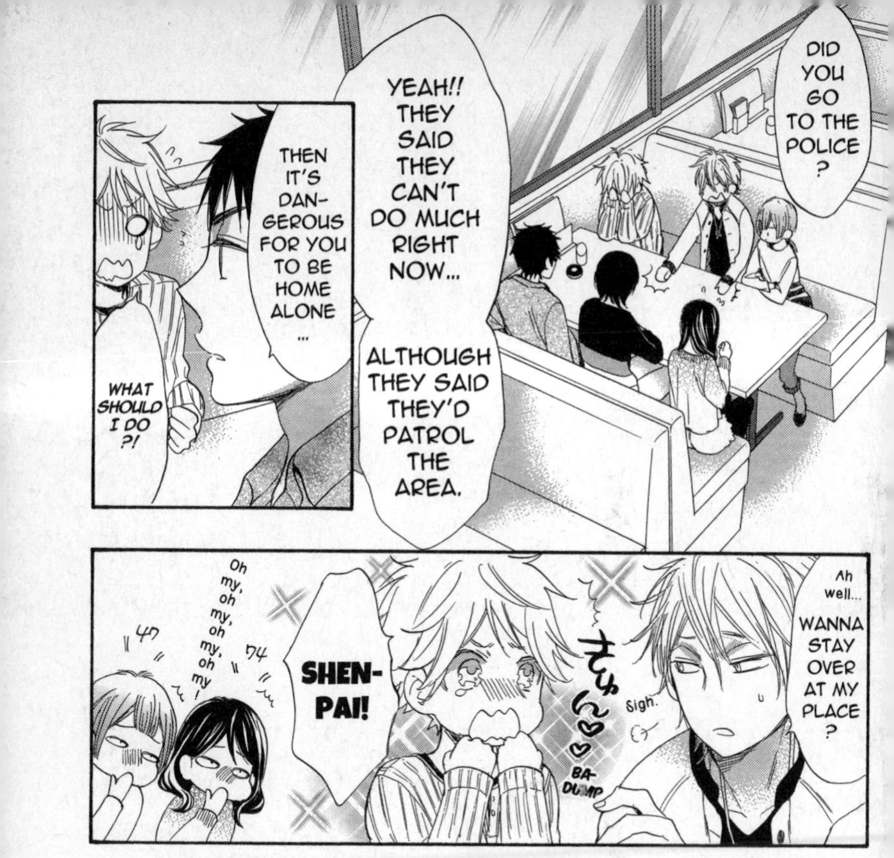
DID YOU GO TO THE POLICE?
YEAH!! THEY SAID THEY CAN'T DO MUCH RIGHT NOW...
ALTHOUGH THEY SAID THEY'D PATROL THE AREA.
THEN IT'S DANGEROUS FOR YOU TO BE HOME ALONE...
WHAT SHOULD I DO?!
Ah well... WANNA STAY OVER AT MY PLACE?
Sigh.
BA-DUMP
SHEN-PAI!
Oh my, oh my, oh my, oh my!

Exclamation: I'm scared of monsters!! Eeek!!

SFX: Aaahhh!! Waaahhh!!

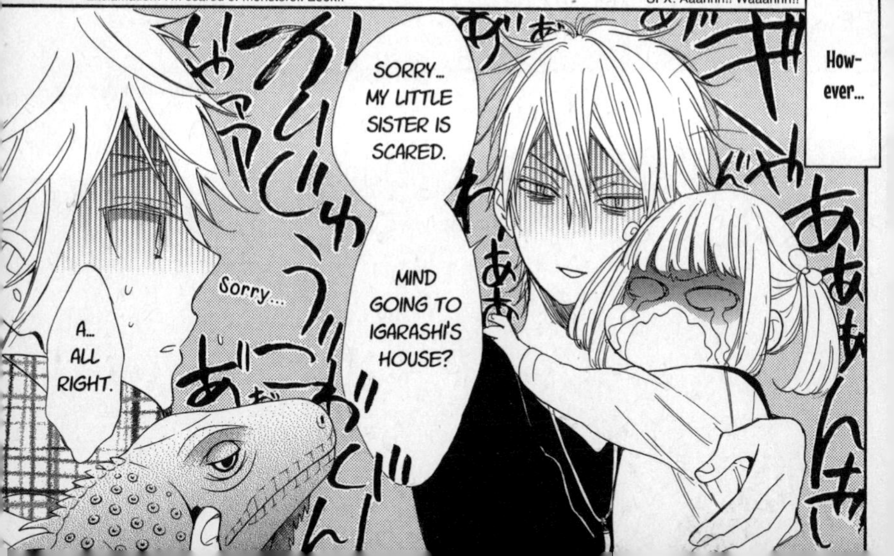
How-ever...
SORRY... MY LITTLE SISTER IS SCARED.
MIND GOING TO IGARASHI'S HOUSE?
Sorry...
A... ALL RIGHT.

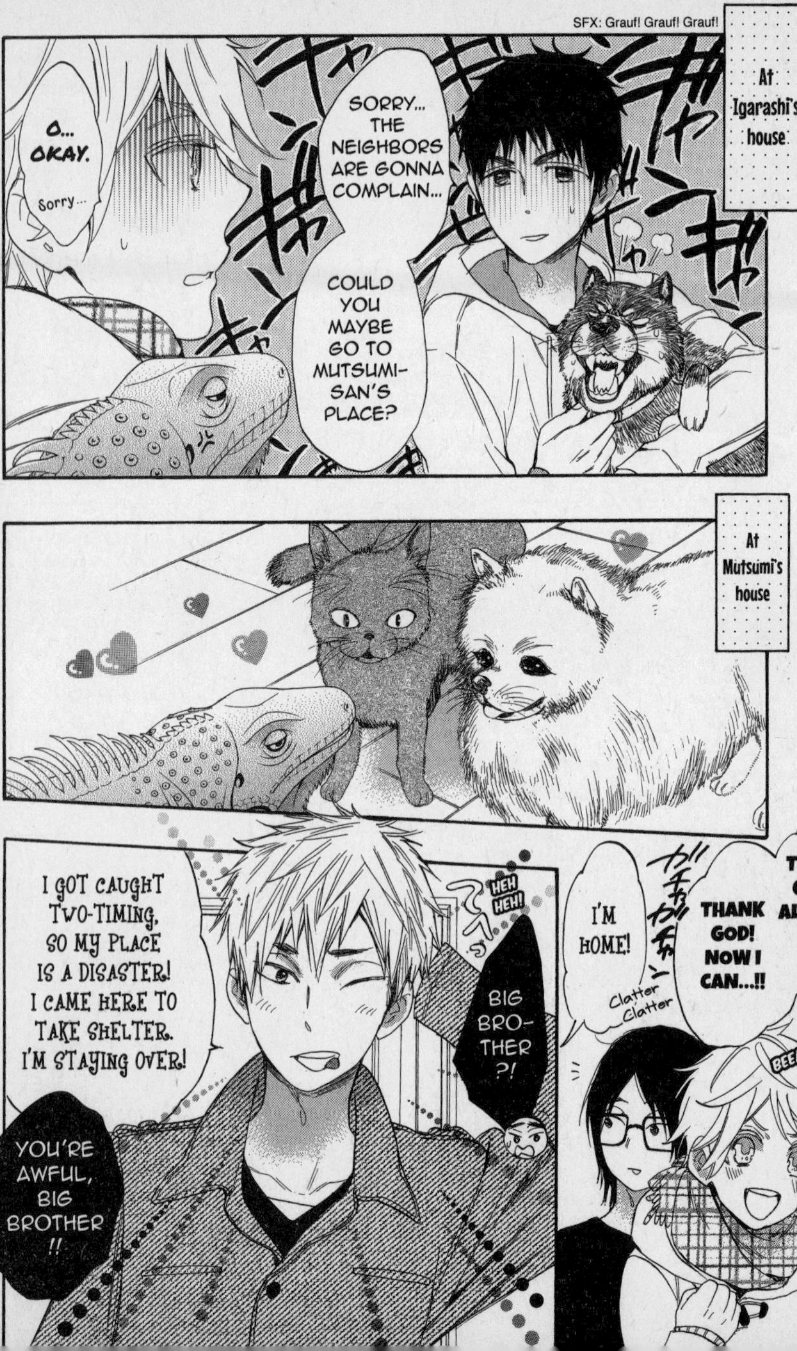
SFX: Grauf! Grauf! Grauf!
At Igarashi's house
SORRY... THE NEIGHBORS ARE GONNA COMPLAIN...
COULD YOU MAYBE GO TO MUTSUMI-SAN'S PLACE?
O... OKAY.
Sorry...
At Mutsumi's house
THEY GET ALONG!!
THANK GOD! NOW I CAN...!!
BEEAM
I'M HOME!
Clatter Clatter
BIG BROTHER?!
HEH HEH!
I GOT CAUGHT TWO-TIMING, SO MY PLACE IS A DISASTER! I CAME HERE TO TAKE SHELTER. I'M STAYING OVER!
YOU'RE AWFUL, BIG BROTHER!!

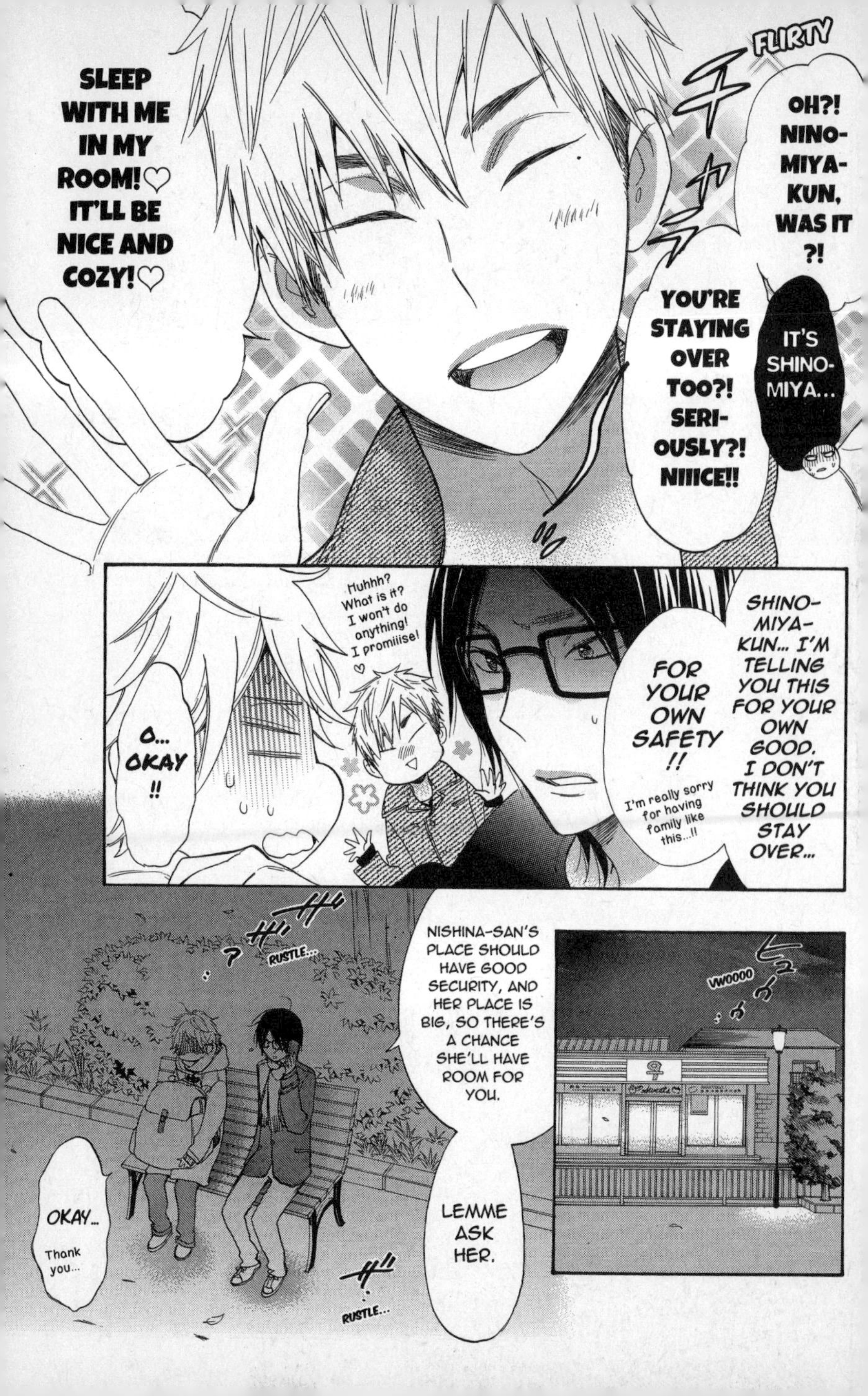
FLIRTY
OH?! NINO-MIYA-KUN, WAS IT ?!
IT'S SHINO-MIYA...
YOU'RE STAYING OVER TOO?! SERI-OUSLY?! NIIICE!!
SLEEP WITH ME IN MY ROOM!♡ IT'LL BE NICE AND COZY!♡
SHINO-MIYA-KUN... I'M TELLING YOU THIS FOR YOUR OWN GOOD. I DON'T THINK YOU SHOULD STAY OVER...
FOR YOUR OWN SAFETY !!
I'm really sorry for having family like this...!!
Huhhh? What is it? I won't do anything! I promiiise! ♡
O... OKAY !!
VWOOOO
NISHINA-SAN'S PLACE SHOULD HAVE GOOD SECURITY, AND HER PLACE IS BIG, SO THERE'S A CHANCE SHE'LL HAVE ROOM FOR YOU.
LEMME ASK HER.
RUSTLE...
OKAY...
Thank you...
RUSTLE...

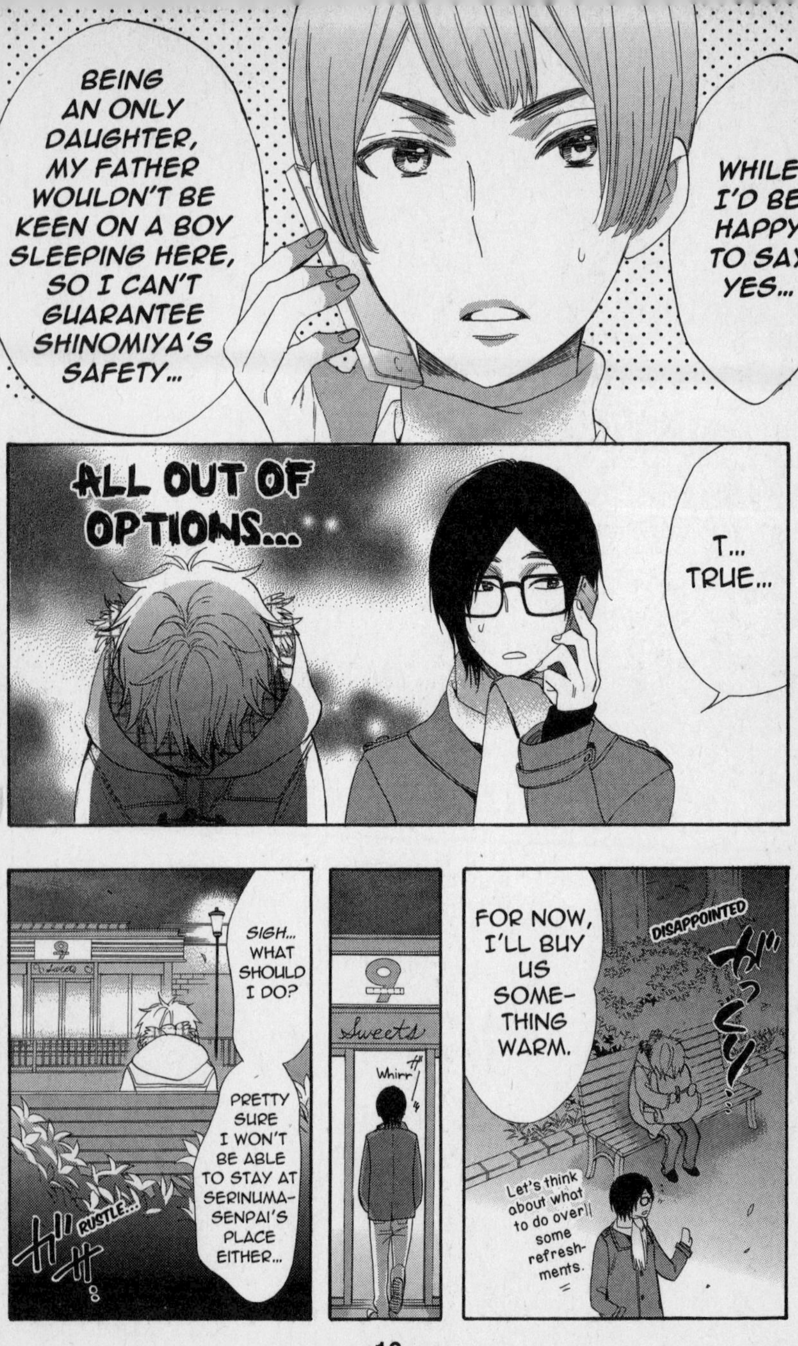
WHILE I'D BE HAPPY TO SAY YES...
BEING AN ONLY DAUGHTER, MY FATHER WOULDN'T BE KEEN ON A BOY SLEEPING HERE, SO I CAN'T GUARANTEE SHINOMIYA'S SAFETY...
T... TRUE...
ALL OUT OF OPTIONS...
DISAPPOINTED
FOR NOW, I'LL BUY US SOMETHING WARM.
Let's think about what to do over some refreshments.
Sweets
Whirr
SIGH... WHAT SHOULD I DO?
PRETTY SURE I WON'T BE ABLE TO STAY AT SERINUMA-SENPAI'S PLACE EITHER...
RUSTLE...

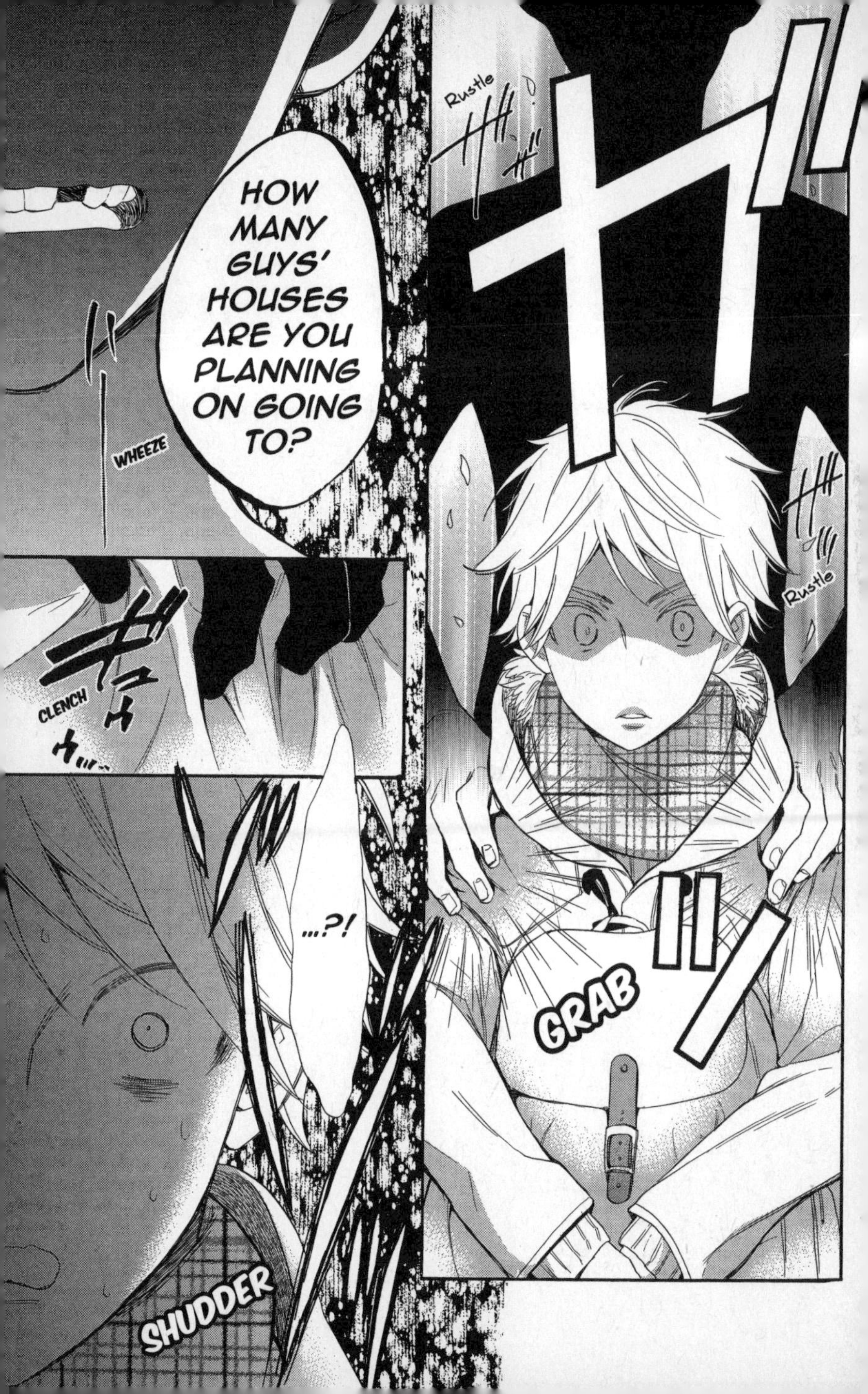
Rustle
Rustle
GRAB
HOW MANY GUYS' HOUSES ARE YOU PLANNING ON GOING TO?
WHEEZE
CLENCH
...?!
SHUDDER

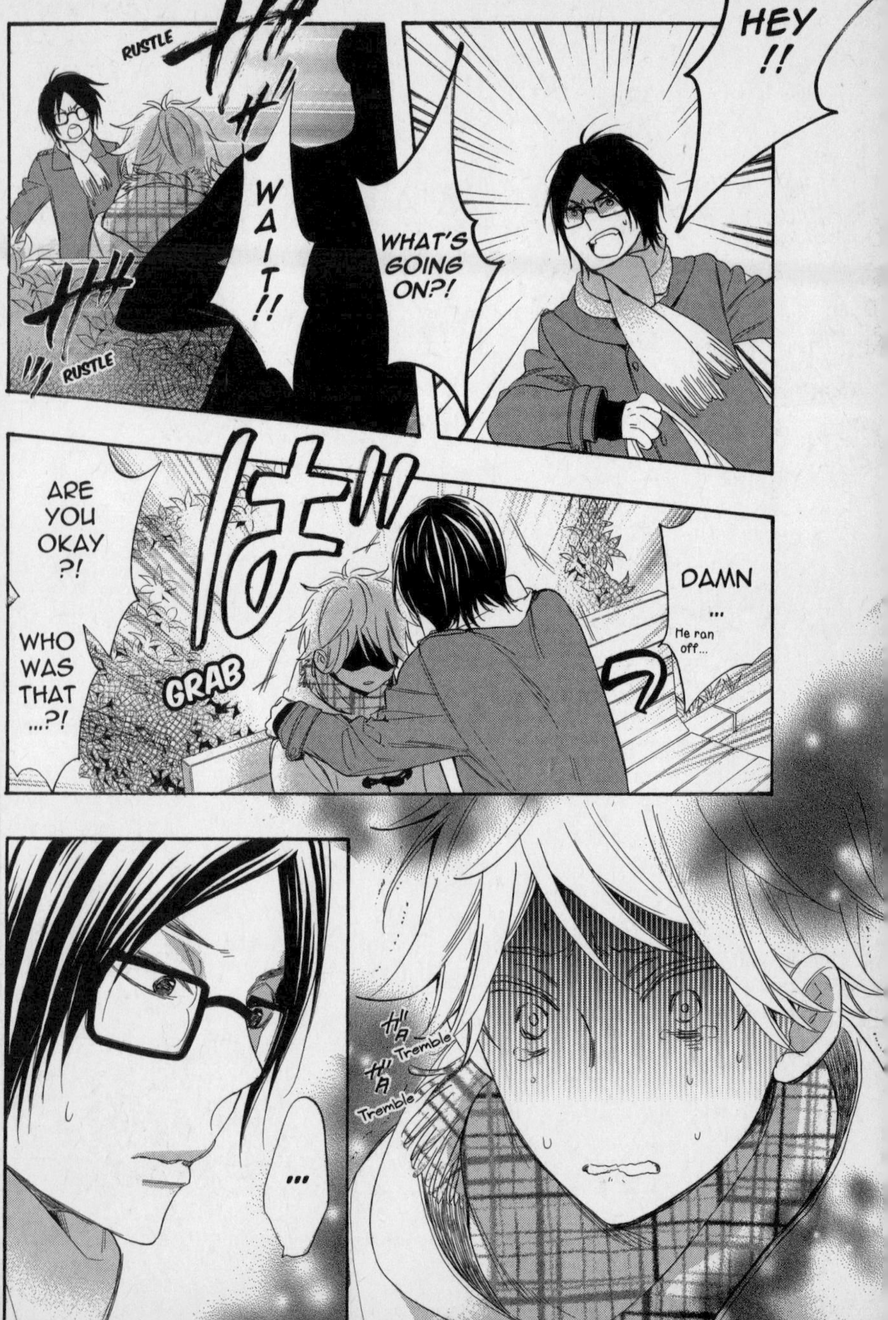
HEY !!
WHAT'S GOING ON?!
WAIT!!
RUSTLE
RUSTLE
DAMN ...
He ran off...
ば
っ
ARE YOU OKAY ?!
WHO WAS THAT ...?!
GRAB
Tremble
Tremble
...

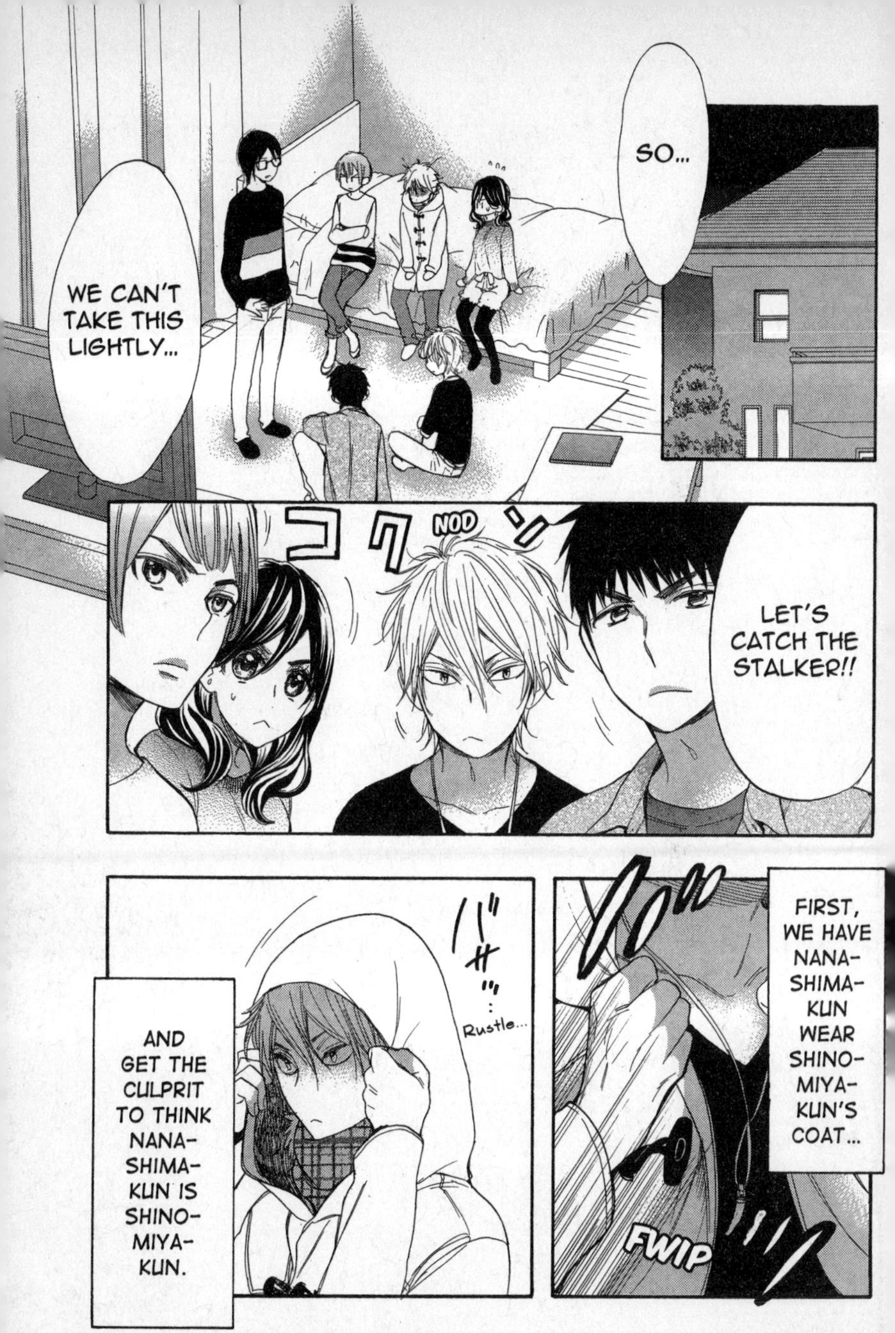
SO...
WE CAN'T TAKE THIS LIGHTLY...
LET'S CATCH THE STALKER!!
NOD
FIRST, WE HAVE NANA-SHIMA-KUN WEAR SHINO-MIYA-KUN'S COAT...
FWIP
Rustle...
AND GET THE CULPRIT TO THINK NANA-SHIMA-KUN IS SHINO-MIYA-KUN.

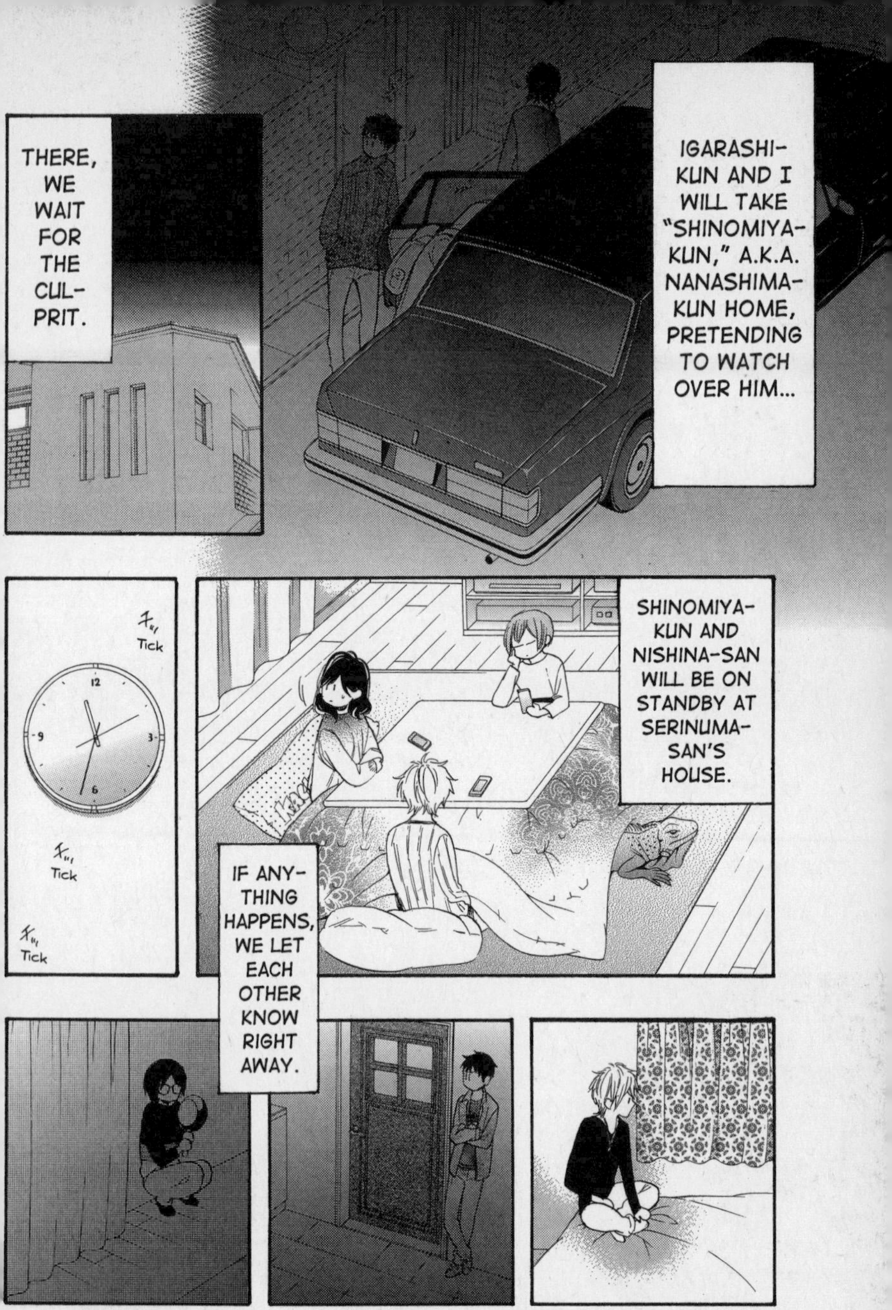
IGARASHI-KUN AND I WILL TAKE "SHINOMIYA-KUN," A.K.A. NANASHIMA-KUN HOME, PRETENDING TO WATCH OVER HIM...
THERE, WE WAIT FOR THE CULPRIT.
SHINOMIYA-KUN AND NISHINA-SAN WILL BE ON STANDBY AT SERINUMA-SAN'S HOUSE.
IF ANYTHING HAPPENS, WE LET EACH OTHER KNOW RIGHT AWAY.
Tick
Tick
Tick

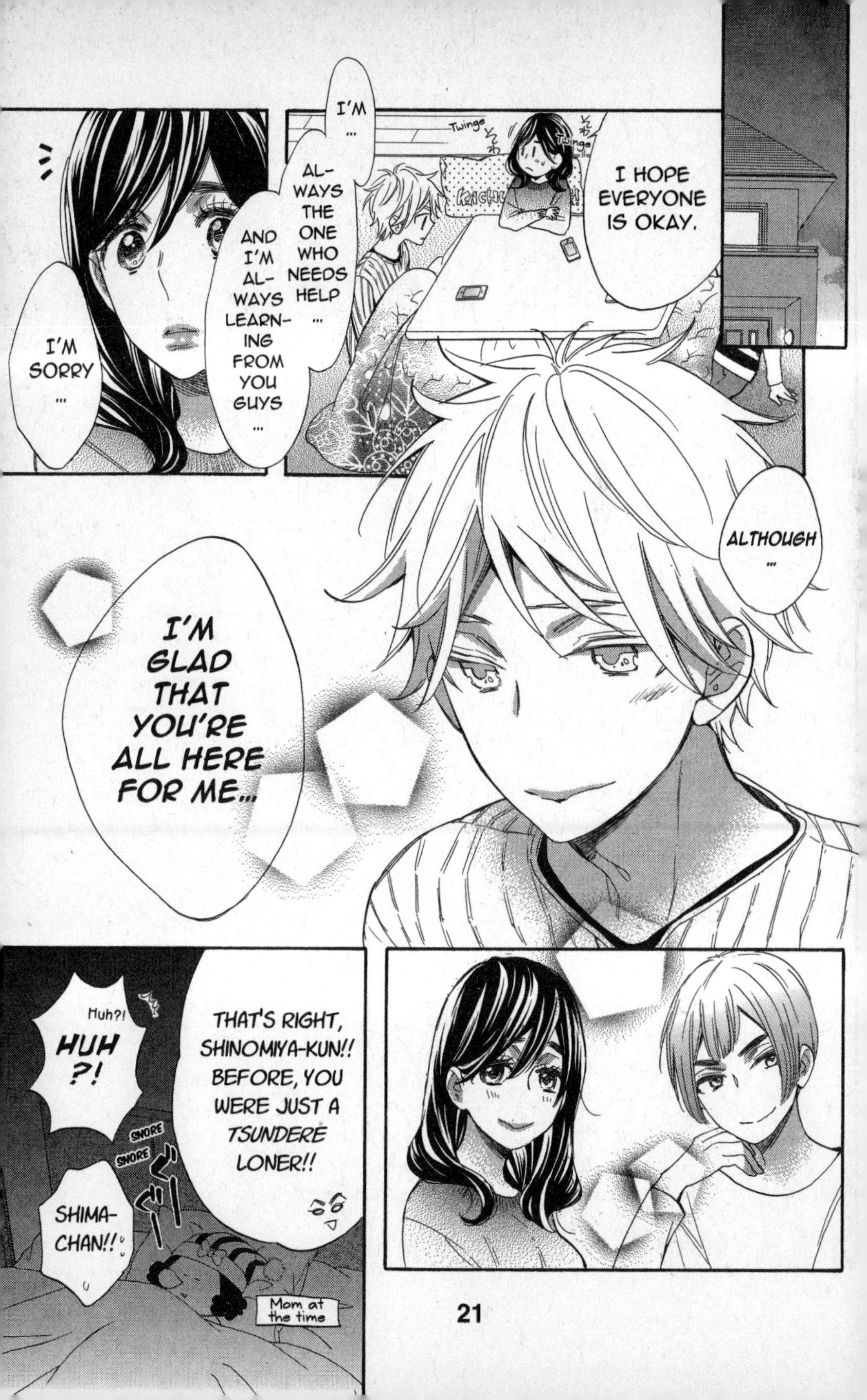
I HOPE EVERYONE IS OKAY.
Twinge
Twinge
I'M ...
ALWAYS THE ONE WHO NEEDS HELP ...
AND I'M ALWAYS LEARNING FROM YOU GUYS ...
I'M SORRY ...
ALTHOUGH ...
I'M GLAD THAT YOU'RE ALL HERE FOR ME...
THAT'S RIGHT, SHINOMIYA-KUN!! BEFORE, YOU WERE JUST A TSUNDERE LONER!!
Huh?!
HUH ?!
SNORE
SNORE
SHIMA-CHAN!!
Mom at the time

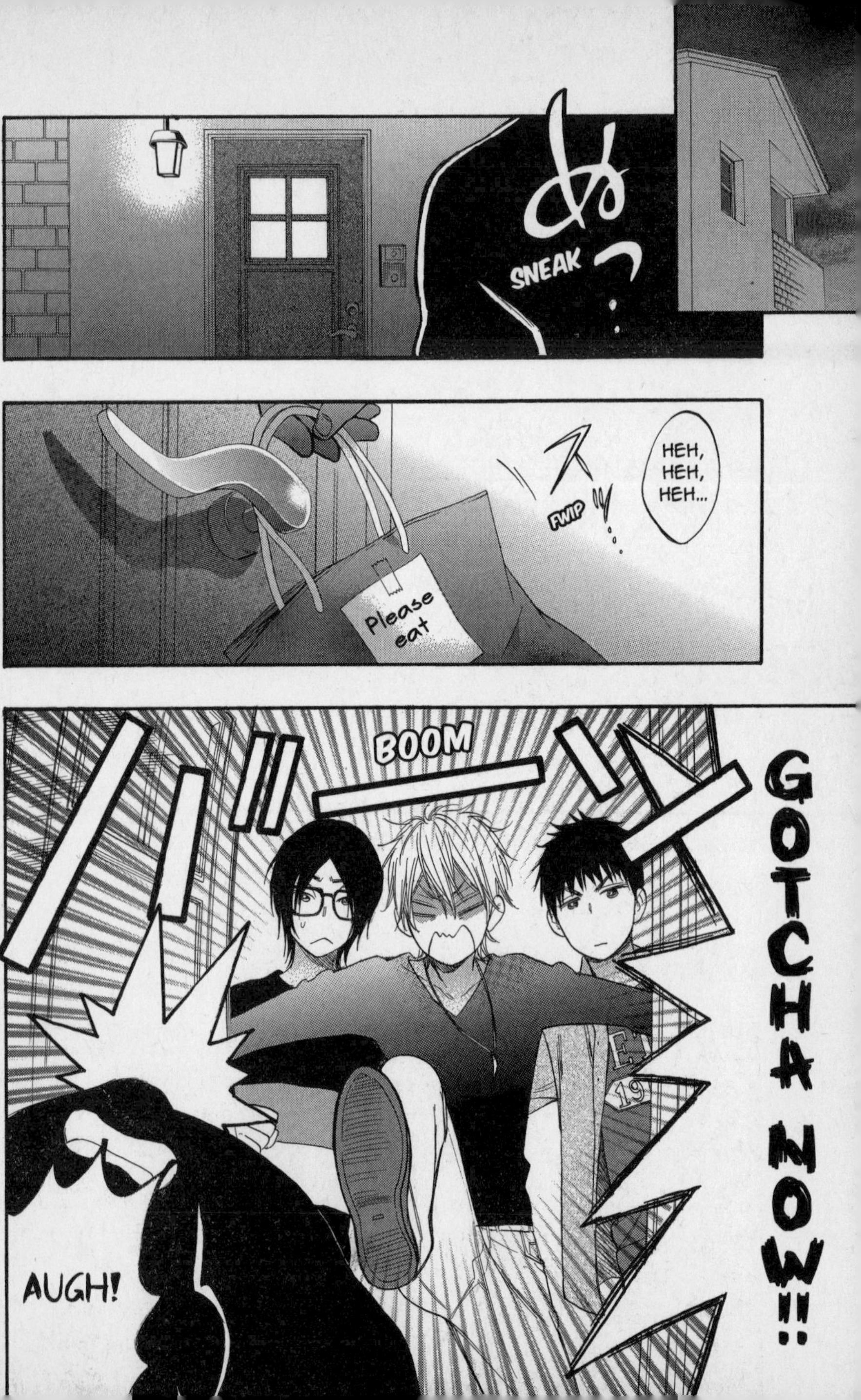
ぬっ
SNEAK
HEH, HEH, HEH...
ス
FWIP
Please eat
BOOM
GOTCHA NOW!!
AUGH!

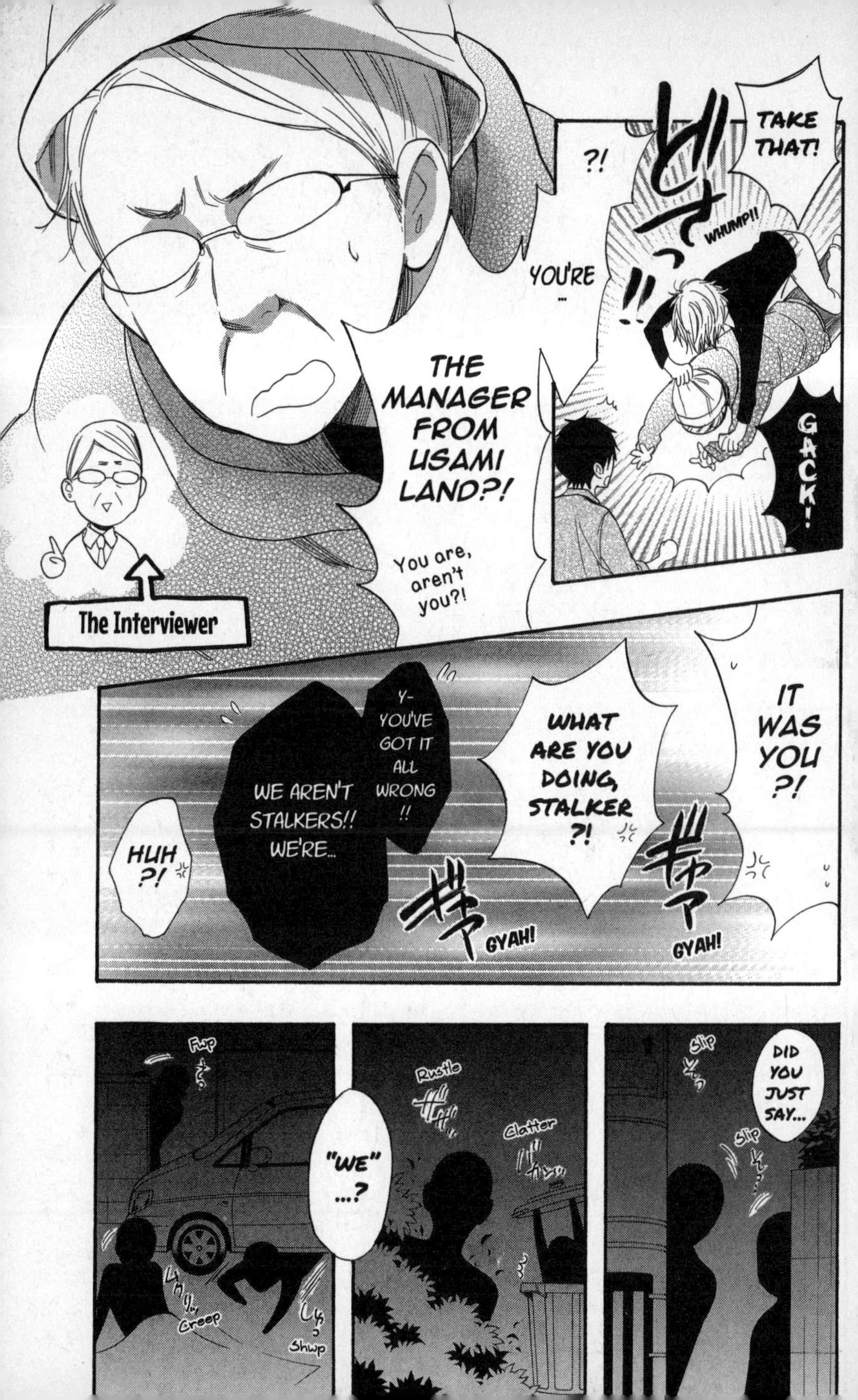
TAKE THAT!
WHUMP!!
?!
YOU'RE ...
GACK!
THE MANAGER FROM USAMI LAND?!
You are, aren't you?!
The Interviewer
IT WAS YOU?!
WHAT ARE YOU DOING, STALKER?!
GYAH!
GYAH!
Y-YOU'VE GOT IT ALL WRONG!!
WE AREN'T STALKERS!! WE'RE...
HUH?!
Slip
DID YOU JUST SAY...
Slip
Rustle
Clatter
"WE" ...?
Fwp
Creep
Shwp

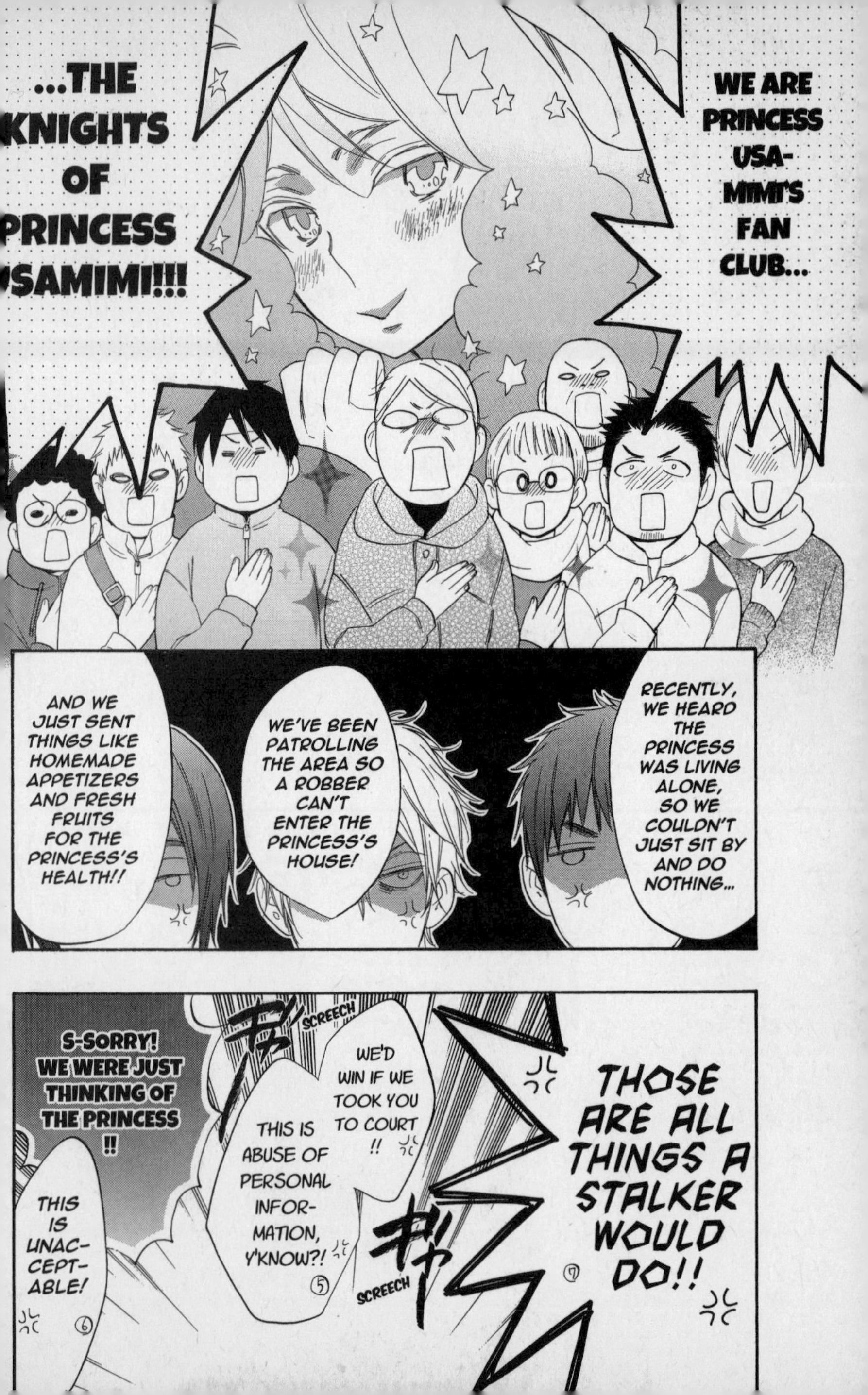
WE ARE PRINCESS USA-MIMI'S FAN CLUB...
...THE KNIGHTS OF PRINCESS USAMIMI!!!
RECENTLY, WE HEARD THE PRINCESS WAS LIVING ALONE, SO WE COULDN'T JUST SIT BY AND DO NOTHING...
WE'VE BEEN PATROLLING THE AREA SO A ROBBER CAN'T ENTER THE PRINCESS'S HOUSE!
AND WE JUST SENT THINGS LIKE HOMEMADE APPETIZERS AND FRESH FRUITS FOR THE PRINCESS'S HEALTH!!
THOSE ARE ALL THINGS A STALKER WOULD DO!!
SCREECH
WE'D WIN IF WE TOOK YOU TO COURT!!
THIS IS ABUSE OF PERSONAL INFOR-MATION, Y'KNOW?!
SCREECH
S-SORRY! WE WERE JUST THINKING OF THE PRINCESS!!
THIS IS UNAC-CEPT-ABLE!

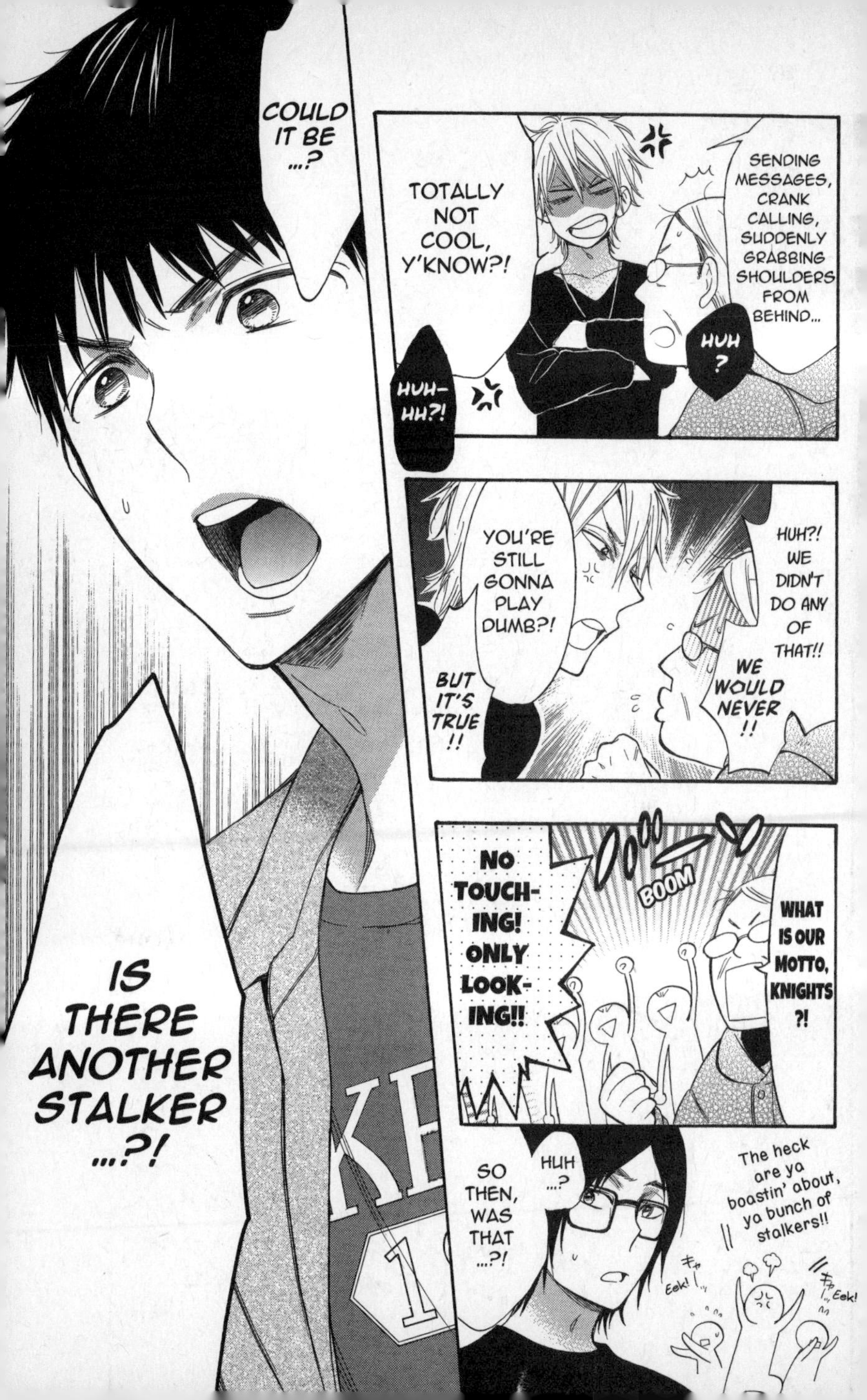
SENDING MESSAGES, CRANK CALLING, SUDDENLY GRABBING SHOULDERS FROM BEHIND...
HUH?
TOTALLY NOT COOL, Y'KNOW?!
HUH-HH?!
HUH?! WE DIDN'T DO ANY OF THAT!!
WE WOULD NEVER!!
YOU'RE STILL GONNA PLAY DUMB?!
BUT IT'S TRUE!!
WHAT IS OUR MOTTO, KNIGHTS?!
BOOM
NO TOUCHING! ONLY LOOKING!!
The heck are ya boastin' about, ya bunch of stalkers!!
Eek!
Eek!
HUH...?
SO THEN, WAS THAT...?!
COULD IT BE...?
IS THERE ANOTHER STALKER...?!

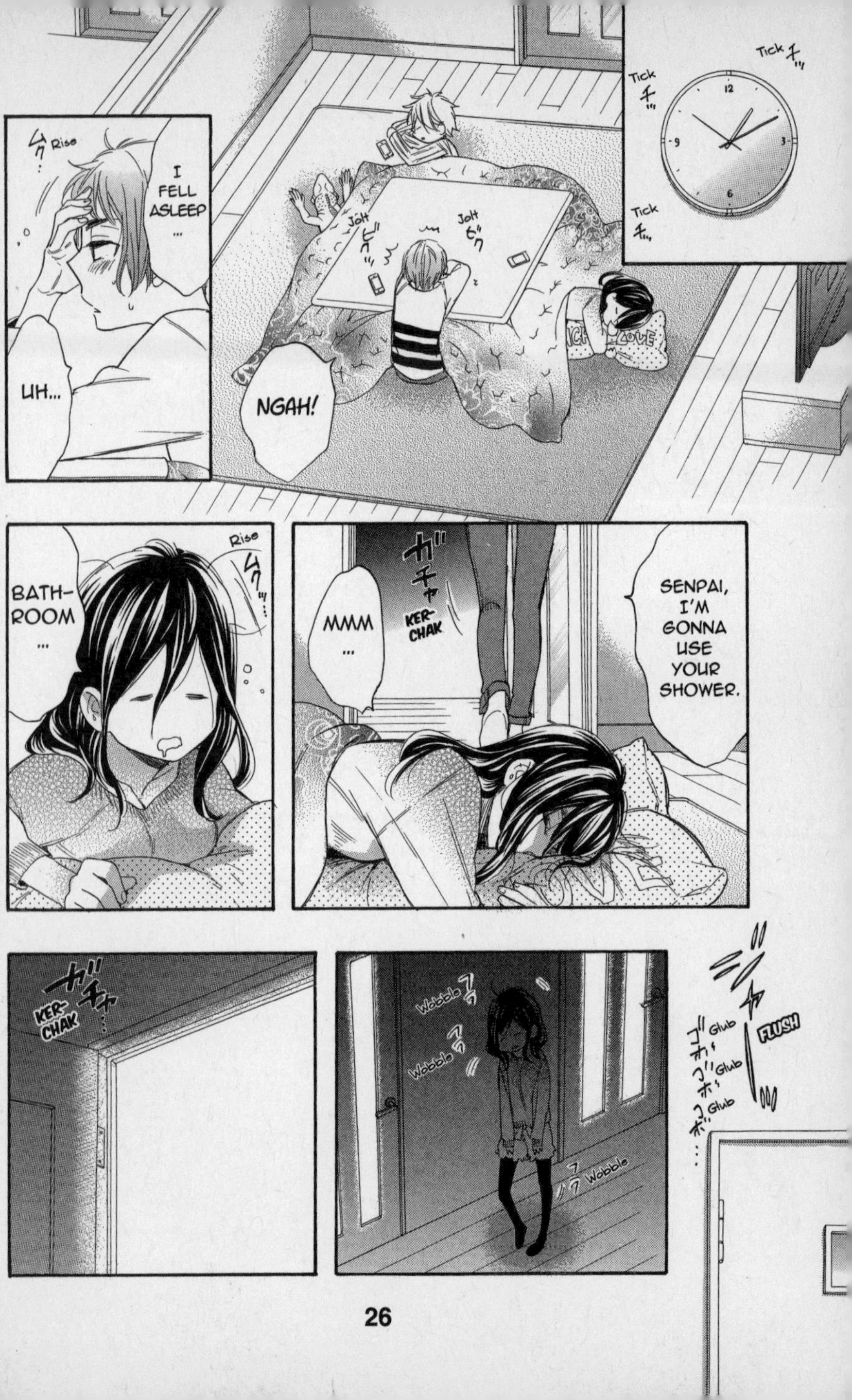
Tick
Tick
Tick
Jolt
Jolt
NGAH!
Rise
I FELL ASLEEP...
UH...
SENPAI, I'M GONNA USE YOUR SHOWER.
KER-CHAK
MMM...
Rise
BATHROOM...
FLUSH
Glub
Glub
Glub
Wobble
Wobble
Wobble
KER-CHAK

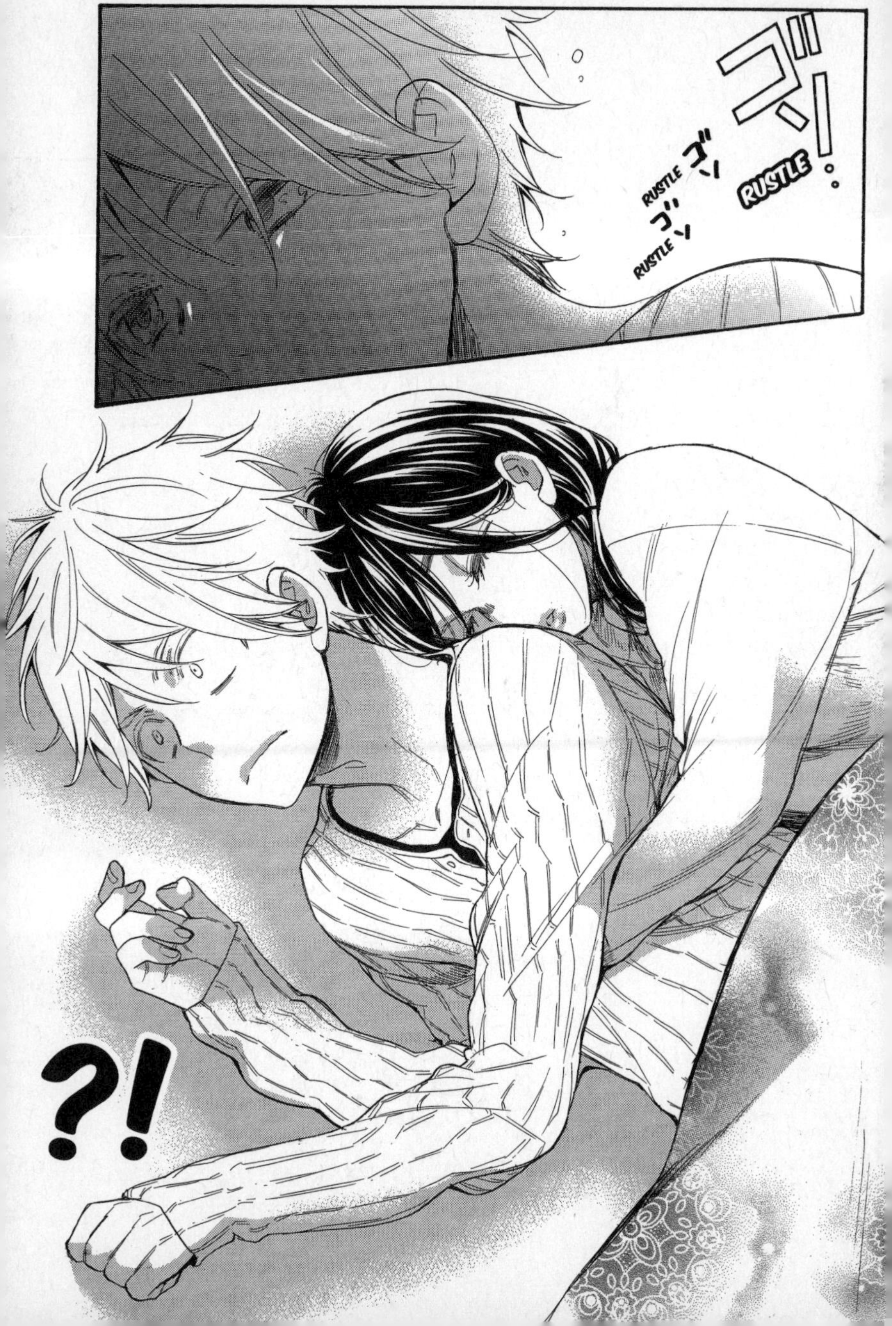
ゴソ!。。
RUSTLE
ゴソ
RUSTLE
ゴソ
RUSTLE
?!

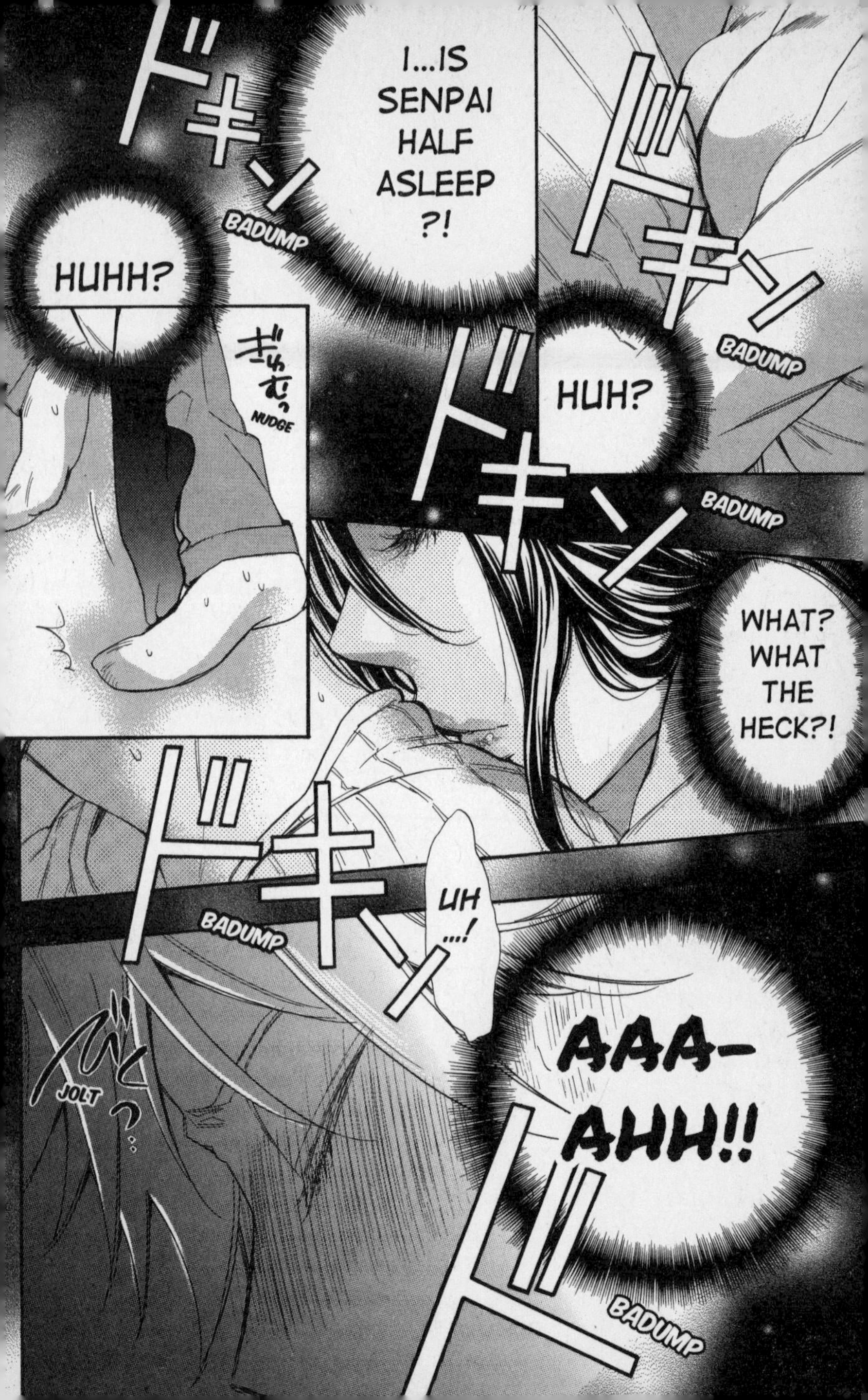

BADUMP
HUH?
I...IS SENPAI HALF ASLEEP?!
BADUMP
HUHH?
BADUMP
WHAT? WHAT THE HECK?!
NUDGE
BADUMP
UH...!
AAA-AHH!!
BADUMP
JOLT

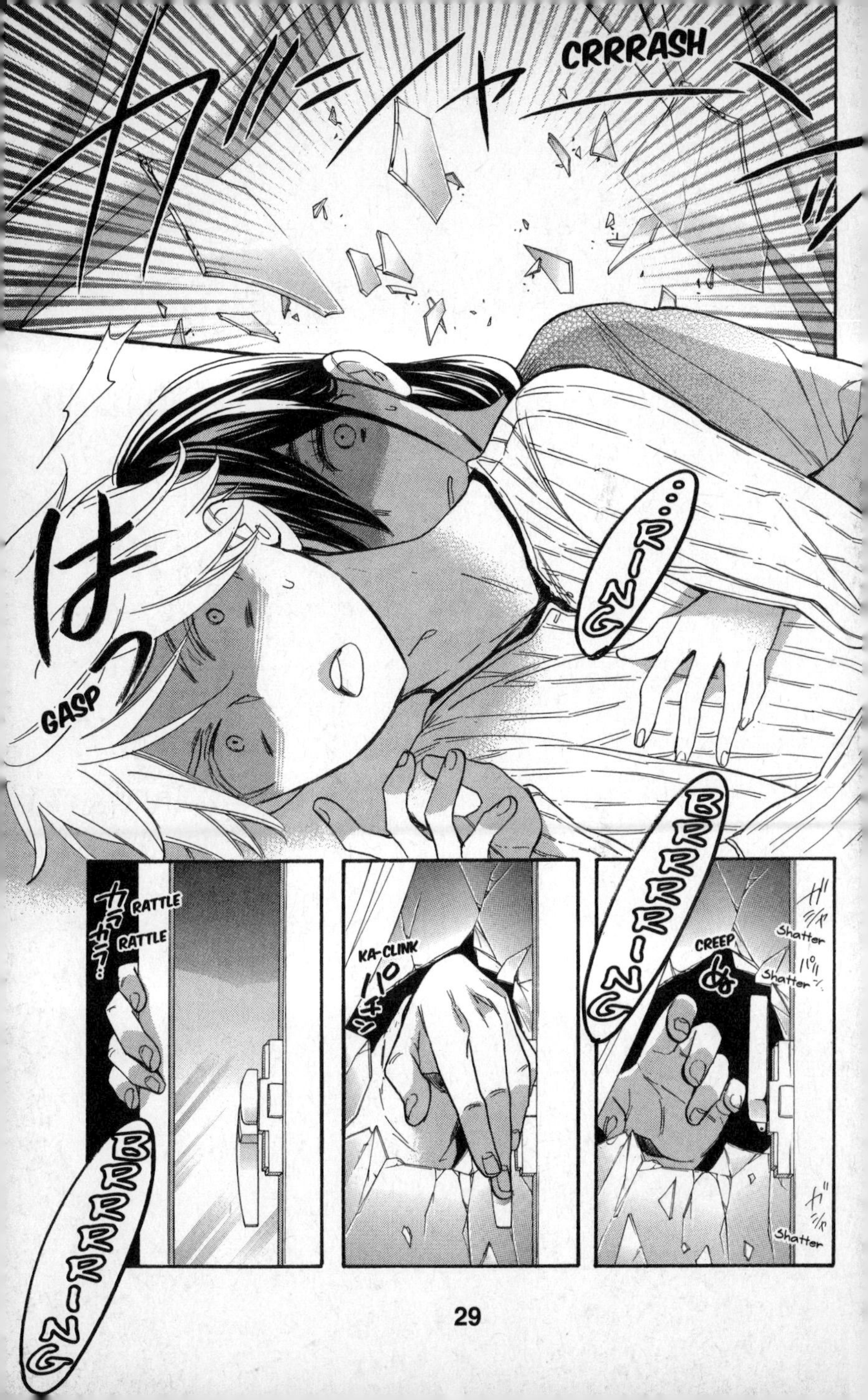
CRRRASH
はっ
GASP
...RI-NG
BRRRRI-NG
CREEP
Shatter
Shatter
Shatter
KA-CLINK
RATTLE
RATTLE
BRRRRI-NG

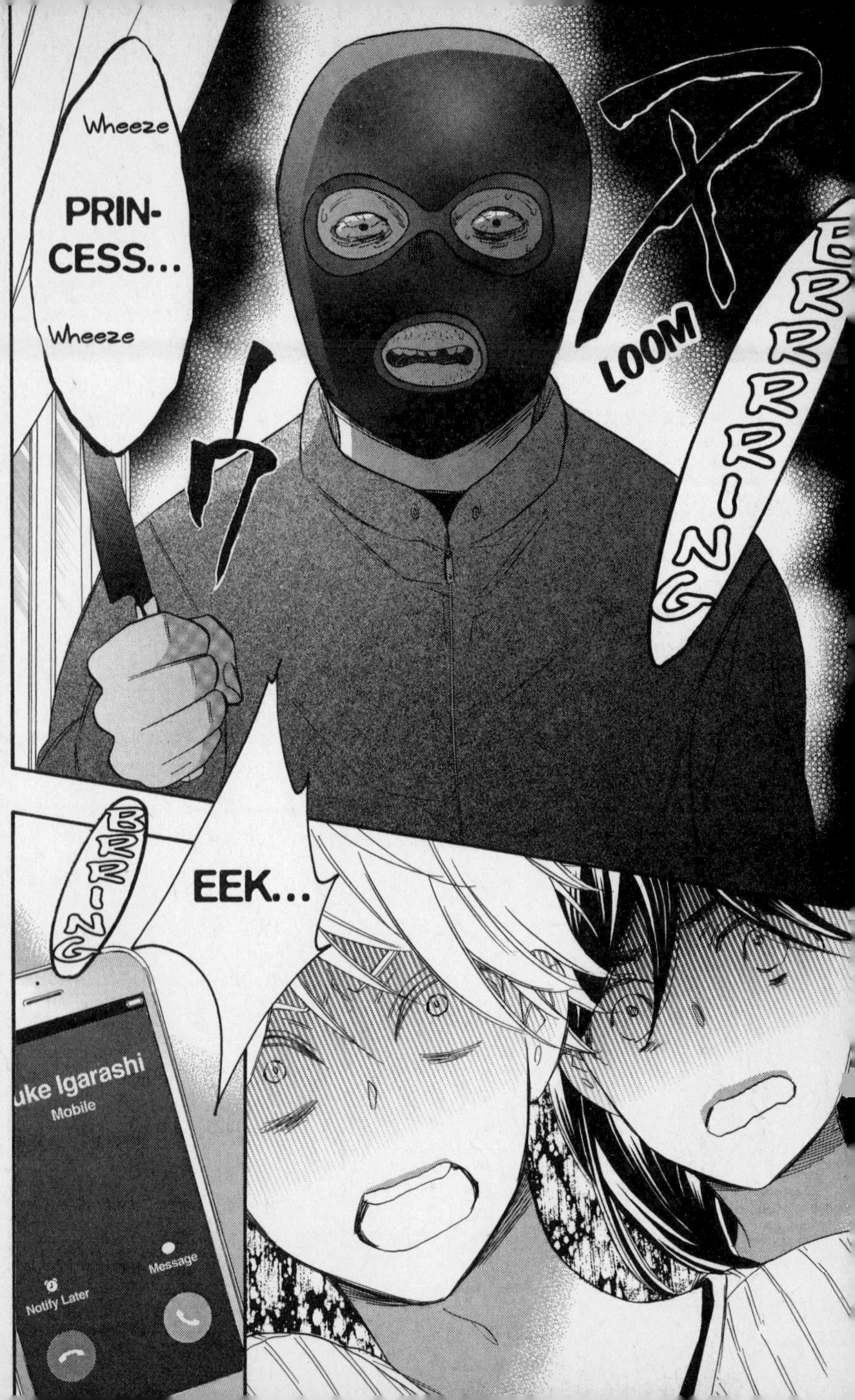
BRRRRING
LOOM
Wheeze
PRIN-
CESS...
Wheeze
EEK...
BRRING
uke Igarashi
Mobile
Message
Notify Later

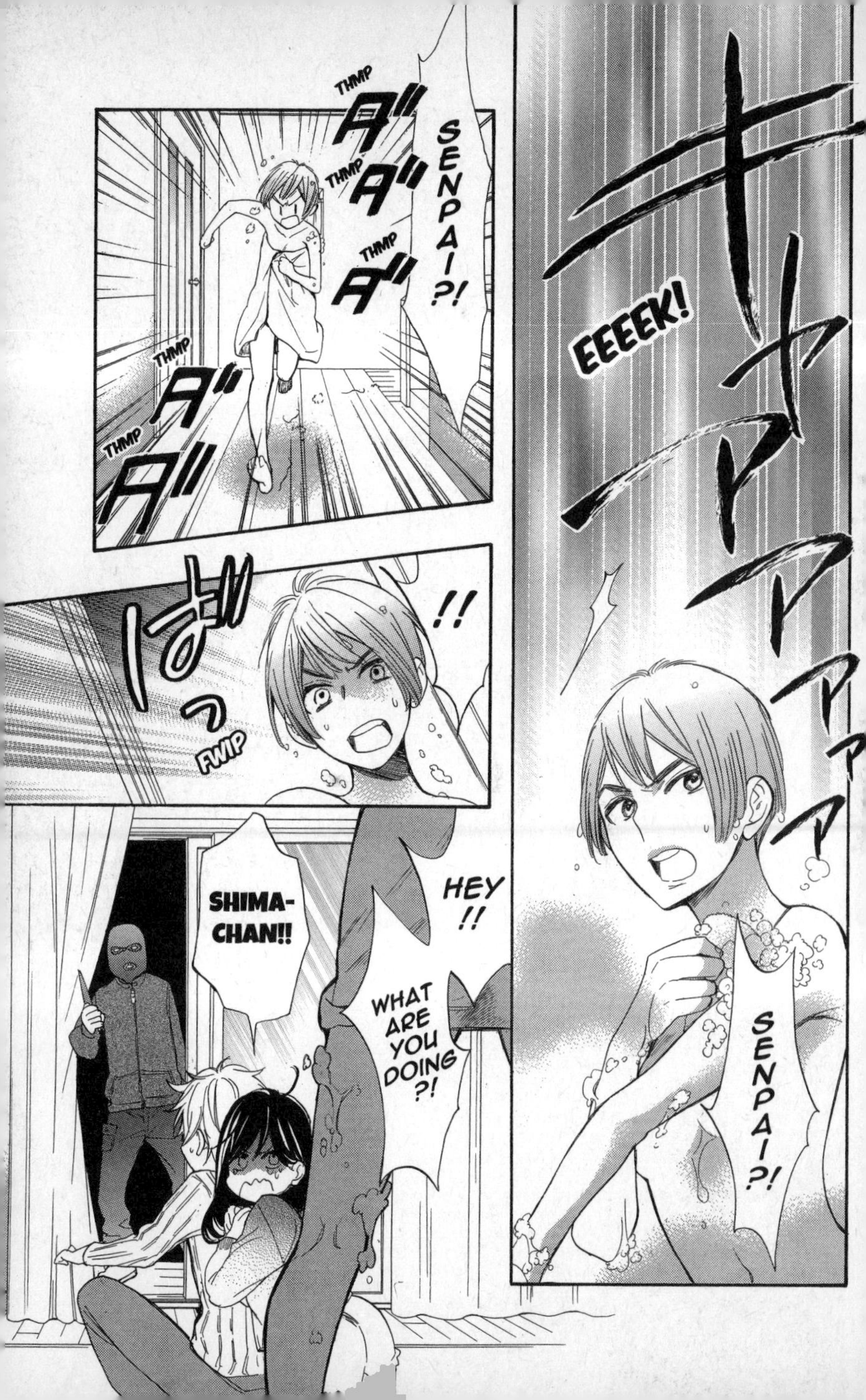
EEEEK!
SENPAI?!
SENPAI?!
THMP
THMP
THMP
THMP
THMP
!!
FWIP
HEY!!
WHAT ARE YOU DOING?!
SHIMA-CHAN!!

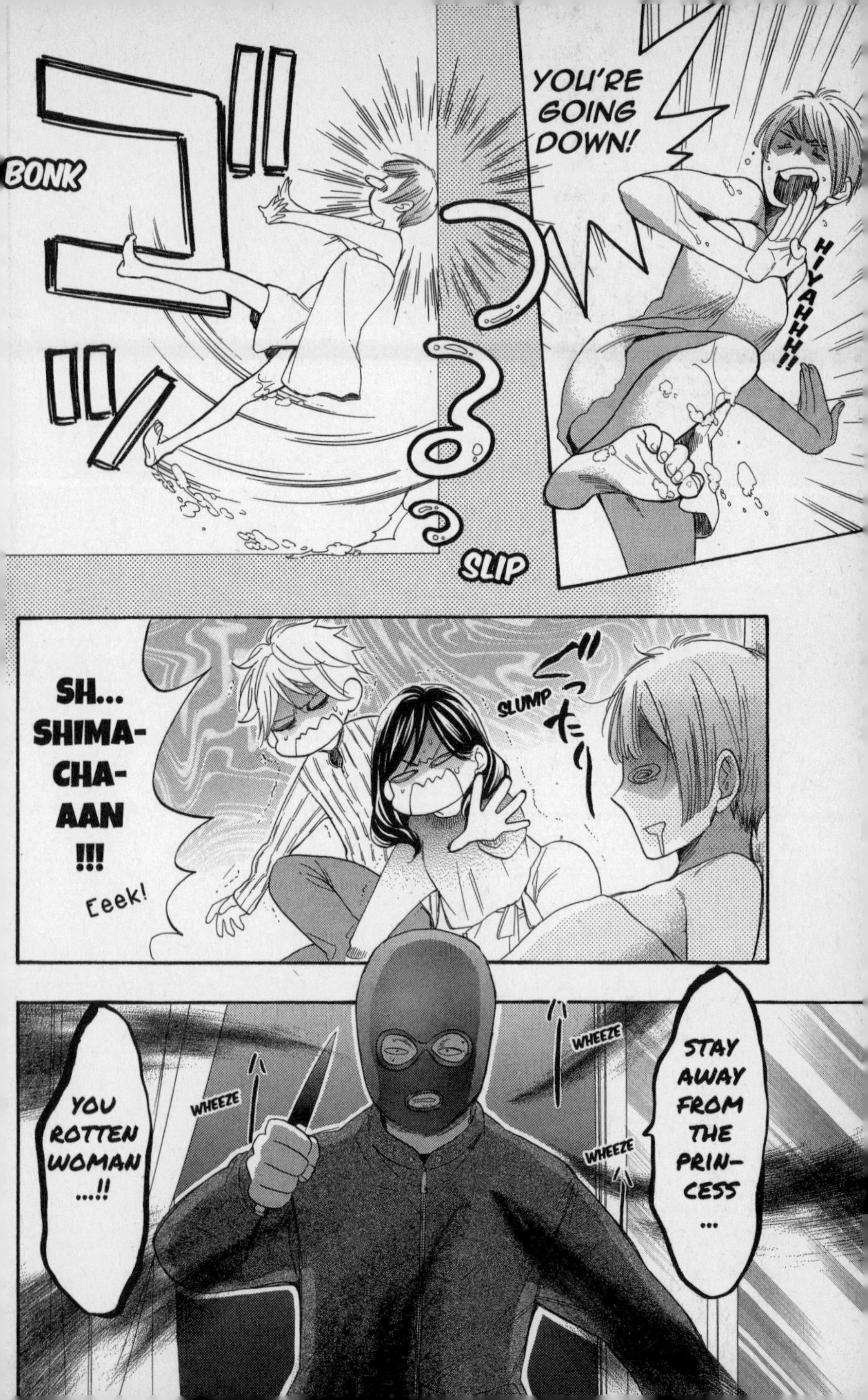
YOU'RE GOING DOWN!
HIYAHHH!!
SLIP
BONK
SLUMP
SH... SHIMA-CHA-AAN!!!
Eeek!
STAY AWAY FROM THE PRIN-CESS ...
WHEEZE
WHEEZE
YOU ROTTEN WOMAN ...!!
WHEEZE

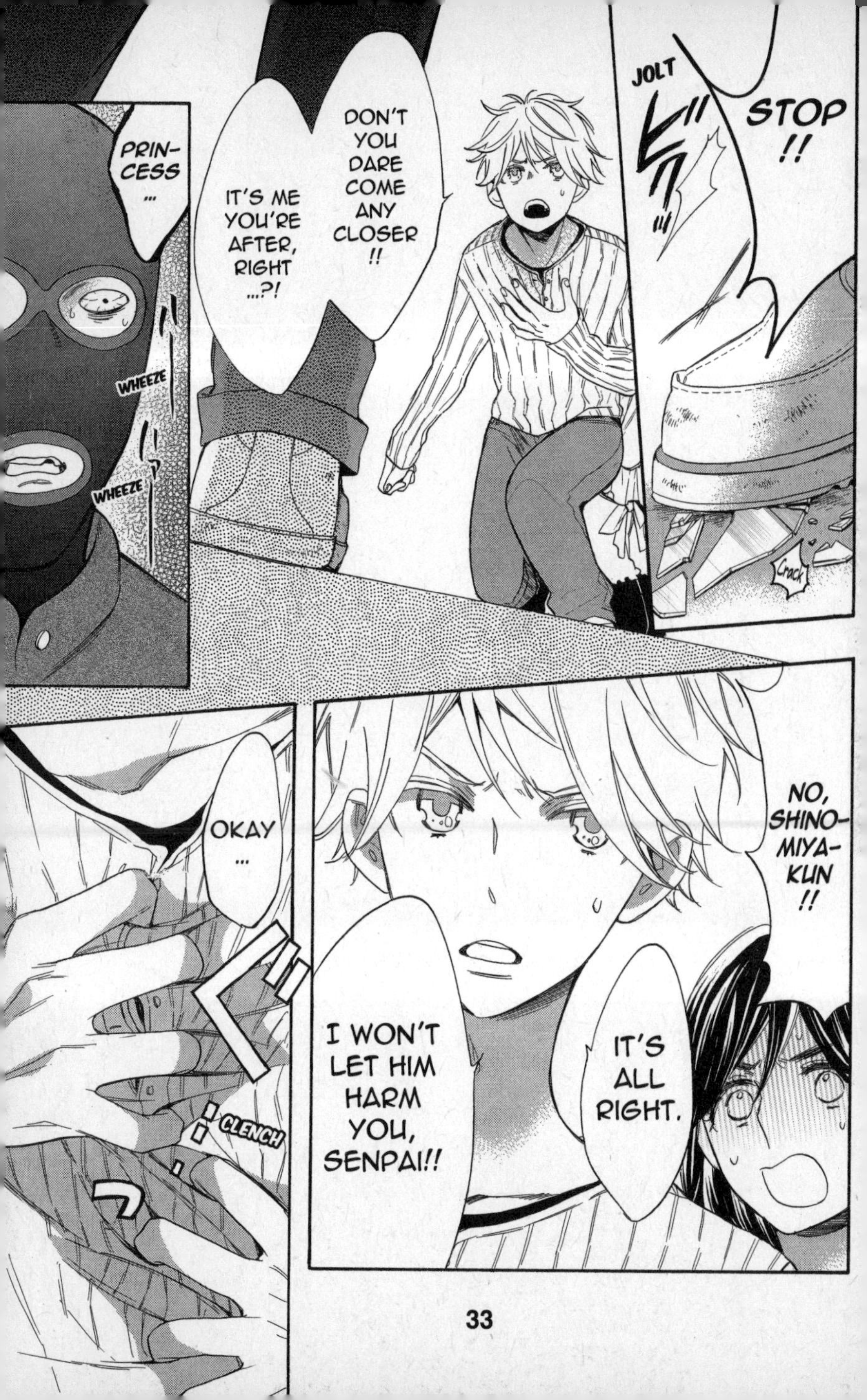
STOP!!
JOLT
Crack
DON'T YOU DARE COME ANY CLOSER!!
IT'S ME YOU'RE AFTER, RIGHT ...?!
PRIN-CESS ...
WHEEZE
WHEEZE
NO, SHINO-MIYA-KUN!!
IT'S ALL RIGHT.
I WON'T LET HIM HARM YOU, SENPAI!!
OKAY ...
CLENCH

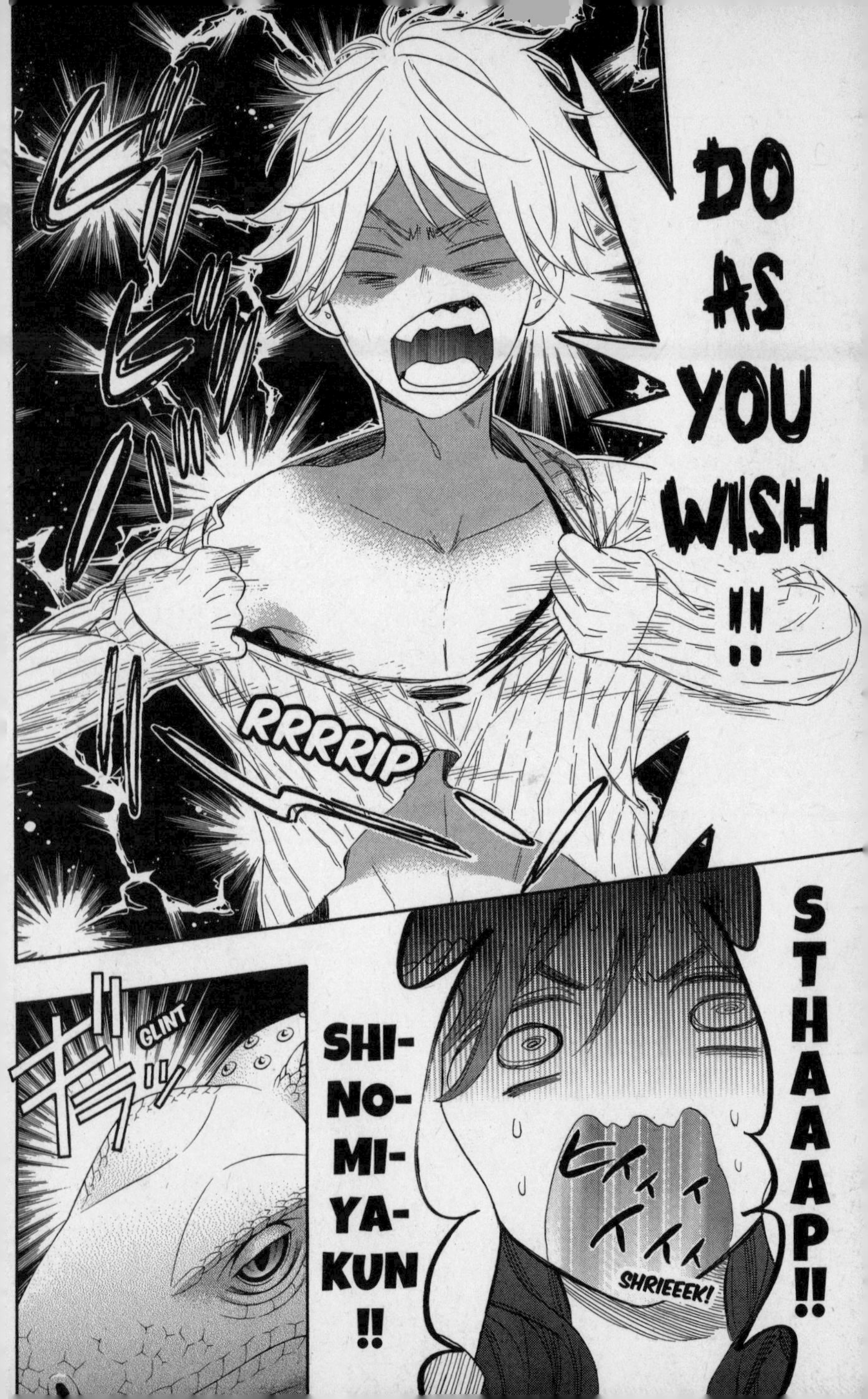
DO AS YOU WISH!!
RRRRIP
STHAAAAP!!
SHRIEEEK!
SHI-NO-MI-YA-KUN!!
GLINT

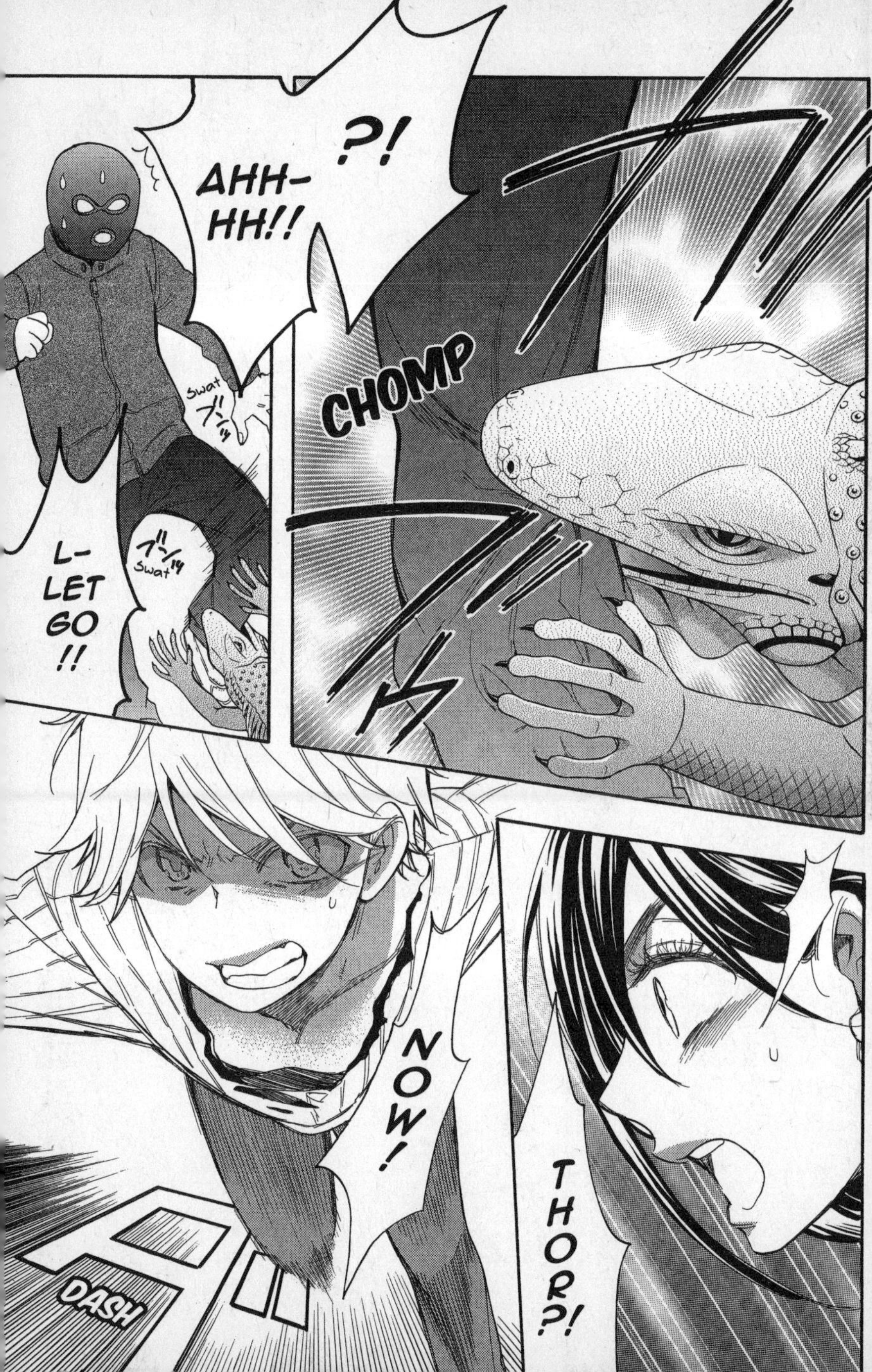
CHOMP
?!
AHHH-HH!!
Swat
Swat
L-LET GO!!
THOR?!
NOW!
DASH

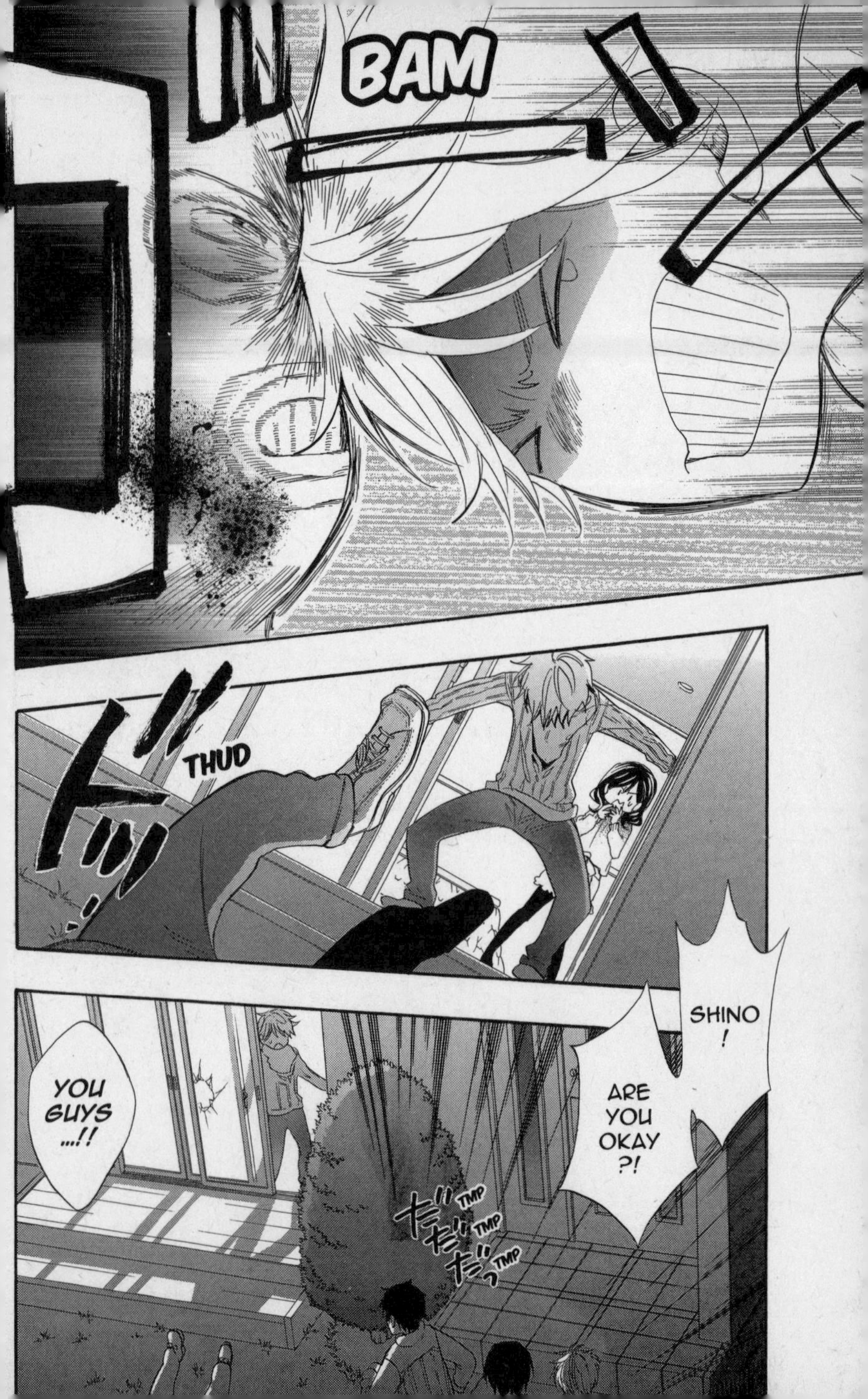
BAM
THUD
SHINO!
ARE YOU OKAY?!
TMP TMP TMP
YOU GUYS ...!!

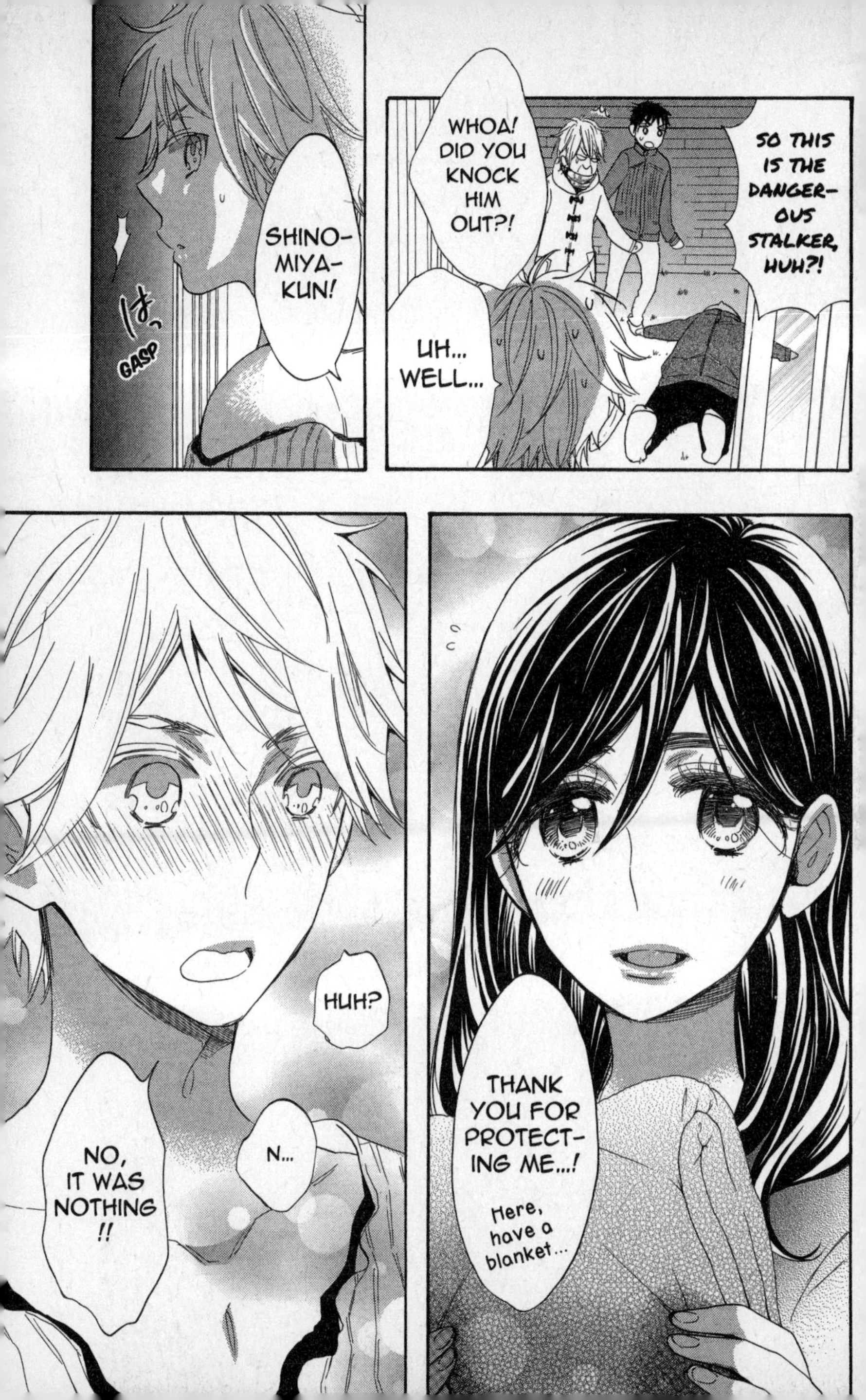
SO THIS IS THE DANGER-OUS STALKER, HUH?!
WHOA! DID YOU KNOCK HIM OUT?!
UH... WELL...
SHINO-MIYA-KUN!
は
GASP
THANK YOU FOR PROTECT-ING ME...!
Here, have a blanket...
HUH?
N...
NO, IT WAS NOTHING !!

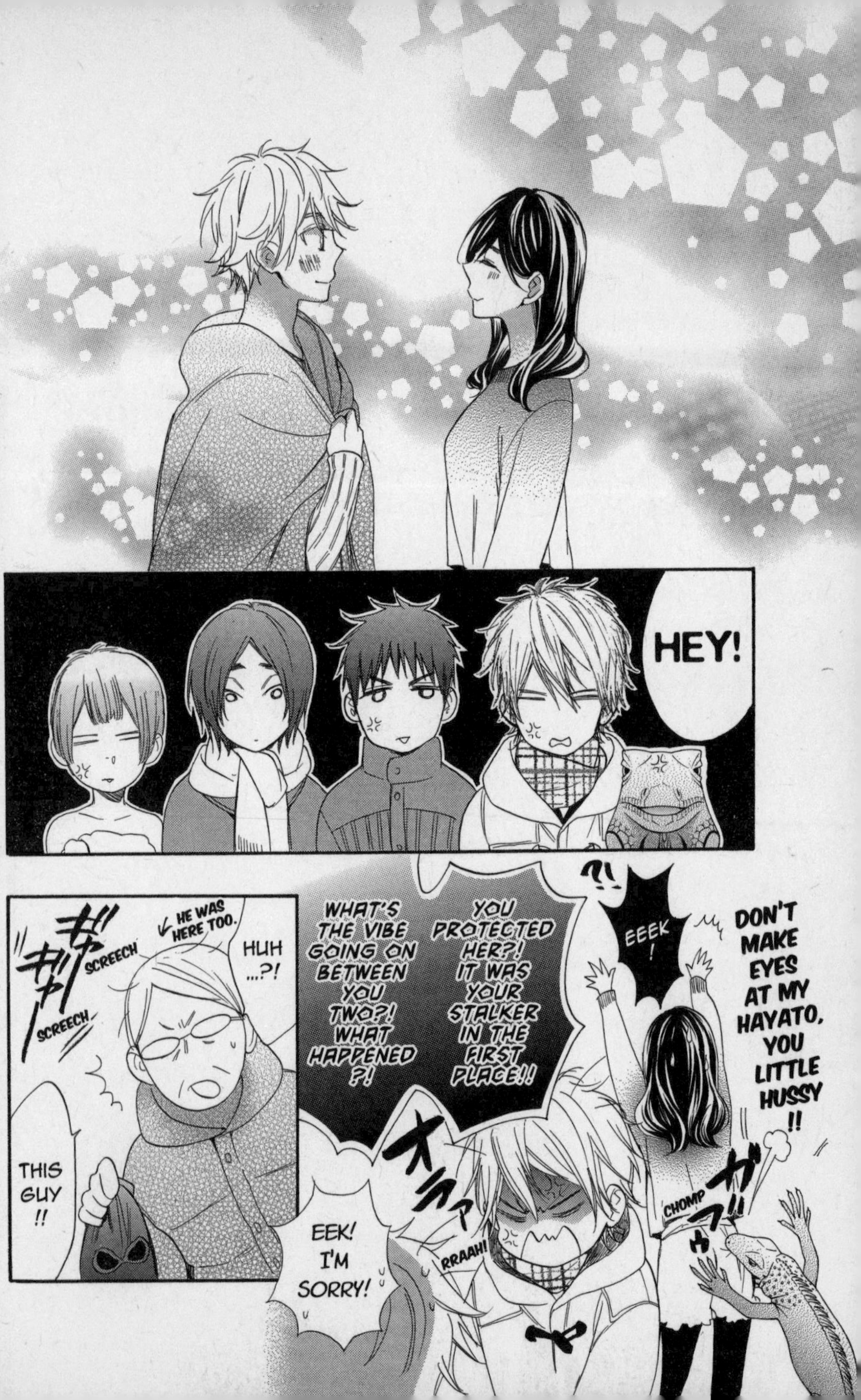
HEY!
?!
EEEK!
DON'T MAKE EYES AT MY HAYATO, YOU LITTLE HUSSY!!
CHOMP
YOU PROTECTED HER?! IT WAS YOUR STALKER IN THE FIRST PLACE!!
WHAT'S THE VIBE GOING ON BETWEEN YOU TWO?! WHAT HAPPENED?!
RRAAH!
EEK! I'M SORRY!
HE WAS HERE TOO.
HUH ...?!
SCREECH
SCREECH
THIS GUY!!

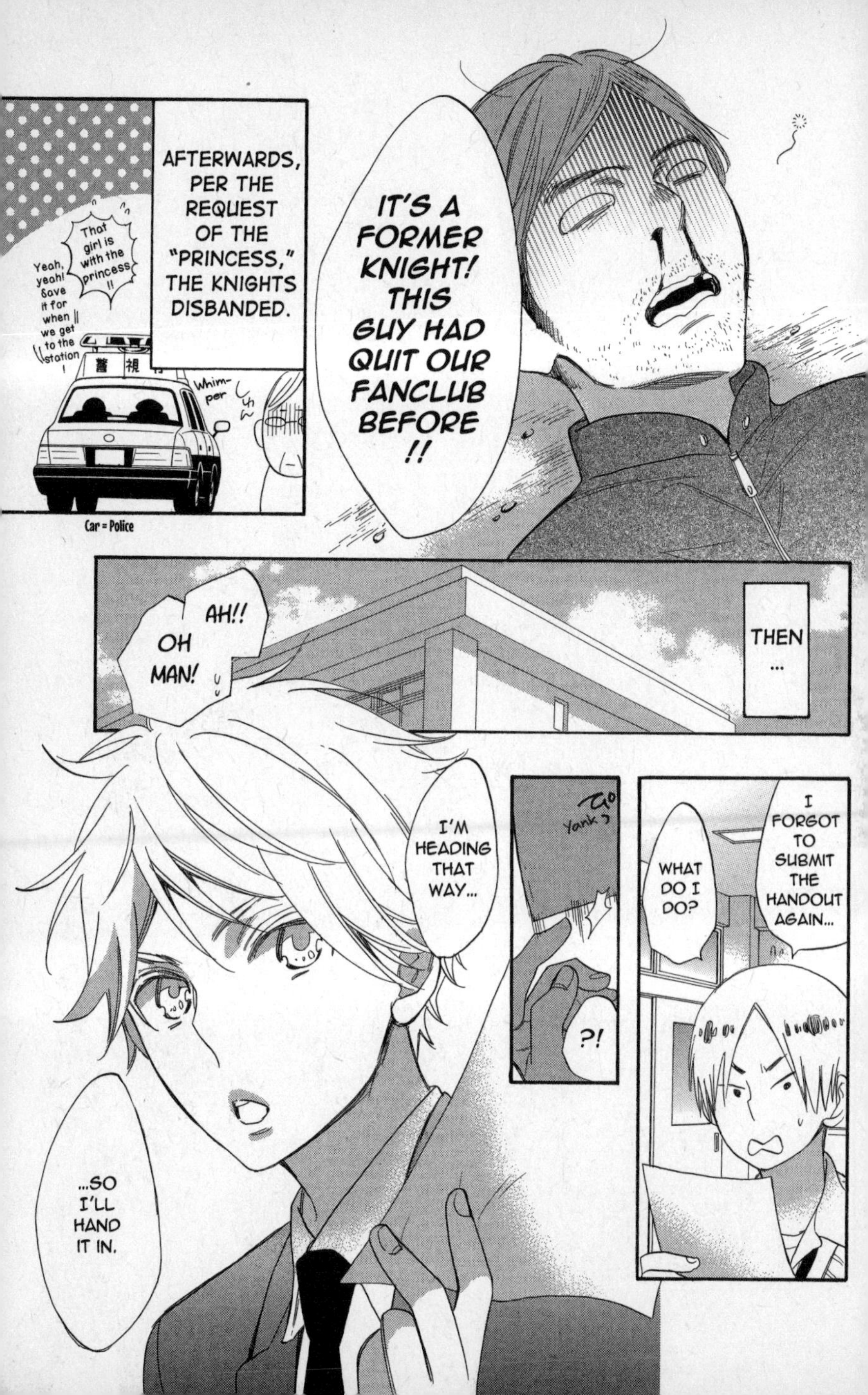
IT'S A FORMER KNIGHT! THIS GUY HAD QUIT OUR FANCLUB BEFORE !!
AFTERWARDS, PER THE REQUEST OF THE "PRINCESS," THE KNIGHTS DISBANDED.
That girl is with the princess !!
Yeah, yeah! Save it for when we get to the station !
Whimper
Car = Police
THEN ...
AH!! OH MAN!
I FORGOT TO SUBMIT THE HANDOUT AGAIN...
WHAT DO I DO?
Yank
?!
I'M HEADING THAT WAY...
...SO I'LL HAND IT IN.

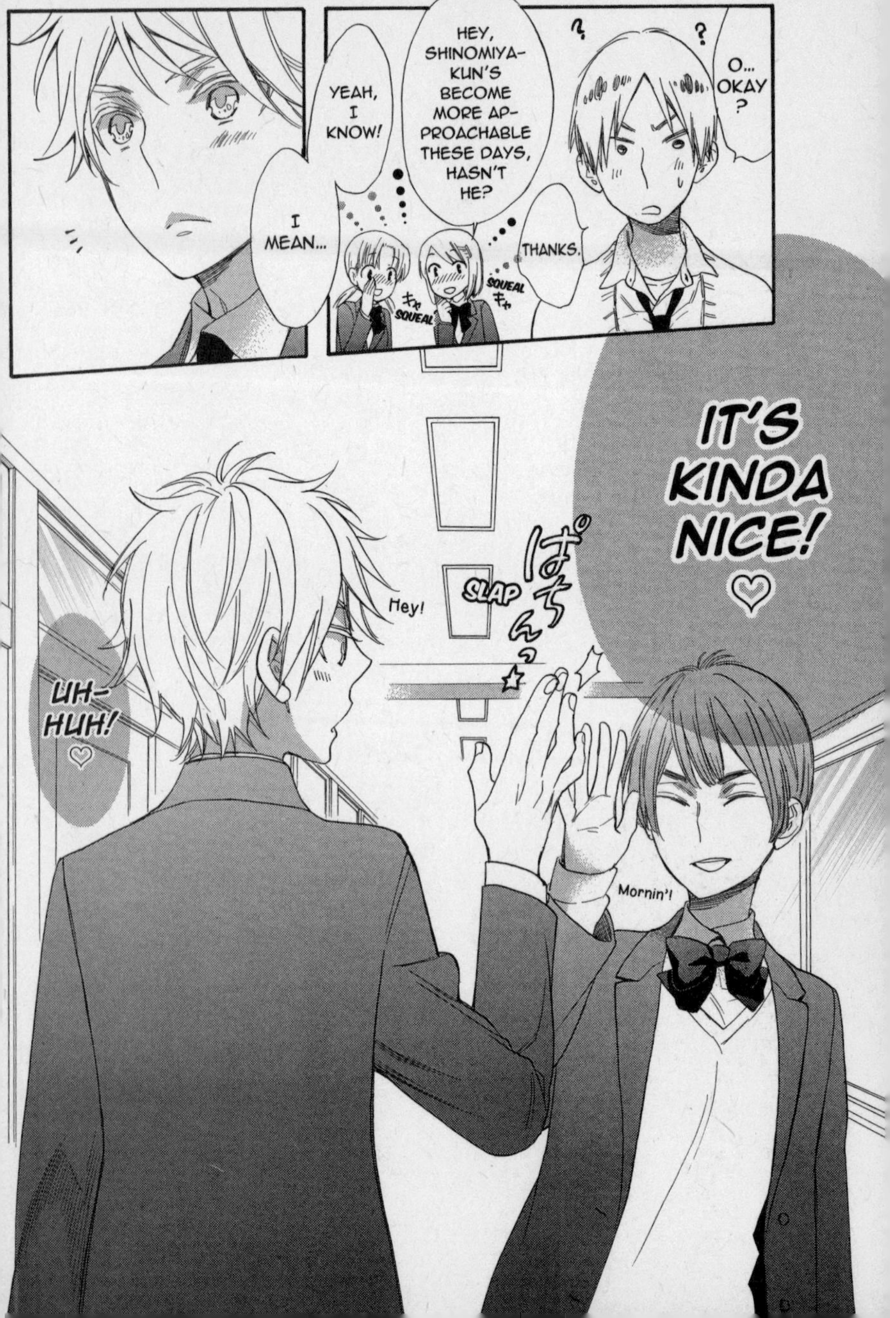

O... OKAY?
HEY, SHINOMIYA-KUN'S BECOME MORE AP-PROACHABLE THESE DAYS, HASN'T HE?
YEAH, I KNOW!
THANKS.
SQUEAL キャ
キャ SQUEAL
I MEAN...
IT'S KINDA NICE! ♡
ぱちんっ
SLAP
Hey!
Mornin'!
UH-HUH! ♡

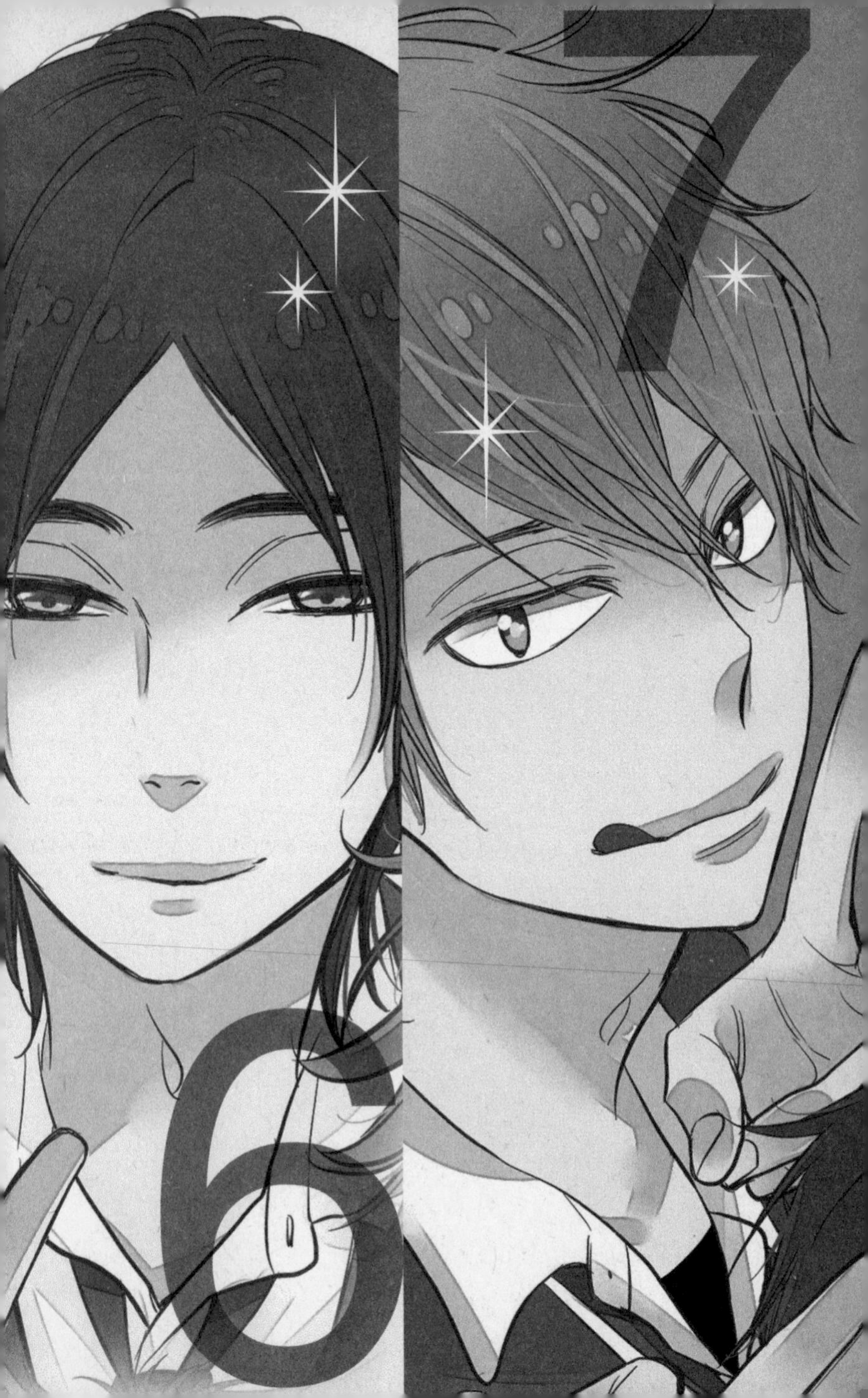
7
6

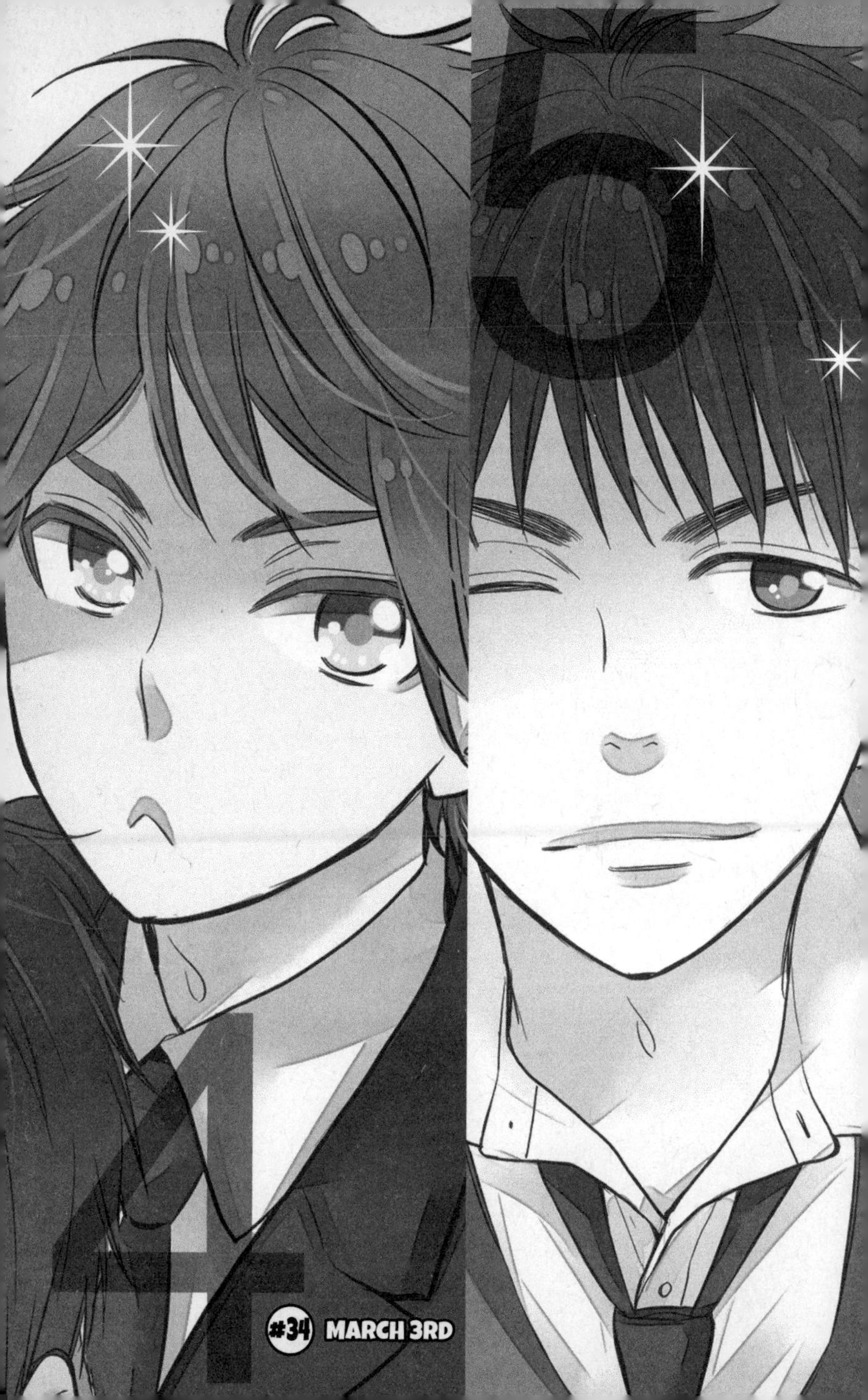
#34 MARCH 3RD

KiSS HiM, NOT ME!

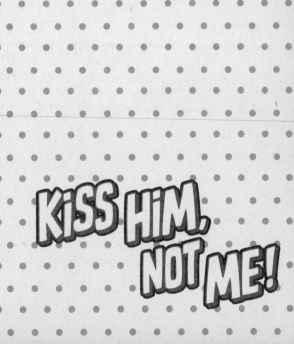

SERI-NUMA-SENPAI!
I HEARD SOME-THING COOL!

WRITE FIVE THINGS YOU WANT ON THIS PAPER, AND PUT IT INSIDE YOUR SCHOOL DESK FOR A NIGHT!!
IF YOU DO... IT'LL COME TRUE!! IT'S LIKE A CHARM TO GET WHAT YOU WANT !!
DREAM

KiSS HiM, NOT ME!

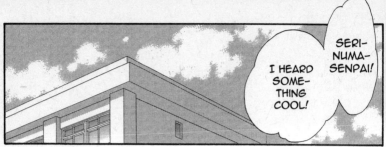

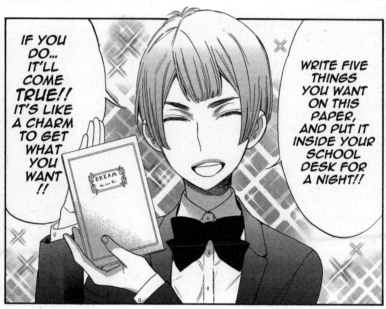

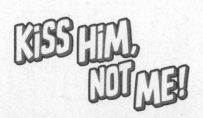

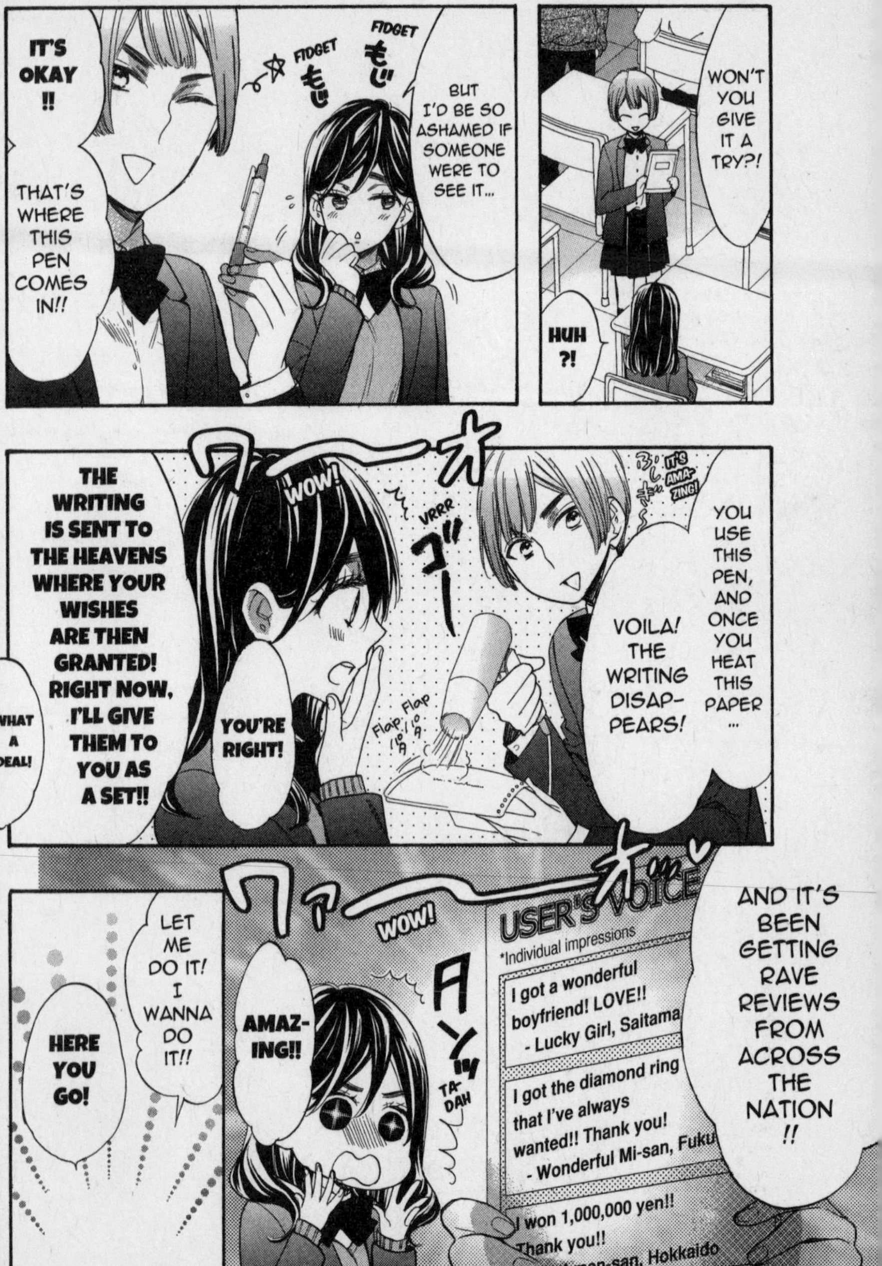
WON'T YOU GIVE IT A TRY?!
HUH ?!
FIDGET
FIDGET
BUT I'D BE SO ASHAMED IF SOMEONE WERE TO SEE IT...
IT'S OKAY !!
THAT'S WHERE THIS PEN COMES IN!!
YOU USE THIS PEN, AND ONCE YOU HEAT THIS PAPER ...
VOILA! THE WRITING DISAP-PEARS!
IT'S AMA-ZING!
VRRR
Flap Flap
WOW!
YOU'RE RIGHT!
THE WRITING IS SENT TO THE HEAVENS WHERE YOUR WISHES ARE THEN GRANTED! RIGHT NOW, I'LL GIVE THEM TO YOU AS A SET!!
WHAT A DEAL!
AND IT'S BEEN GETTING RAVE REVIEWS FROM ACROSS THE NATION !!
USER'S VOICE
*Individual impressions
I got a wonderful boyfriend! LOVE!! - Lucky Girl, Saitama
I got the diamond ring that I've always wanted!! Thank you! - Wonderful Mi-san, Fuku
I won 1,000,000 yen!! Thank you!! - Richman-san, Hokkaido
WOW!
TA-DAH
AMAZ-ING!!
LET ME DO IT! I WANNA DO IT!!
HERE YOU GO!

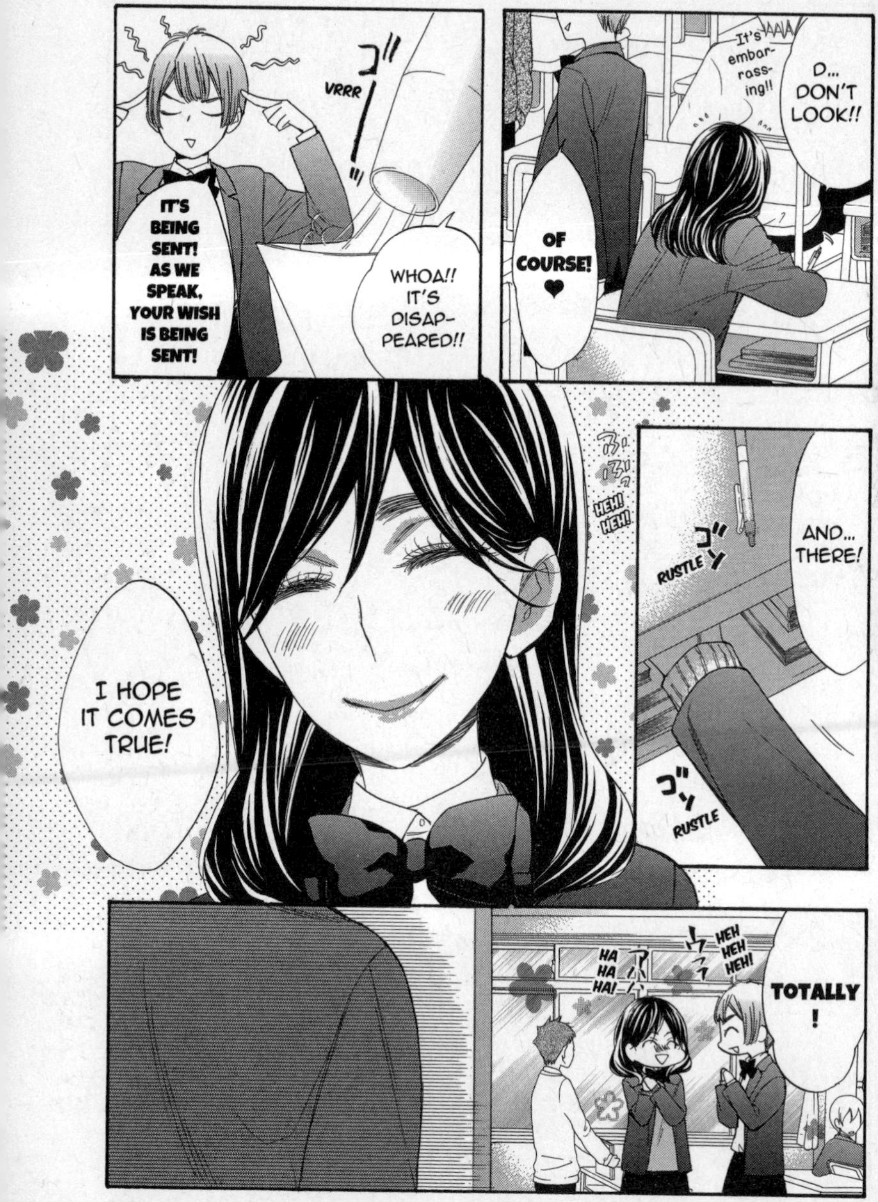
D... DON'T LOOK!!
It's embarrassing!!
OF COURSE! ♥
VRRR
IT'S BEING SENT! AS WE SPEAK, YOUR WISH IS BEING SENT!
WHOA!! IT'S DISAPPEARED!!
AND... THERE!
RUSTLE
RUSTLE
HEH! HEH!
I HOPE IT COMES TRUE!
TOTALLY!
HEH HEH HEH!
HA HA HA!

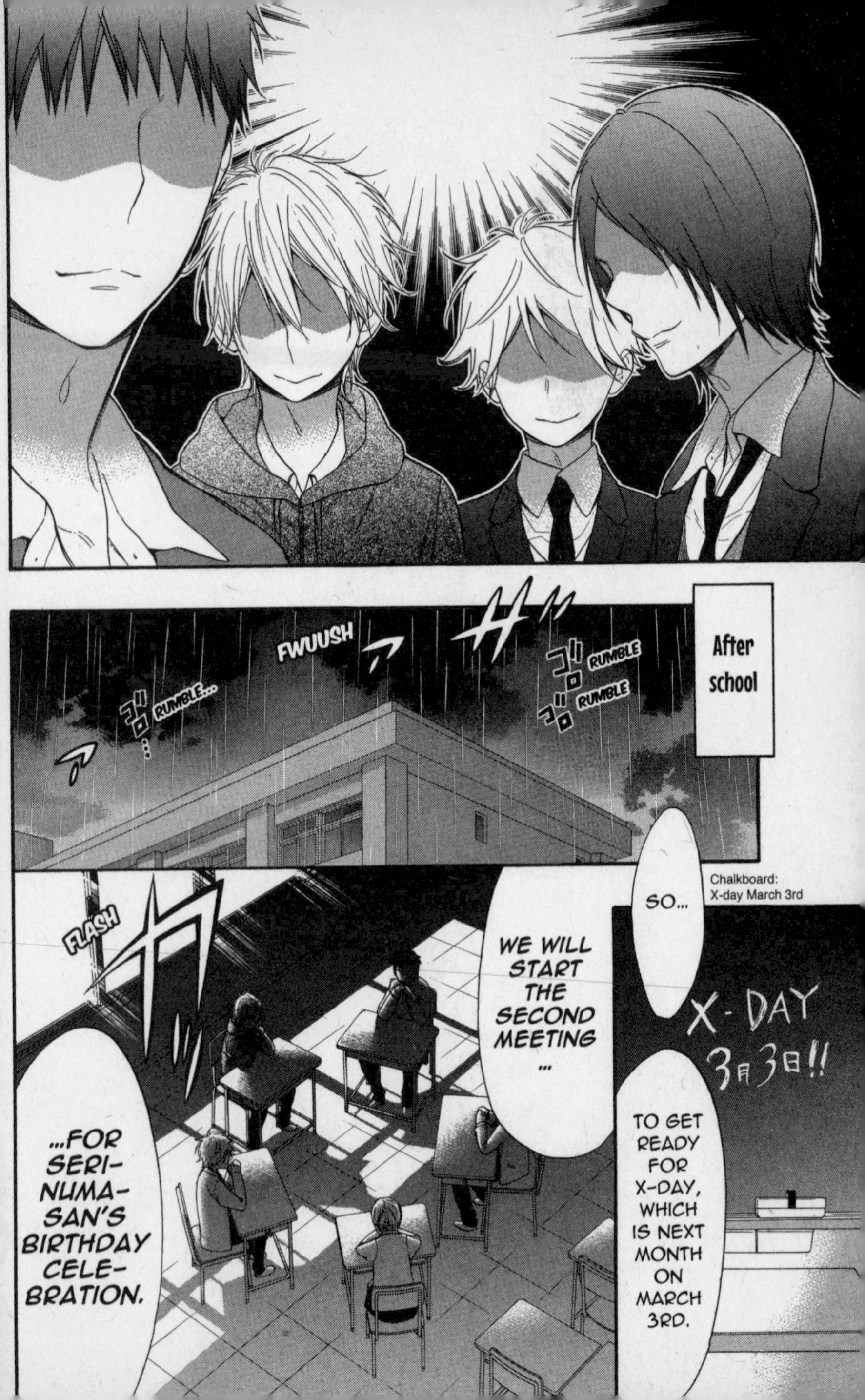
After school
RUMBLE
RUMBLE
FWUUSH
RUMBLE...
SO...
Chalkboard: X-day March 3rd
X-DAY 3月3日!!
TO GET READY FOR X-DAY, WHICH IS NEXT MONTH ON MARCH 3RD.
WE WILL START THE SECOND MEETING...
FLASH
...FOR SERI-NUMA-SAN'S BIRTHDAY CELE-BRATION.

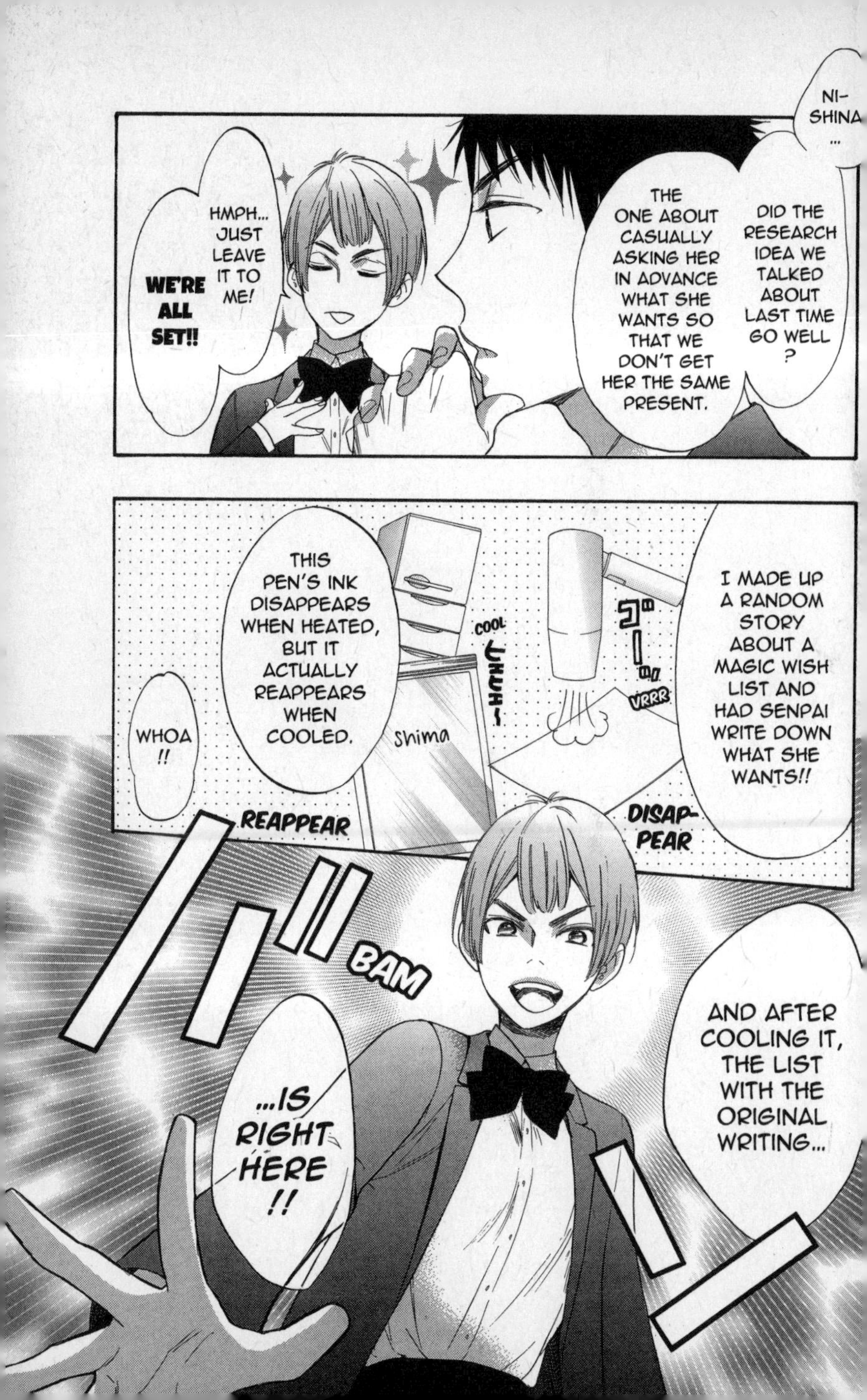
NI-SHINA...
DID THE RESEARCH IDEA WE TALKED ABOUT LAST TIME GO WELL?
THE ONE ABOUT CASUALLY ASKING HER IN ADVANCE WHAT SHE WANTS SO THAT WE DON'T GET HER THE SAME PRESENT.
HMPH... JUST LEAVE IT TO ME!
WE'RE ALL SET!!
I MADE UP A RANDOM STORY ABOUT A MAGIC WISH LIST AND HAD SENPAI WRITE DOWN WHAT SHE WANTS!!
VRRR
DISAP-PEAR
COOL
THIS PEN'S INK DISAPPEARS WHEN HEATED, BUT IT ACTUALLY REAPPEARS WHEN COOLED.
Shima
REAPPEAR
WHOA!!
AND AFTER COOLING IT, THE LIST WITH THE ORIGINAL WRITING...
BAM
...IS RIGHT HERE!!

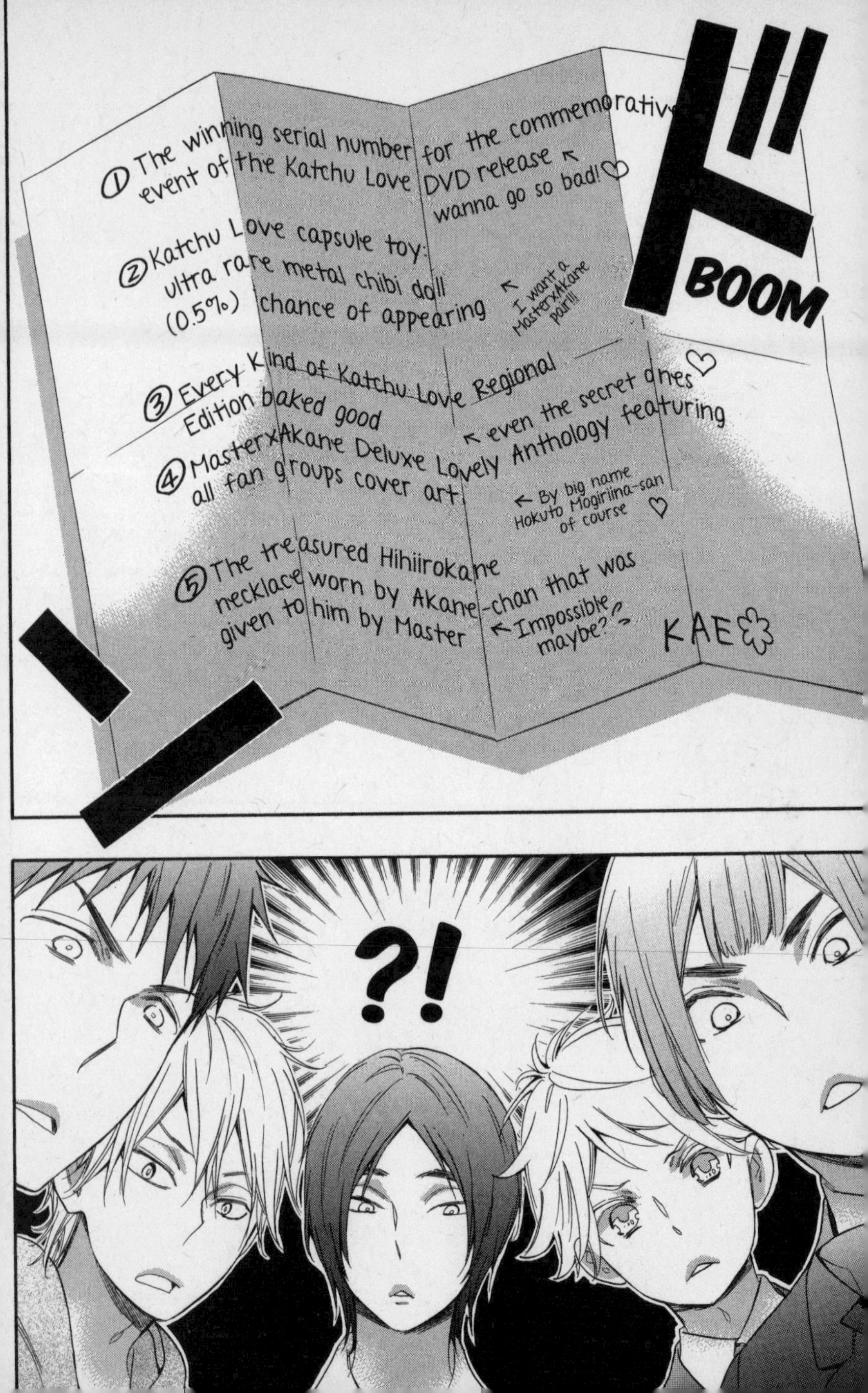

① The winning serial number for the commemorative event of the Katchu Love DVD release
← wanna go so bad! ♡
② Katchu Love capsule toy: ultra rare metal chibi doll (0.5%) chance of appearing
← I want a Master×Akane pair!!!
③ Every kind of Katchu Love Regional Edition baked good
← even the secret ones ♡
④ Master×Akane Deluxe Lovely Anthology featuring all fan groups cover art
← By big name Hokuto Mogiriina-san of course ♡
⑤ The treasured Hihiirokane necklace worn by Akane-chan that was given to him by Master
← Impossible maybe?
KAE
ド
BOOM
?!

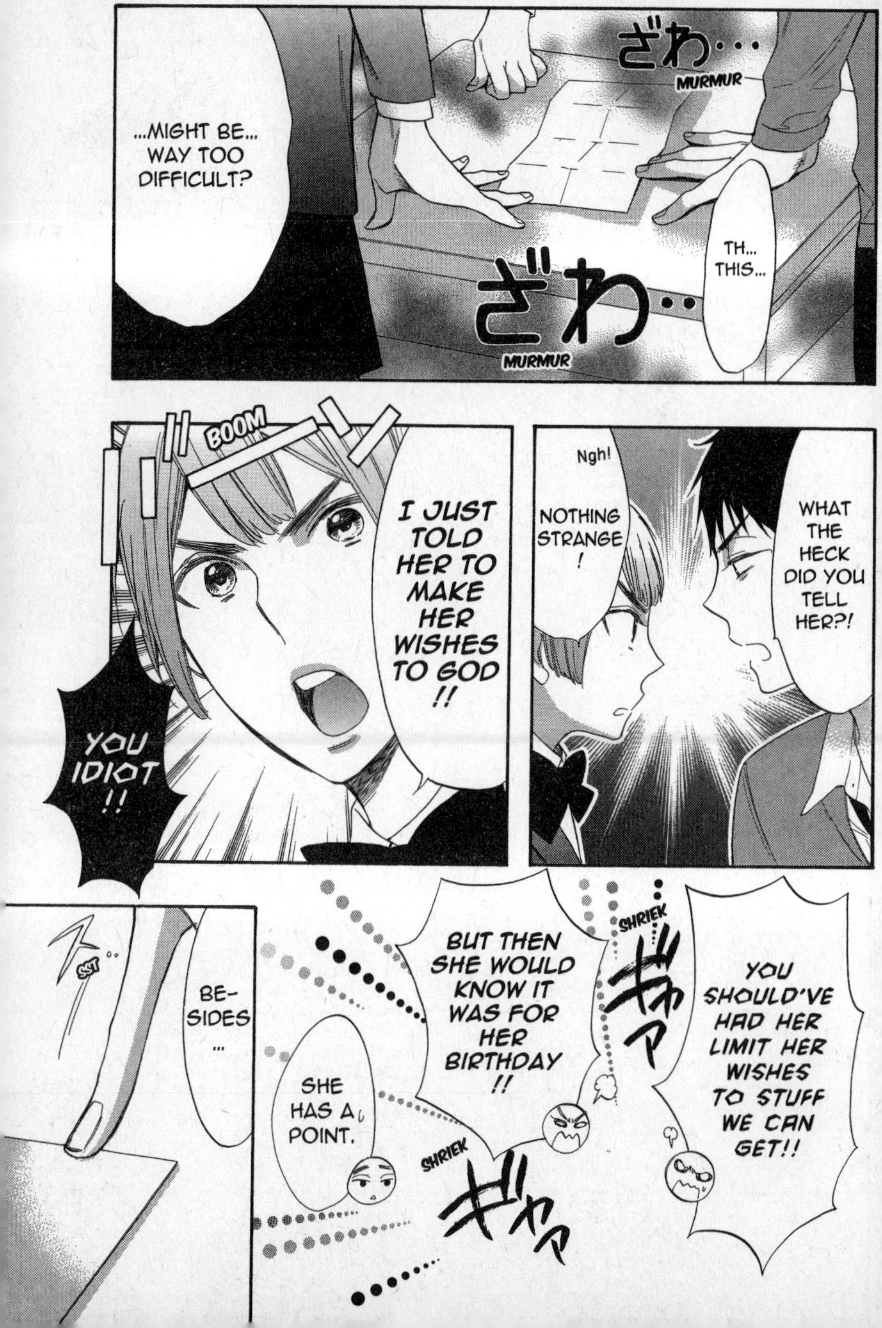
ざわ…
MURMUR
TH... THIS...
...MIGHT BE... WAY TOO DIFFICULT?
ざわ‥
MURMUR
WHAT THE HECK DID YOU TELL HER?!
Ngh!
NOTHING STRANGE!
BOOM
I JUST TOLD HER TO MAKE HER WISHES TO GOD!!
YOU IDIOT!!
YOU SHOULD'VE HAD HER LIMIT HER WISHES TO STUFF WE CAN GET!!
SHRIEK
ギャア
BUT THEN SHE WOULD KNOW IT WAS FOR HER BIRTHDAY!!
SHE HAS A POINT.
SHRIEK
ギャア
BE-SIDES...
SST

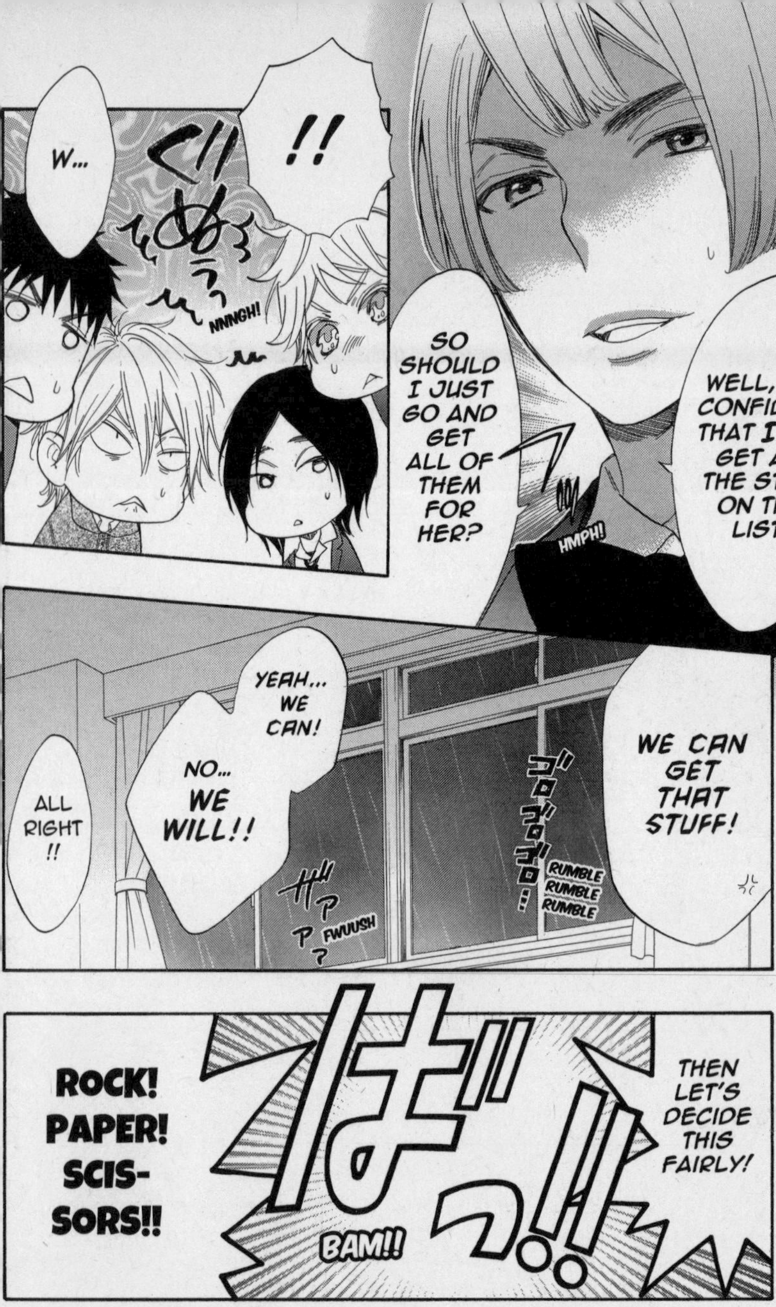
WELL, I'M CONFIDENT THAT I CAN GET ALL THE STUFF ON THIS LIST...
HMPH!
SO SHOULD I JUST GO AND GET ALL OF THEM FOR HER?
!!
W...
NNNGH!
WE CAN GET THAT STUFF!
RUMBLE RUMBLE RUMBLE
FWUUSH
YEAH... WE CAN!
NO... WE WILL!!
ALL RIGHT !!
THEN LET'S DECIDE THIS FAIRLY!
BAM!!
ROCK! PAPER! SCIS-SORS!!

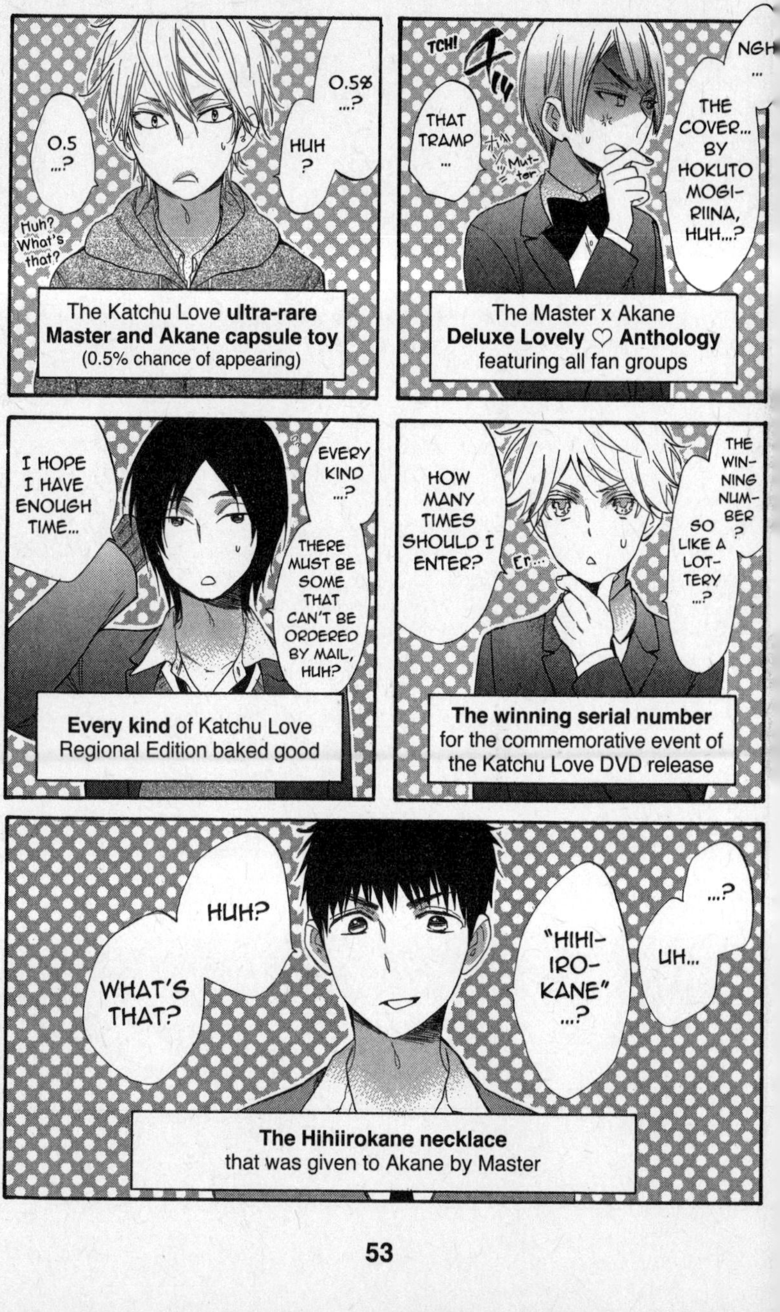
NGH ...
THE COVER... BY HOKUTO MOGI-RIINA, HUH...?
TCH!
THAT TRAMP ...
Mut-ter.
The Master x Akane **Deluxe Lovely ♡ Anthology** featuring all fan groups
0.5% ...?
HUH ?
0.5 ...?
Huh? What's that?
The Katchu Love **ultra-rare Master and Akane capsule toy** (0.5% chance of appearing)
THE WIN-NING NUM-BER ?
SO LIKE A LOT-TERY ...?
Er...
HOW MANY TIMES SHOULD I ENTER?
The winning serial number for the commemorative event of the Katchu Love DVD release
EVERY KIND ...?
THERE MUST BE SOME THAT CAN'T BE ORDERED BY MAIL, HUH?
I HOPE I HAVE ENOUGH TIME...
Every kind of Katchu Love Regional Edition baked good
...?
UH...
"HIHI-IRO-KANE" ...?
HUH?
WHAT'S THAT?
The Hihiirokane necklace that was given to Akane by Master

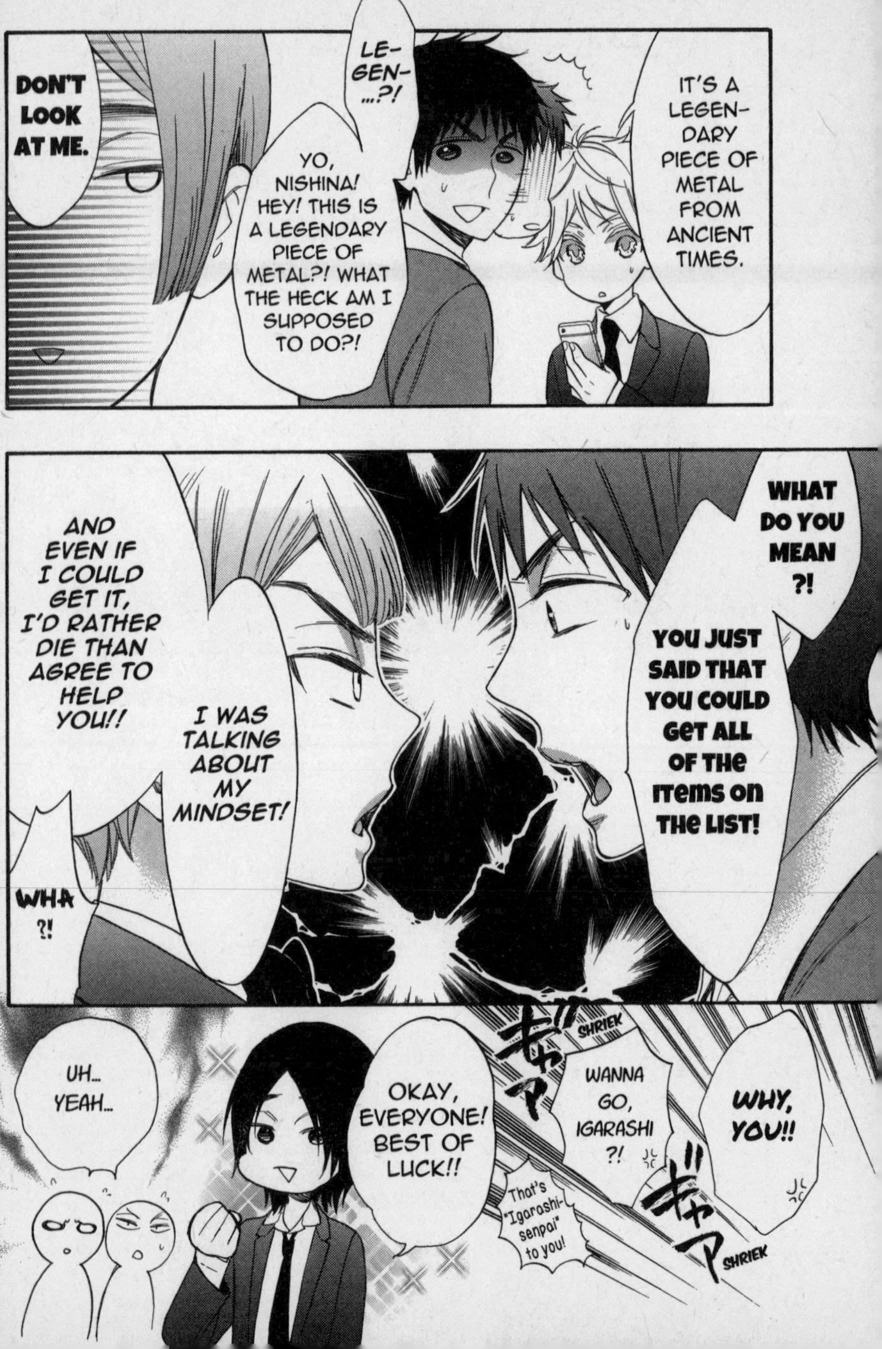
IT'S A LEGENDARY PIECE OF METAL FROM ANCIENT TIMES.
LE-GEN-...?!
YO, NISHINA! HEY! THIS IS A LEGENDARY PIECE OF METAL?! WHAT THE HECK AM I SUPPOSED TO DO?!
DON'T LOOK AT ME.
WHAT DO YOU MEAN?!
YOU JUST SAID THAT YOU COULD GET ALL OF THE ITEMS ON THE LIST!
I WAS TALKING ABOUT MY MINDSET!
AND EVEN IF I COULD GET IT, I'D RATHER DIE THAN AGREE TO HELP YOU!!
WHA?!
WHY, YOU!!
SHRIEK
WANNA GO, IGARASHI?!
That's "Igarashi-senpai" to you!
SHRIEK
OKAY, EVERYONE! BEST OF LUCK!!
UH... YEAH...

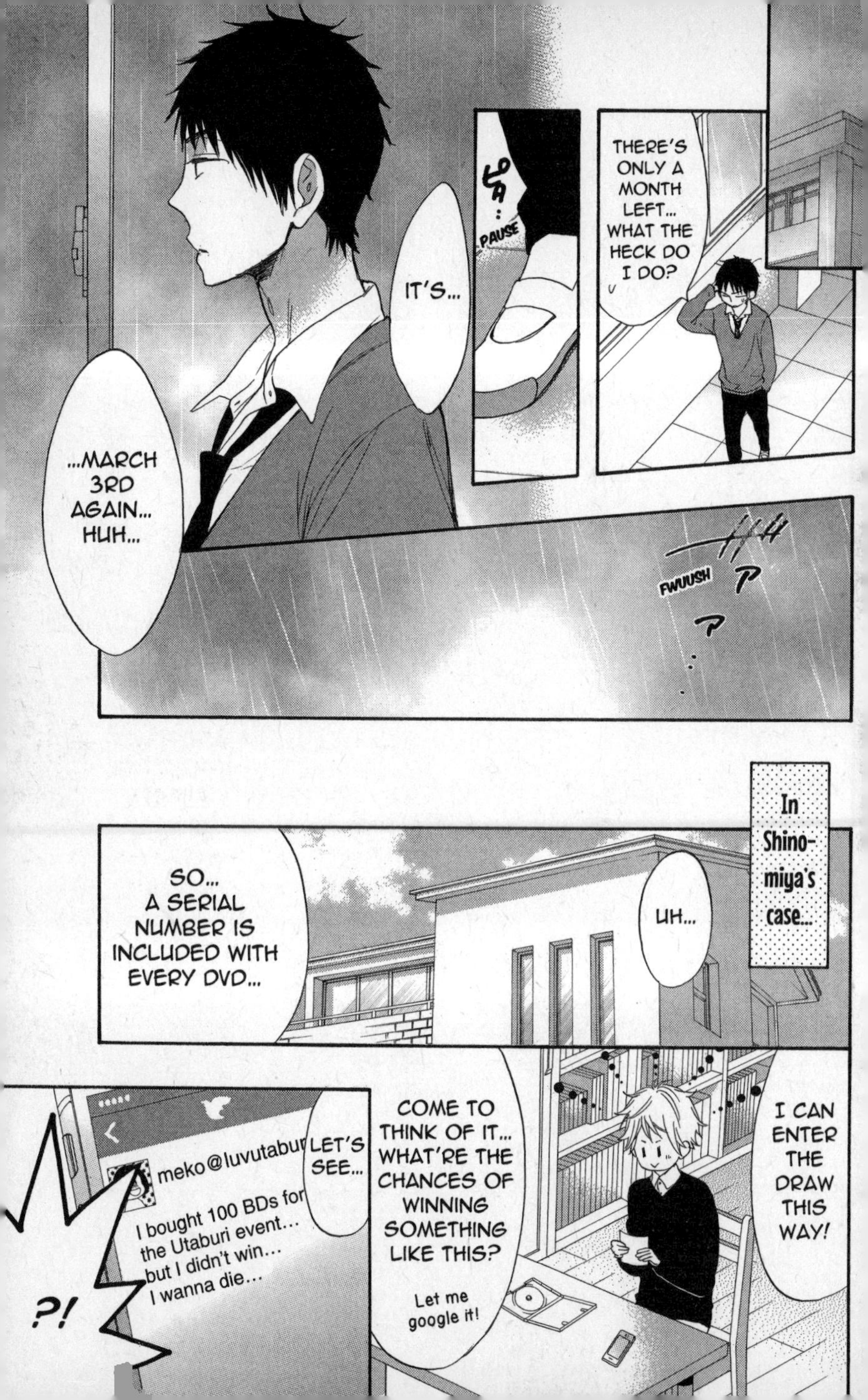
THERE'S ONLY A MONTH LEFT... WHAT THE HECK DO I DO?
PAUSE
IT'S...
...MARCH 3RD AGAIN... HUH...
FWUUSH
In Shino-miya's case...
UH...
SO... A SERIAL NUMBER IS INCLUDED WITH EVERY DVD...
I CAN ENTER THE DRAW THIS WAY!
COME TO THINK OF IT... WHAT'RE THE CHANCES OF WINNING SOMETHING LIKE THIS?
Let me google it!
LET'S SEE...
meko@luvutabur
I bought 100 BDs for the Utaburi event… but I didn't win… I wanna die…
?!

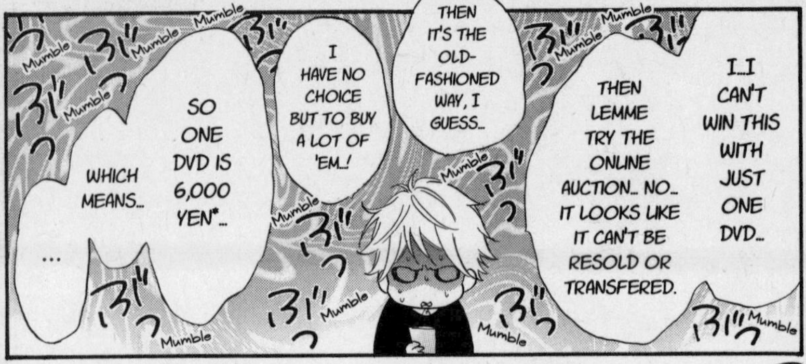
Mumble
I...I CAN'T WIN THIS WITH JUST ONE DVD...
THEN LEMME TRY THE ONLINE AUCTION... NO... IT LOOKS LIKE IT CAN'T BE RESOLD OR TRANSFERED.
Mumble
Mumble
THEN IT'S THE OLD-FASHIONED WAY, I GUESS...
Mumble
I HAVE NO CHOICE BUT TO BUY A LOT OF 'EM...!
Mumble
Mumble
SO ONE DVD IS 6,000 YEN*...
Mumble
Mumble
WHICH MEANS... ...
Mumble
Mumble

*About 60 USD

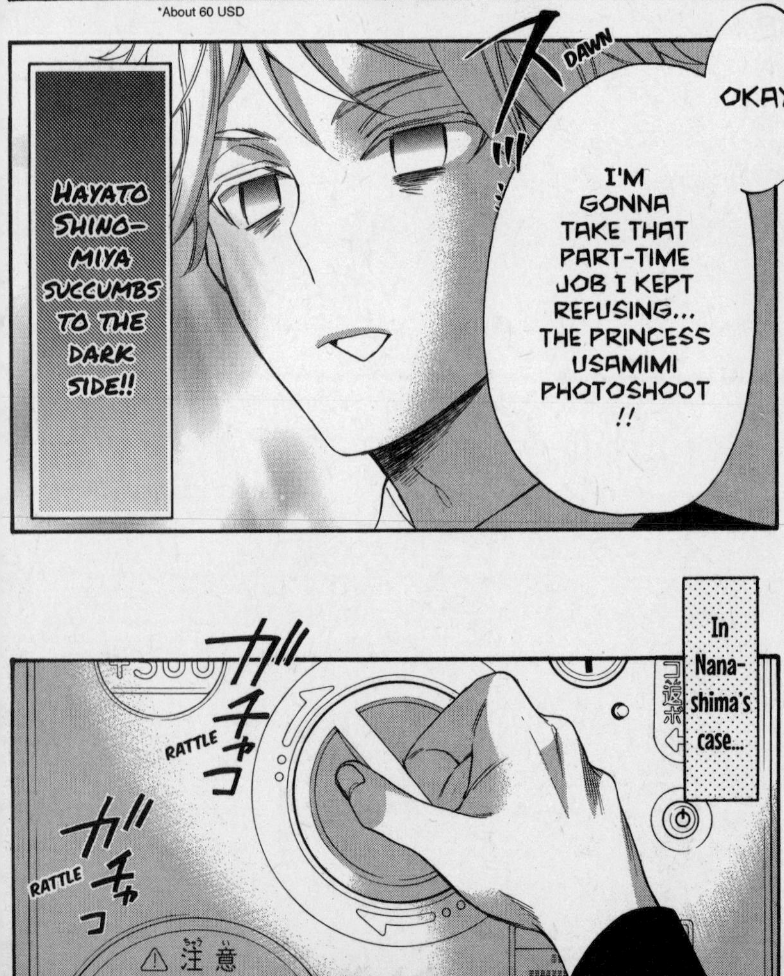
DAWN
OKAY!
I'M GONNA TAKE THAT PART-TIME JOB I KEPT REFUSING... THE PRINCESS USAMIMI PHOTOSHOOT!!
HAYATO SHINO-MIYA SUCCUMBS TO THE DARK SIDE!!
In Nana-shima's case...
RATTLE
RATTLE

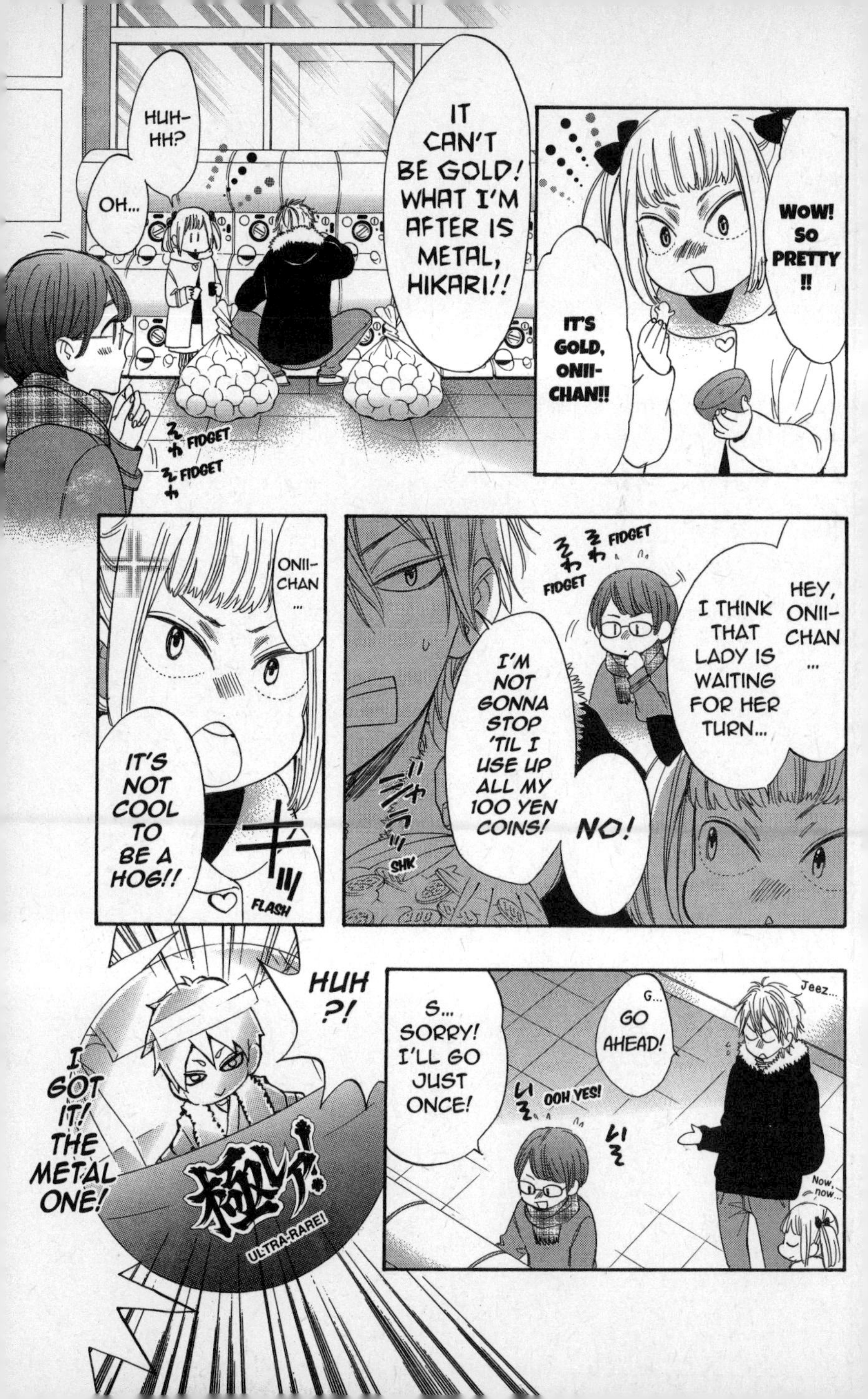
WOW! SO PRETTY!!
IT'S GOLD, ONII-CHAN!!
IT CAN'T BE GOLD! WHAT I'M AFTER IS METAL, HIKARI!!
HUH-HH?
OH...
FIDGET
FIDGET
HEY, ONII-CHAN...
I THINK THAT LADY IS WAITING FOR HER TURN...
FIDGET
FIDGET
NO!
I'M NOT GONNA STOP 'TIL I USE UP ALL MY 100 YEN COINS!
SHK
ONII-CHAN...
IT'S NOT COOL TO BE A HOG!!
FLASH
Jeez...
G... GO AHEAD!
S... SORRY! I'LL GO JUST ONCE!
OOH YES!
Now, now...
HUH?!
I GOT IT! THE METAL ONE!
極レア!
ULTRA-RARE!

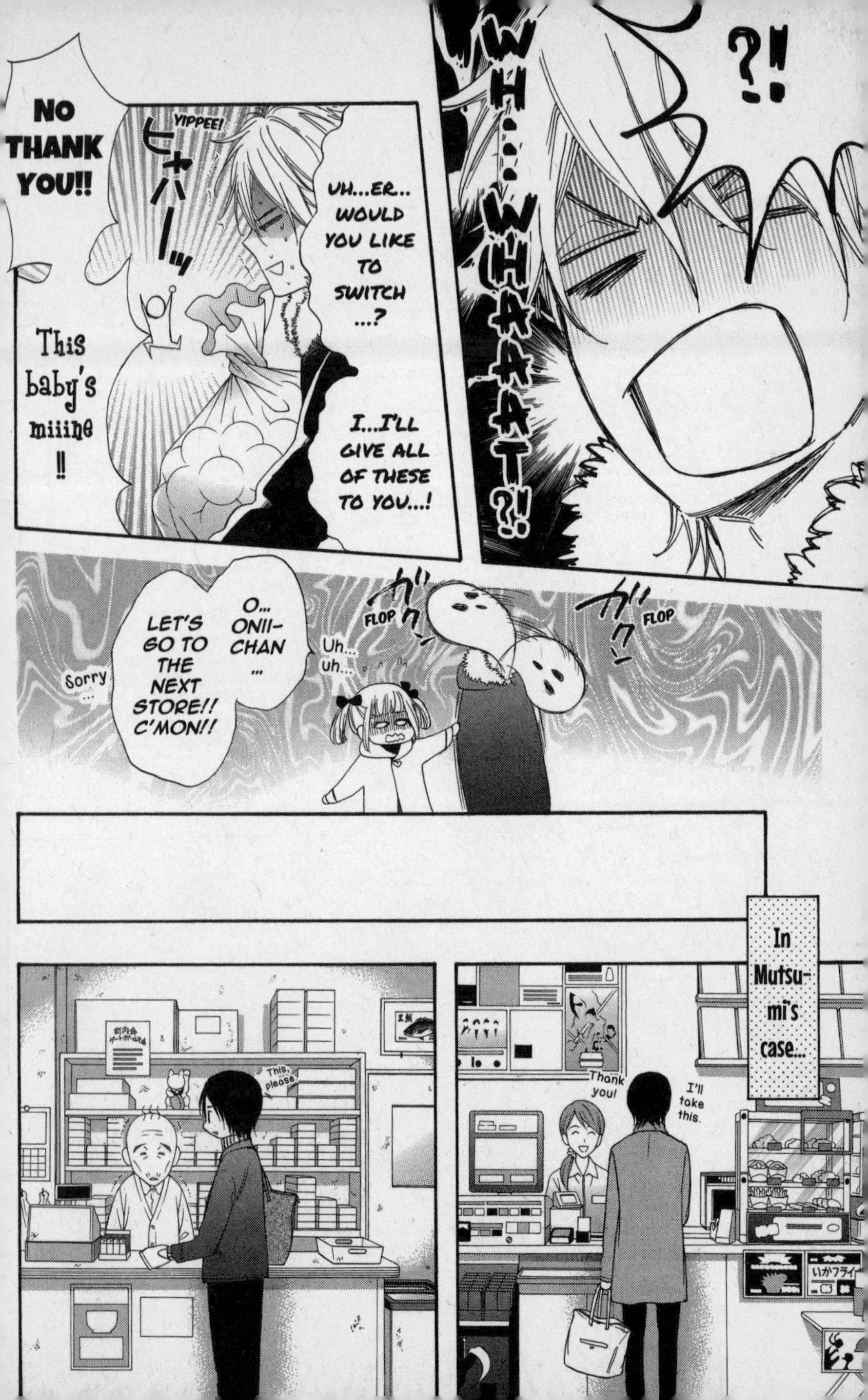
?!!
WH...WHAAAT?!!
UH...ER... WOULD YOU LIKE TO SWITCH ...?
I...I'LL GIVE ALL OF THESE TO YOU...!
NO THANK YOU!!
YIPPEE!
ヒャハーッ
This baby's miiine!!
FLOP
FLOP
Uh... uh...
O... ONII-CHAN ...
LET'S GO TO THE NEXT STORE!! C'MON!!
Sorry ...
In Mutsu-mi's case...
I'll take this.
Thank you!
いかフライ
This, please.

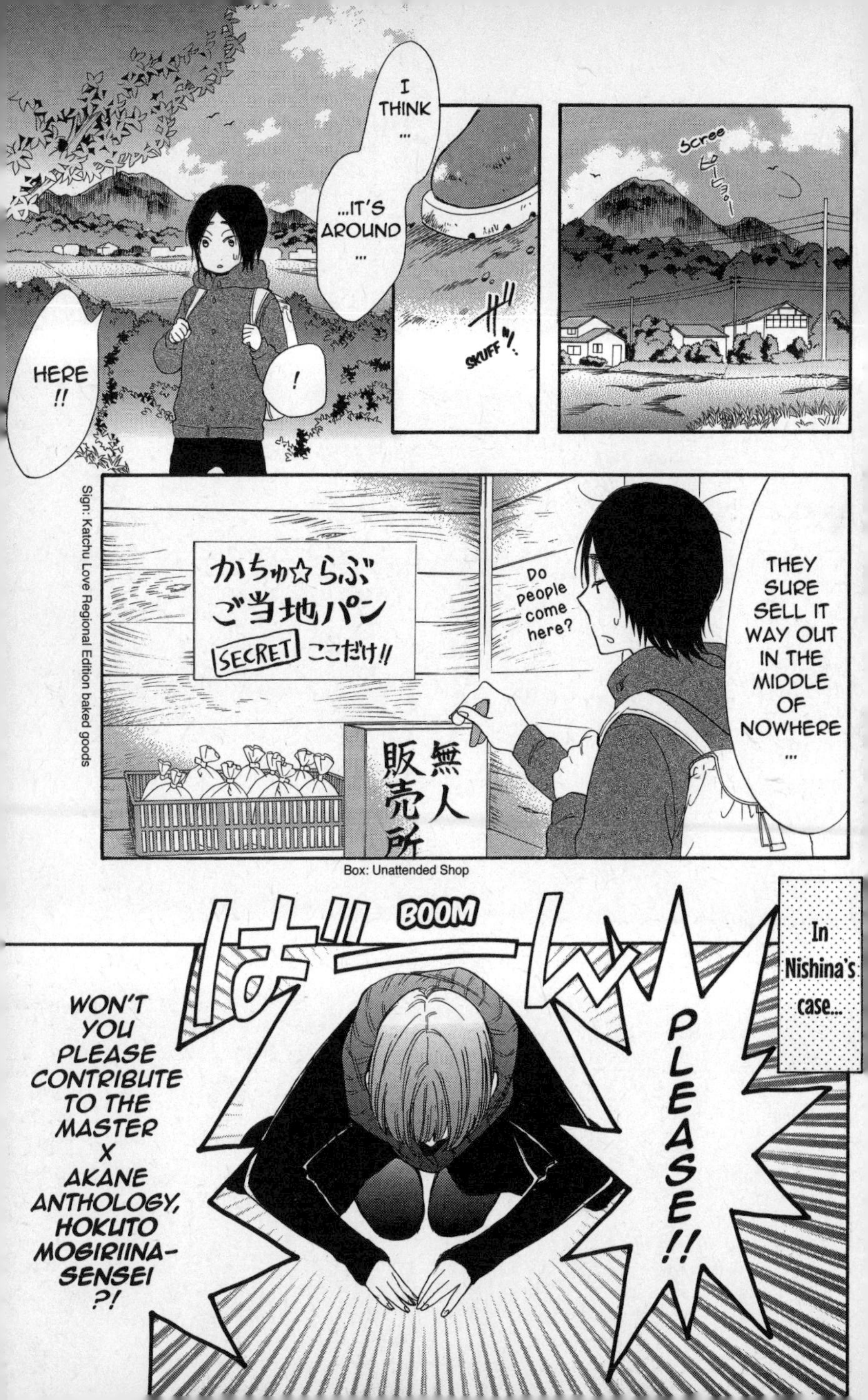
Scree
ピーヒョー
SKUFF
ザッ
I THINK ...
...IT'S AROUND ...
HERE!!
!
THEY SURE SELL IT WAY OUT IN THE MIDDLE OF NOWHERE ...
Do people come here?
かちゅ☆らぶ
ご当地パン
SECRET ここだけ!!
無人販売所
In Nishina's case...
BOOM
ばーん
PLEASE!!
WON'T YOU PLEASE CONTRIBUTE TO THE MASTER X AKANE ANTHOLOGY, HOKUTO MOGIRIINA-SENSEI ?!
Sign: Katchu Love Regional Edition baked goods
Box: Unattended Shop

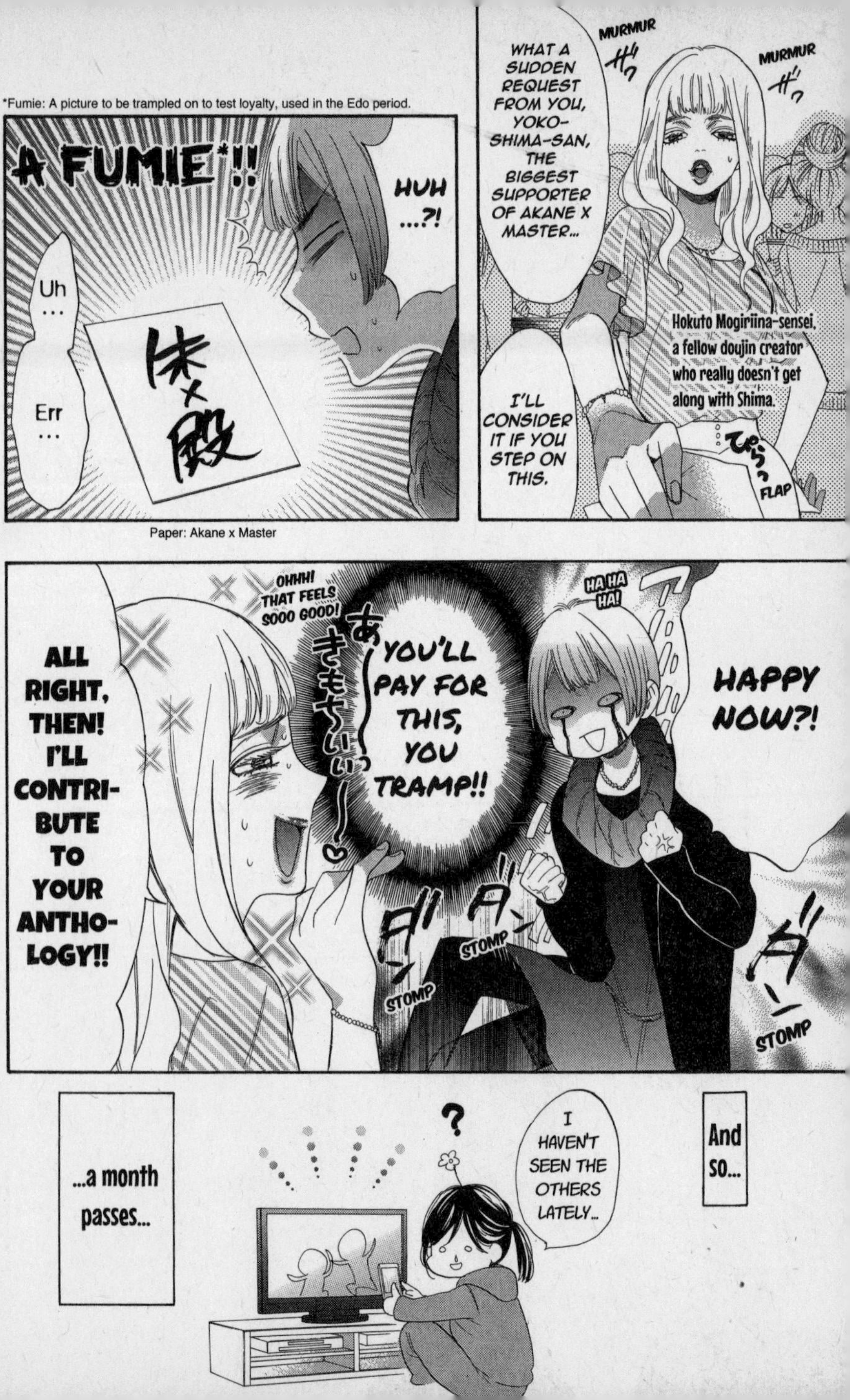

MURMUR
MURMUR
WHAT A SUDDEN REQUEST FROM YOU, YOKO-SHIMA-SAN, THE BIGGEST SUPPORTER OF AKANE X MASTER...
Hokuto Mogiriina-sensei, a fellow doujin creator who really doesn't get along with Shima.
I'LL CONSIDER IT IF YOU STEP ON THIS.
FLAP
*Fumie: A picture to be trampled on to test loyalty, used in the Edo period.
A FUMIE*!!
HUH ...?!
Uh ...
Err ...
Paper: Akane x Master
HAPPY NOW?!
HA HA HA!
YOU'LL PAY FOR THIS, YOU TRAMP!!
あ～きもちいい～っ♥
OHHH! THAT FEELS SOOO GOOD!
ALL RIGHT, THEN! I'LL CONTRI-BUTE TO YOUR ANTHO-LOGY!!
STOMP
STOMP
STOMP
And so...
I HAVEN'T SEEN THE OTHERS LATELY...
?
...a month passes...

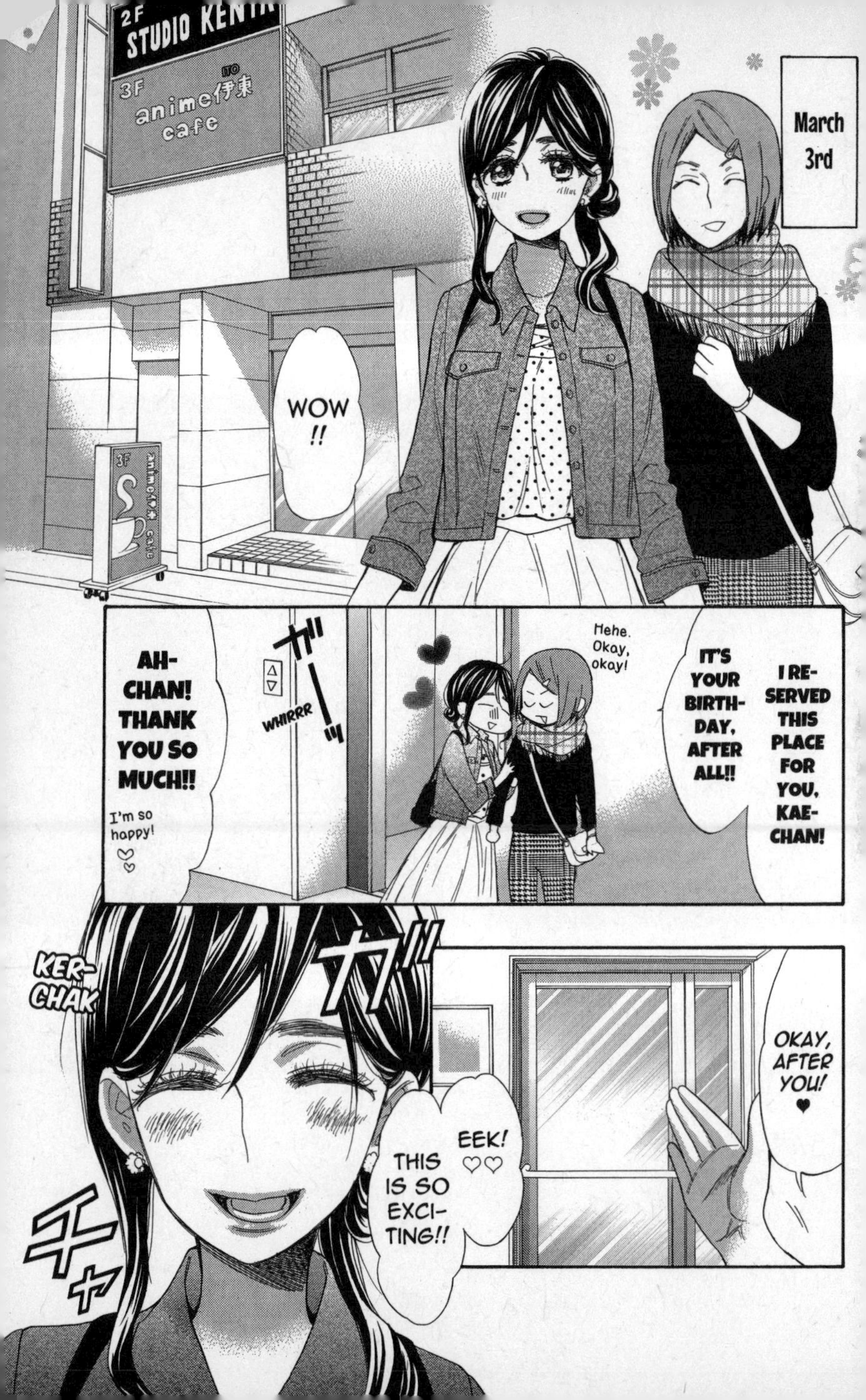
March 3rd
2F STUDIO KENTR
3F anime伊東 cafe
ITO
WOW!!
I RE-SERVED THIS PLACE FOR YOU, KAE-CHAN!
IT'S YOUR BIRTH-DAY, AFTER ALL!!
Hehe. Okay, okay!
ガーッ
WHIRRR
AH-CHAN! THANK YOU SO MUCH!!
I'm so happy! ♡♡
OKAY, AFTER YOU! ♥
ガ
KER-CHAK
チャ
EEK! ♡♡
THIS IS SO EXCI-TING!!

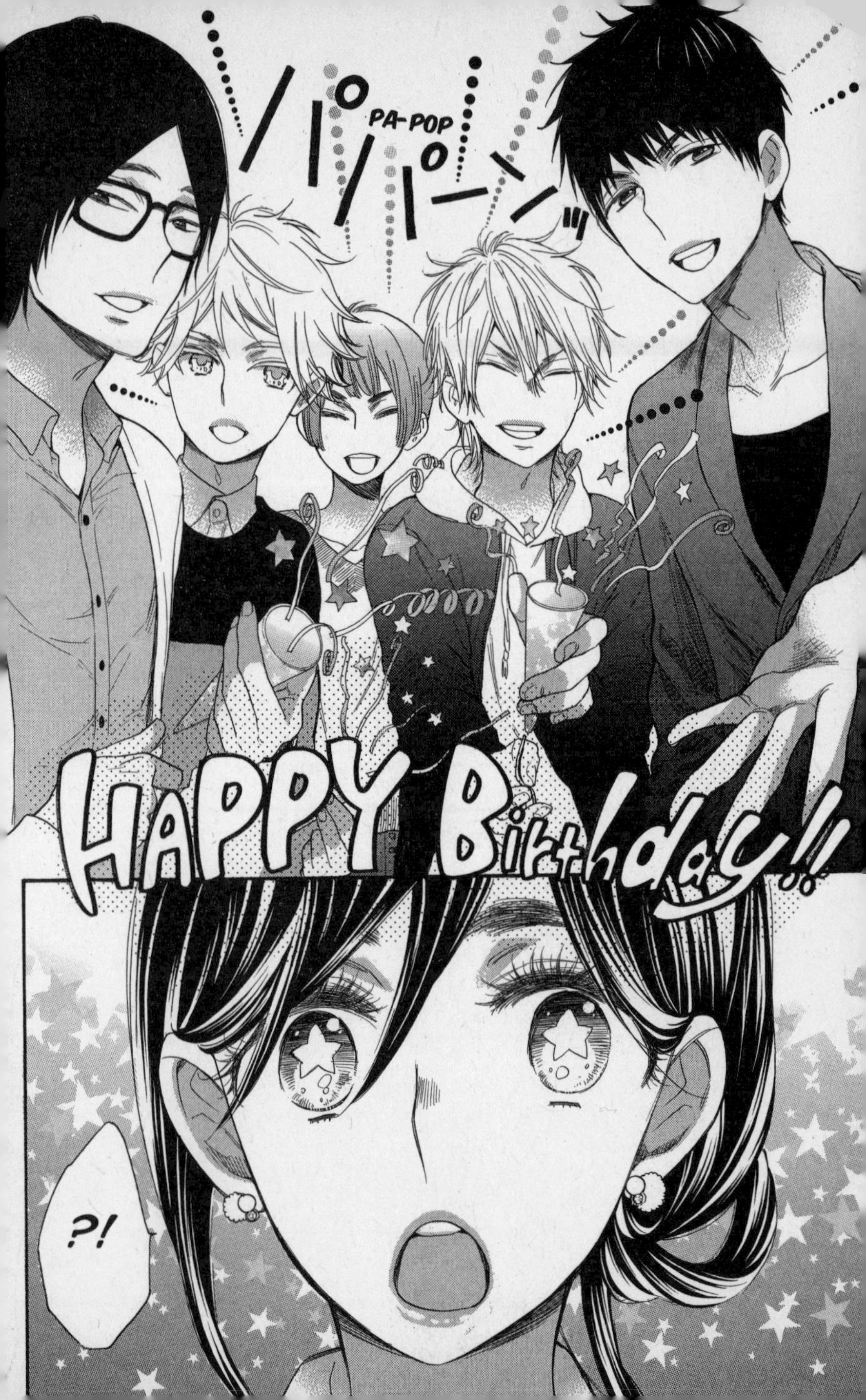
パパーンッ
PA-POP
HAPPY Birthday!!
?!

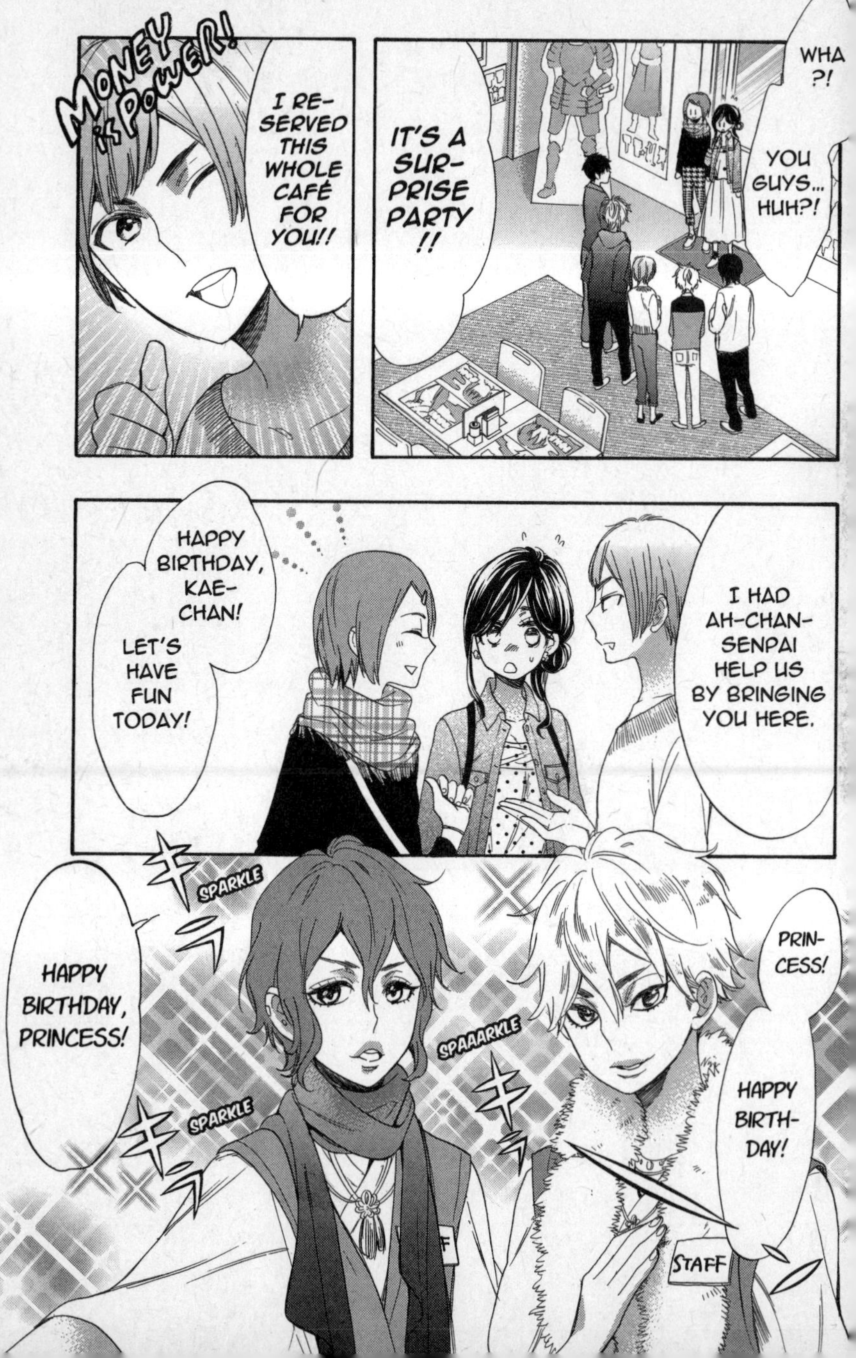
WHA?!
YOU GUYS... HUH?!
IT'S A SURPRISE PARTY!!
I RESERVED THIS WHOLE CAFÉ FOR YOU!!
MONEY is POWER!
I HAD AH-CHAN-SENPAI HELP US BY BRINGING YOU HERE.
HAPPY BIRTHDAY, KAE-CHAN!
LET'S HAVE FUN TODAY!
PRINCESS!
HAPPY BIRTHDAY!
STAFF
SPAAARKLE
SPARKLE
SPARKLE
HAPPY BIRTHDAY, PRINCESS!

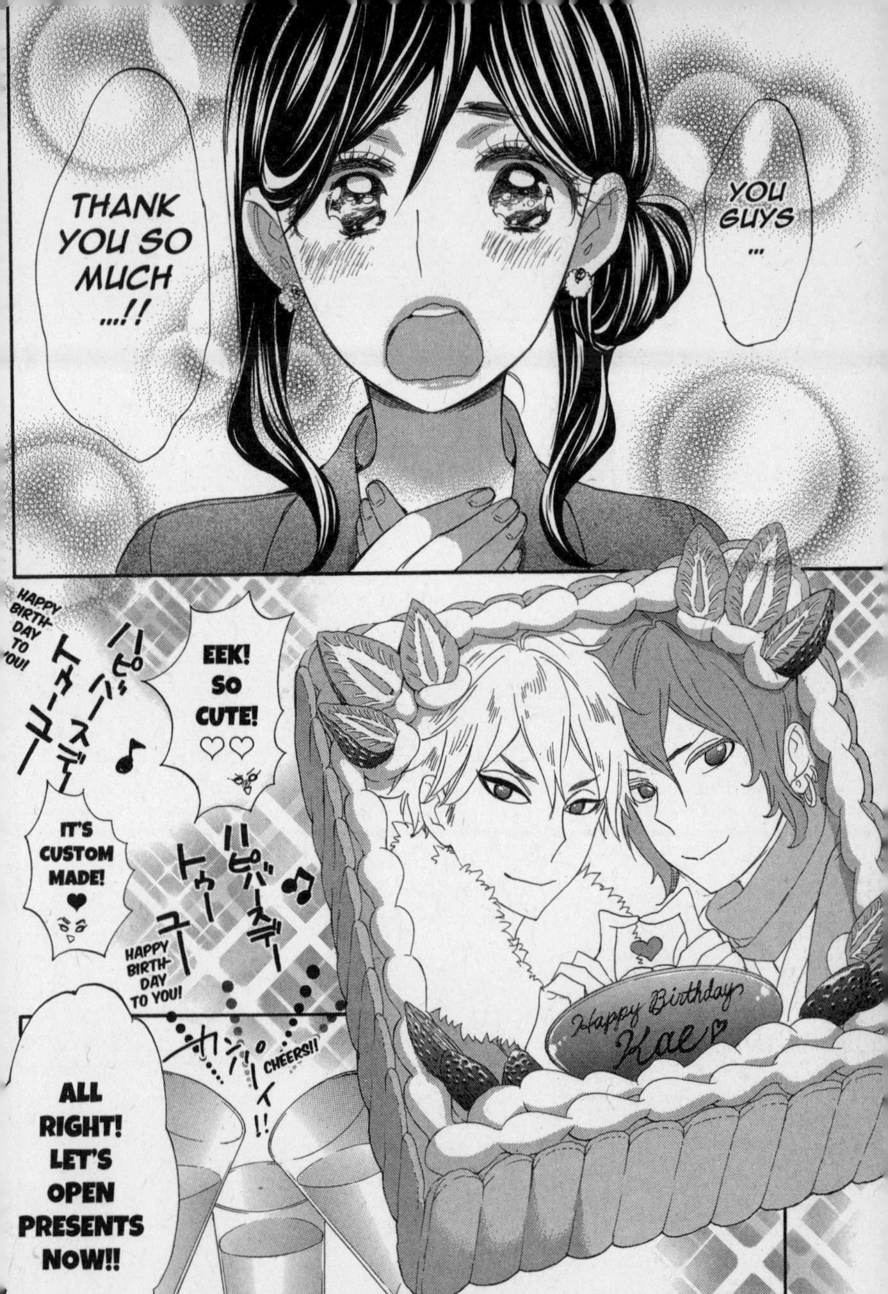
YOU GUYS ...
THANK YOU SO MUCH ...!!
Happy Birthday Kae♥
EEK! SO CUTE! ♡♡
ハピバースデー トゥーユー
HAPPY BIRTHDAY TO YOU!
ハピバースデー トゥーユー
HAPPY BIRTHDAY TO YOU!
IT'S CUSTOM MADE! ♥
カンパーイ!!
CHEERS!!
ALL RIGHT! LET'S OPEN PRESENTS NOW!!

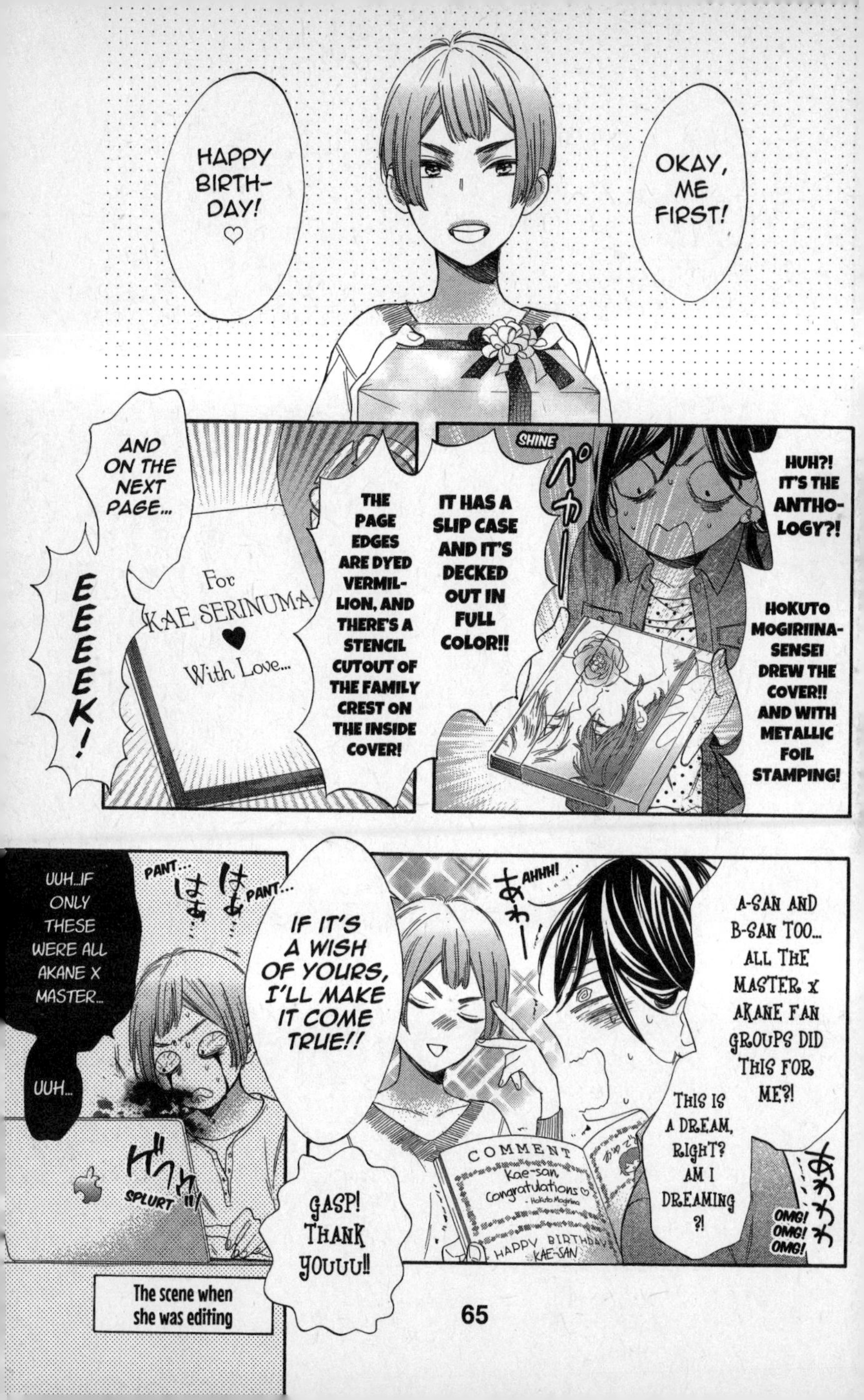
OKAY, ME FIRST!
HAPPY BIRTHDAY! ♡
SHINE
HUH?! IT'S THE ANTHOLOGY?!
HOKUTO MOGIRIINA-SENSEI DREW THE COVER!! AND WITH METALLIC FOIL STAMPING!
IT HAS A SLIP CASE AND IT'S DECKED OUT IN FULL COLOR!!
THE PAGE EDGES ARE DYED VERMILLION, AND THERE'S A STENCIL CUTOUT OF THE FAMILY CREST ON THE INSIDE COVER!
For KAE SERINUMA ♥ With Love...
AND ON THE NEXT PAGE...
EEEEEK!
AHHH!
A-SAN AND B-SAN TOO... ALL THE MASTER x AKANE FAN GROUPS DID THIS FOR ME?!
THIS IS A DREAM, RIGHT? AM I DREAMING?!
OMG! OMG! OMG!
COMMENT
Kae-san, Congratulations ♡ - Hokuto Mogirina
HAPPY BIRTHDAY KAE-SAN
IF IT'S A WISH OF YOURS, I'LL MAKE IT COME TRUE!!
GASP! THANK YOUUU!!
UUH...IF ONLY THESE WERE ALL AKANE X MASTER...
PANT... PANT...
UUH...
SPLURT
The scene when she was editing

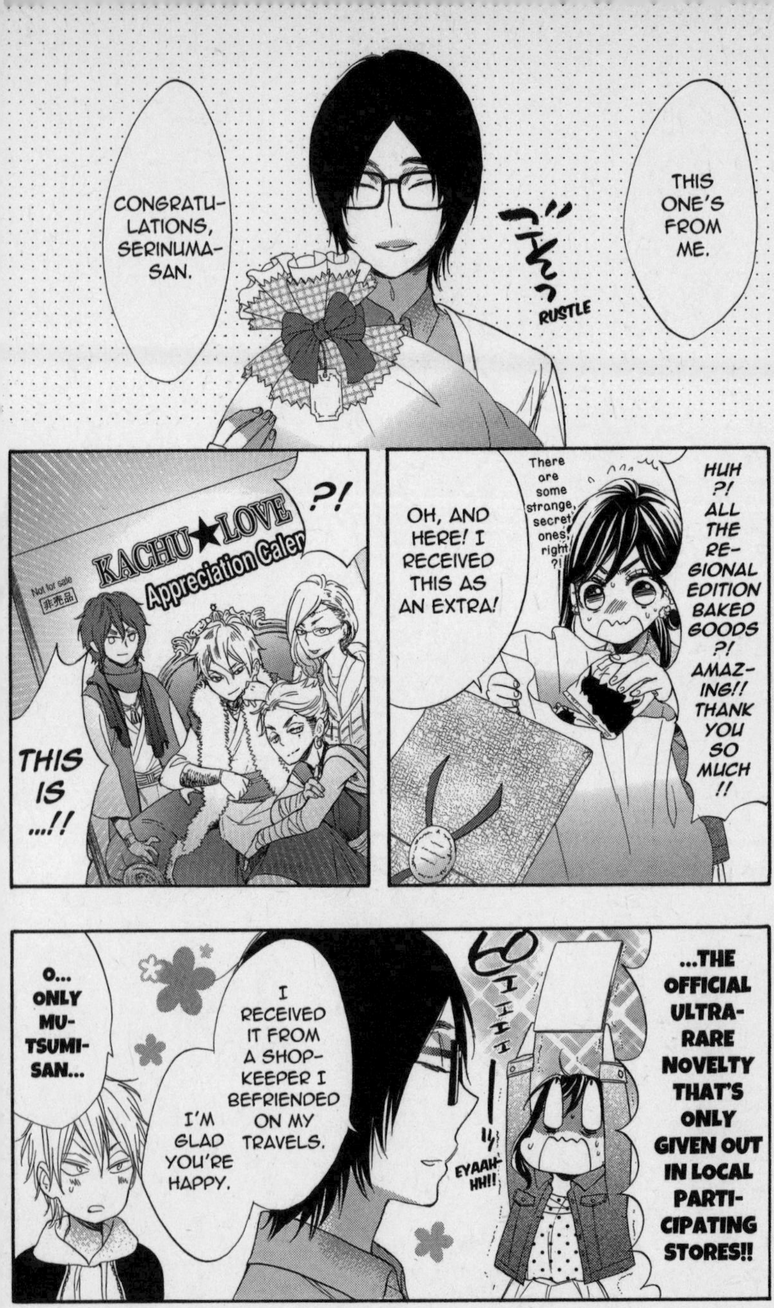
THIS ONE'S FROM ME.
RUSTLE
CONGRATULATIONS, SERINUMA-SAN.
HUH?! ALL THE REGIONAL EDITION BAKED GOODS?! AMAZING!! THANK YOU SO MUCH!!
There are some strange, secret ones, right?!
OH, AND HERE! I RECEIVED THIS AS AN EXTRA!
?!
KACHU★LOVE
Appreciation Calen
Not for sale
非売品
THIS IS ...!!
...THE OFFICIAL ULTRA-RARE NOVELTY THAT'S ONLY GIVEN OUT IN LOCAL PARTICIPATING STORES!!
EYAAHHH!!
I RECEIVED IT FROM A SHOPKEEPER I BEFRIENDED ON MY TRAVELS.
I'M GLAD YOU'RE HAPPY.
O... ONLY MUTSUMI-SAN...

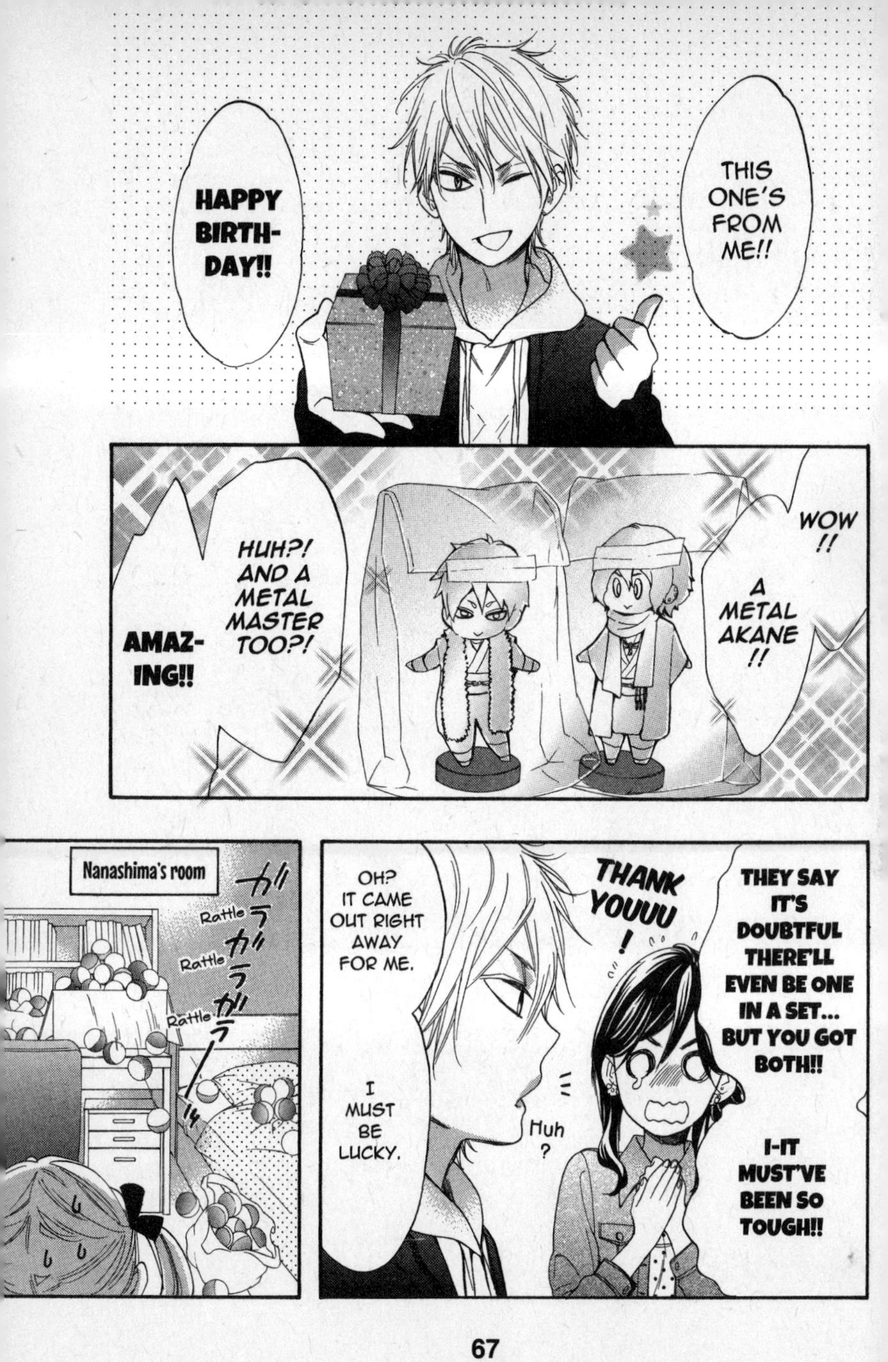
THIS ONE'S FROM ME!!
HAPPY BIRTH-DAY!!
WOW!!
A METAL AKANE!!
HUH?! AND A METAL MASTER TOO?!
AMAZ-ING!!
THEY SAY IT'S DOUBTFUL THERE'LL EVEN BE ONE IN A SET... BUT YOU GOT BOTH!!
THANK YOUUU!
OH? IT CAME OUT RIGHT AWAY FOR ME.
I-IT MUST'VE BEEN SO TOUGH!!
Huh?
I MUST BE LUCKY.
Nanashima's room
Rattle
Rattle
Rattle

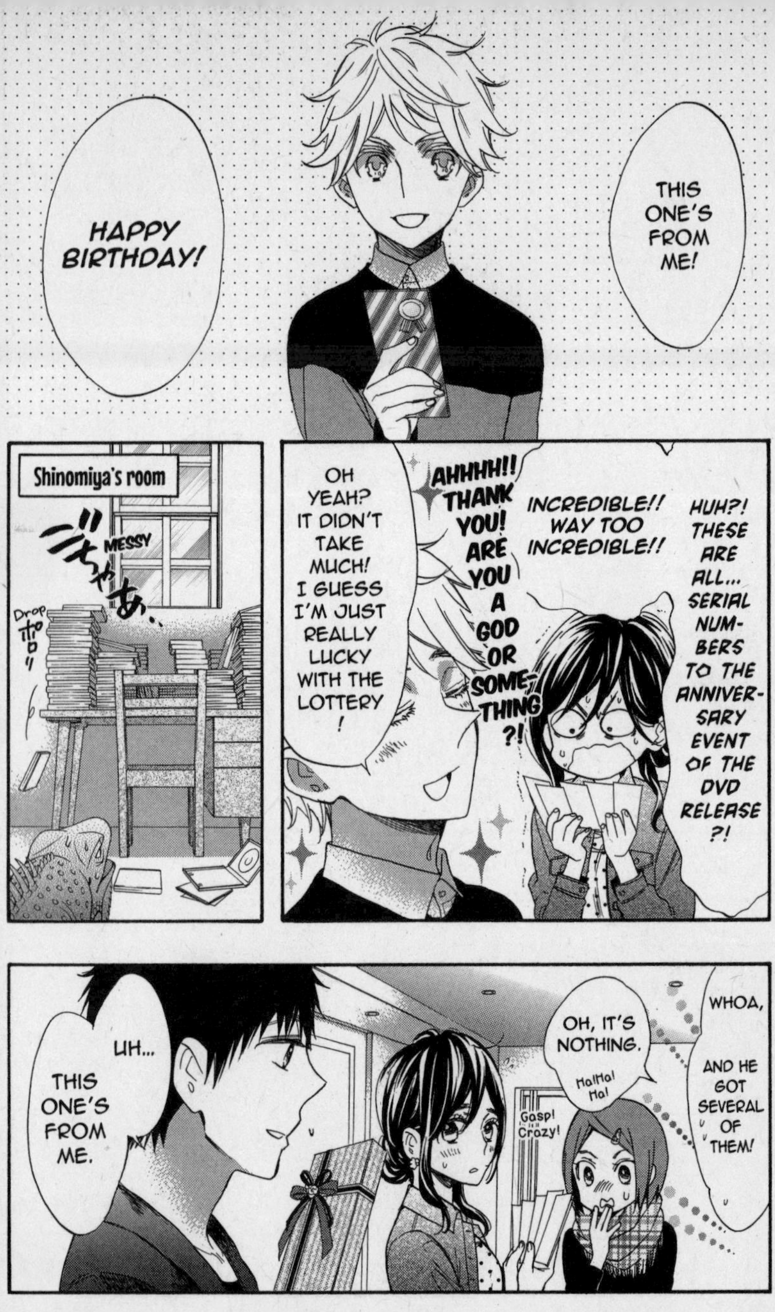
THIS ONE'S FROM ME!
HAPPY BIRTHDAY!
HUH?! THESE ARE ALL... SERIAL NUMBERS TO THE ANNIVERSARY EVENT OF THE DVD RELEASE?!
INCREDIBLE!! WAY TOO INCREDIBLE!!
AHHHH!! THANK YOU! ARE YOU A GOD OR SOMETHING?!
OH YEAH? IT DIDN'T TAKE MUCH! I GUESS I'M JUST REALLY LUCKY WITH THE LOTTERY!
Shinomiya's room
MESSY
Drop
WHOA, AND HE GOT SEVERAL OF THEM!
OH, IT'S NOTHING.
HaHa! Ha!
Gasp! Crazy!
UH... THIS ONE'S FROM ME.

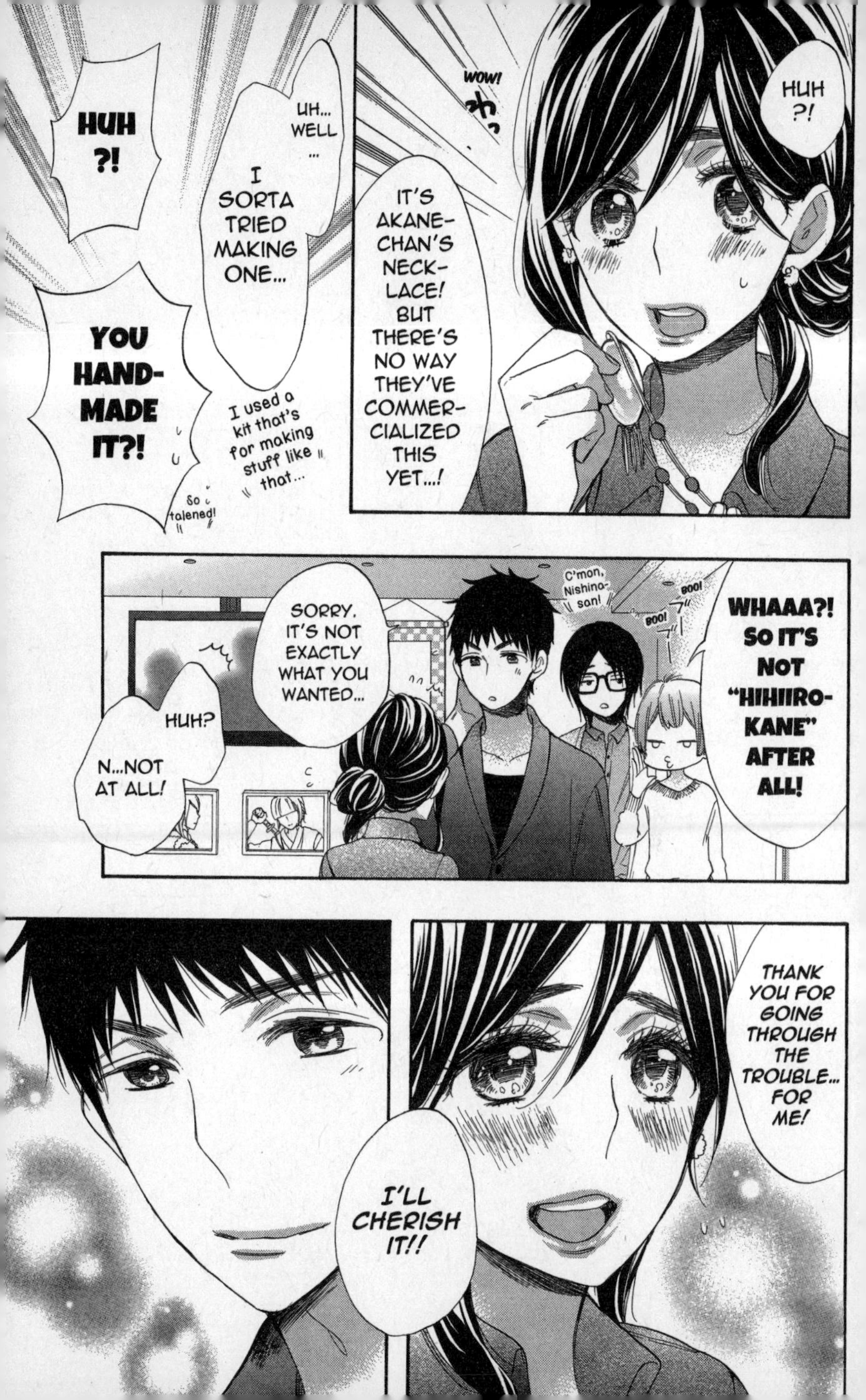
HUH ?!
WOW!
IT'S AKANE-CHAN'S NECK-LACE! BUT THERE'S NO WAY THEY'VE COMMER-CIALIZED THIS YET...!
UH... WELL ...
I SORTA TRIED MAKING ONE...
HUH ?!
YOU HAND-MADE IT?!
I used a kit that's for making stuff like that...
So talened!
WHAAA?! SO IT'S NOT "HIHIIRO-KANE" AFTER ALL!
BOO!
BOO!
C'mon, Nishino-san!
SORRY. IT'S NOT EXACTLY WHAT YOU WANTED...
HUH?
N...NOT AT ALL!
THANK YOU FOR GOING THROUGH THE TROUBLE... FOR ME!
I'LL CHERISH IT!!

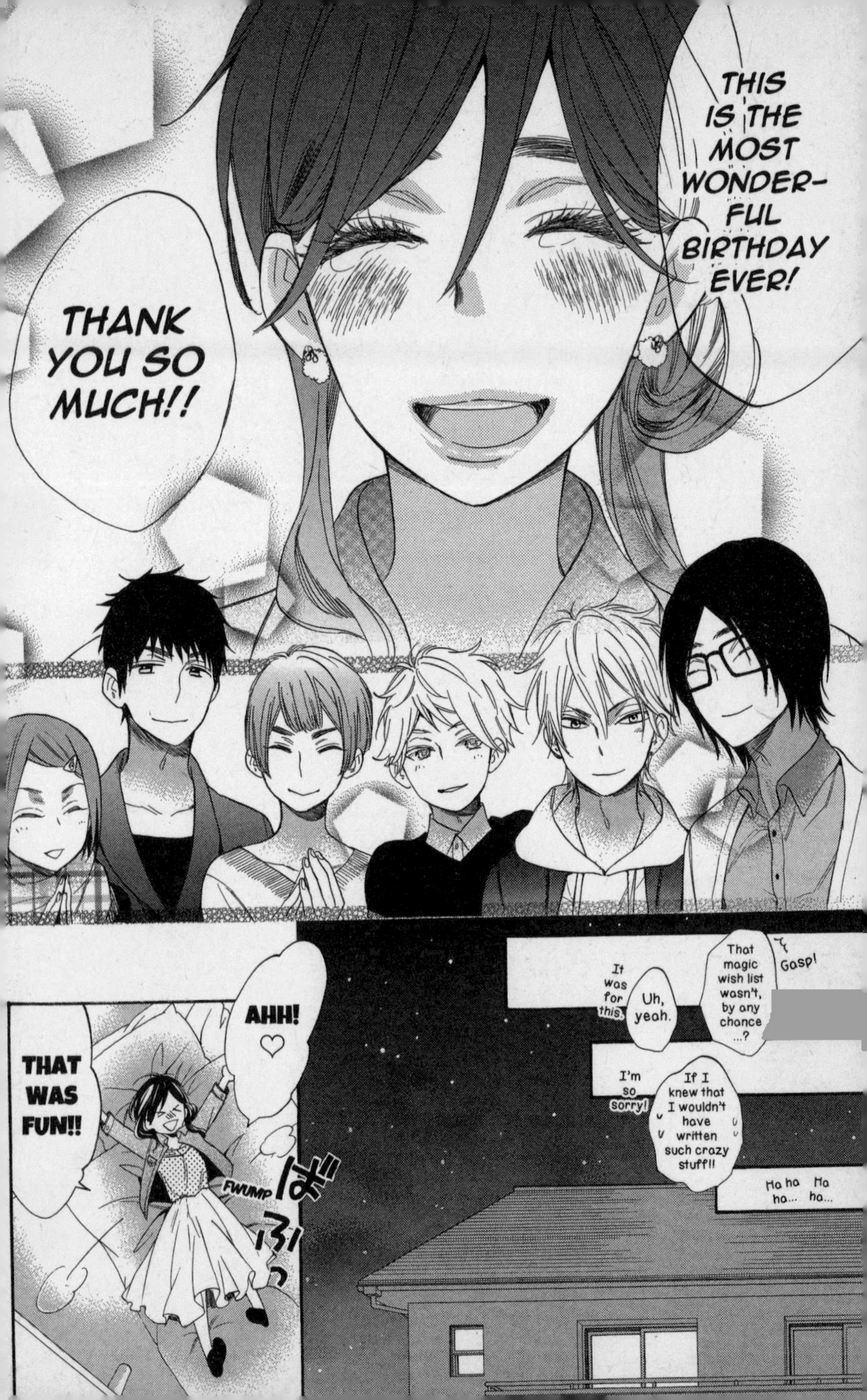
THIS IS THE MOST WONDERFUL BIRTHDAY EVER!
THANK YOU SO MUCH!!
Gasp!
That magic wish list wasn't, by any chance ...?
Uh, yeah.
It was for this.
If I knew that I wouldn't have written such crazy stuff!!
I'm so sorry!
Ha ha ha... Ha ha...
AHH! ♡
THAT WAS FUN!!
FWUMP

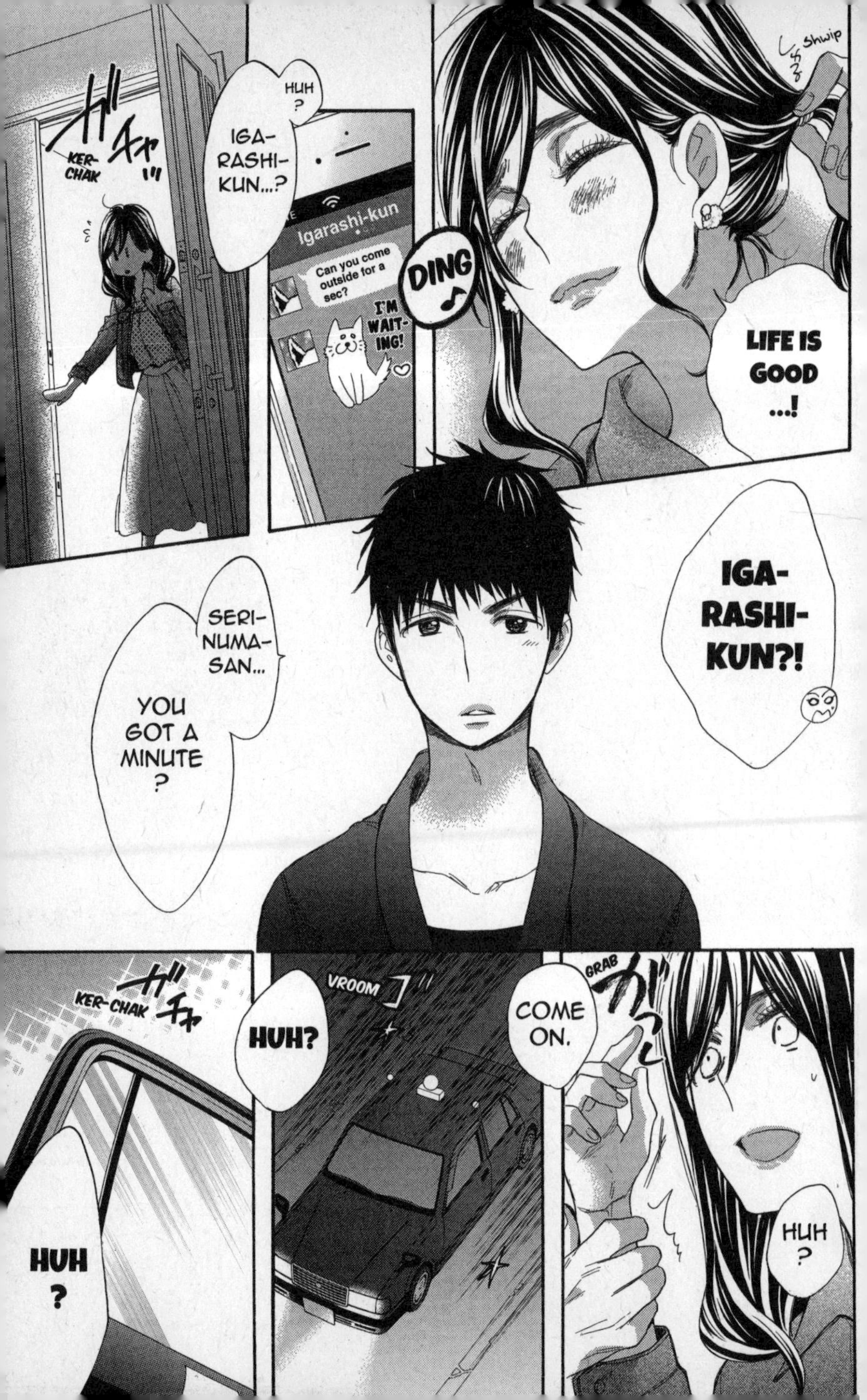
Shwip
DING
LIFE IS GOOD ...!
HUH ?
IGA-RASHI-KUN...?
Igarashi-kun
Can you come outside for a sec?
I'M WAIT-ING!
KER-CHAK
IGA-RASHI-KUN?!
SERI-NUMA-SAN...
YOU GOT A MINUTE ?
GRAB
COME ON.
HUH ?
VROOM
HUH?
KER-CHAK
HUH ?

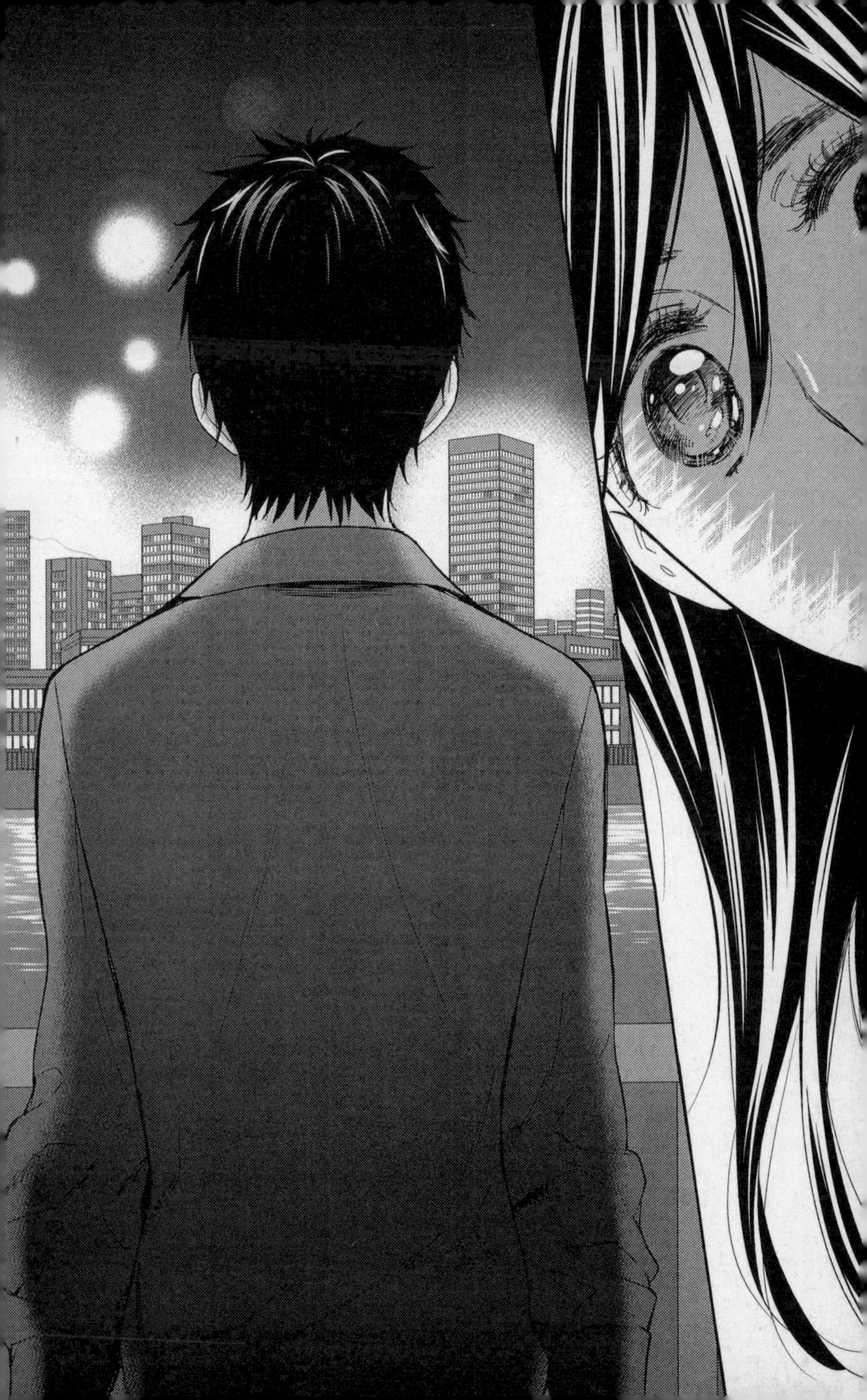

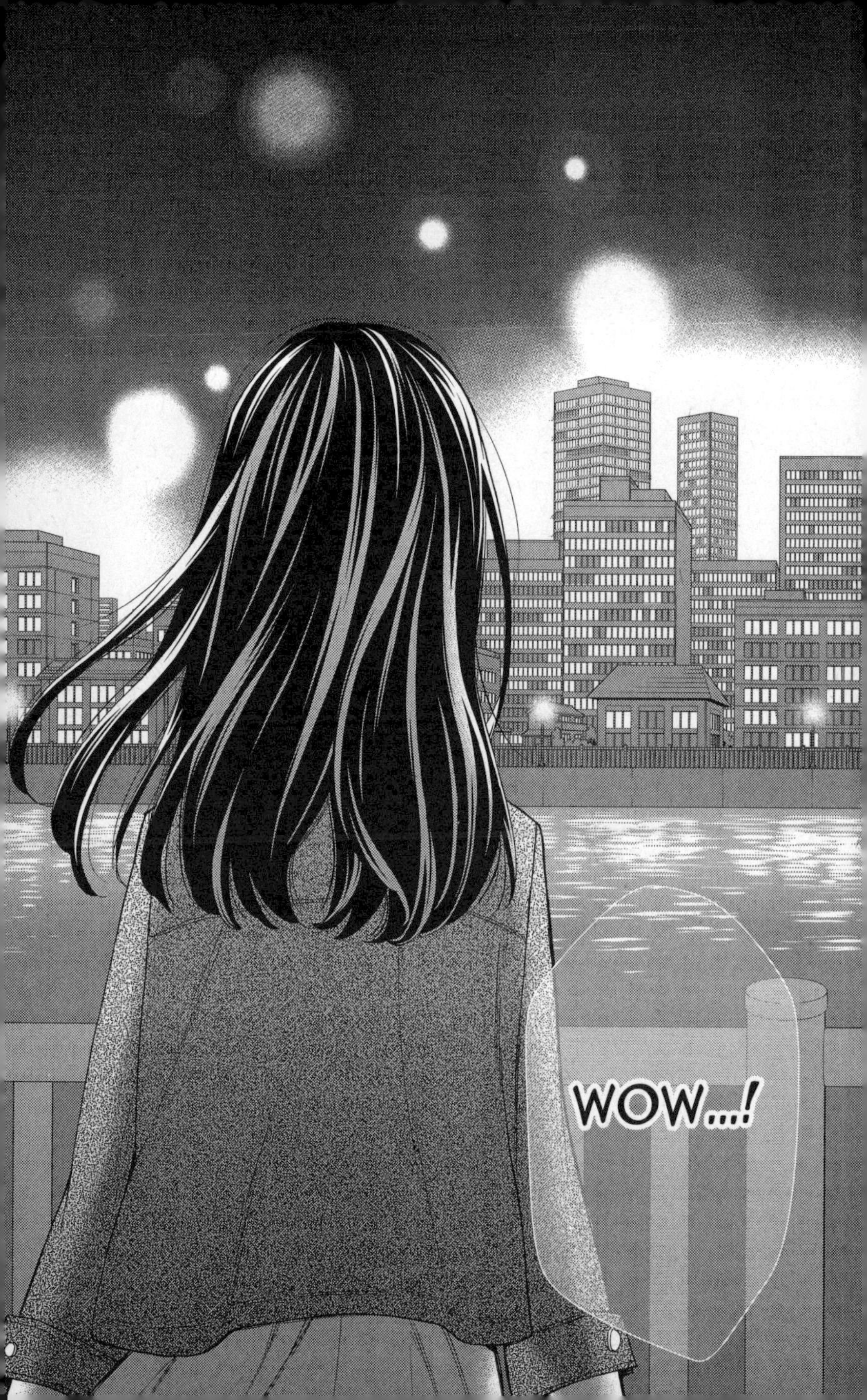
WOW...!

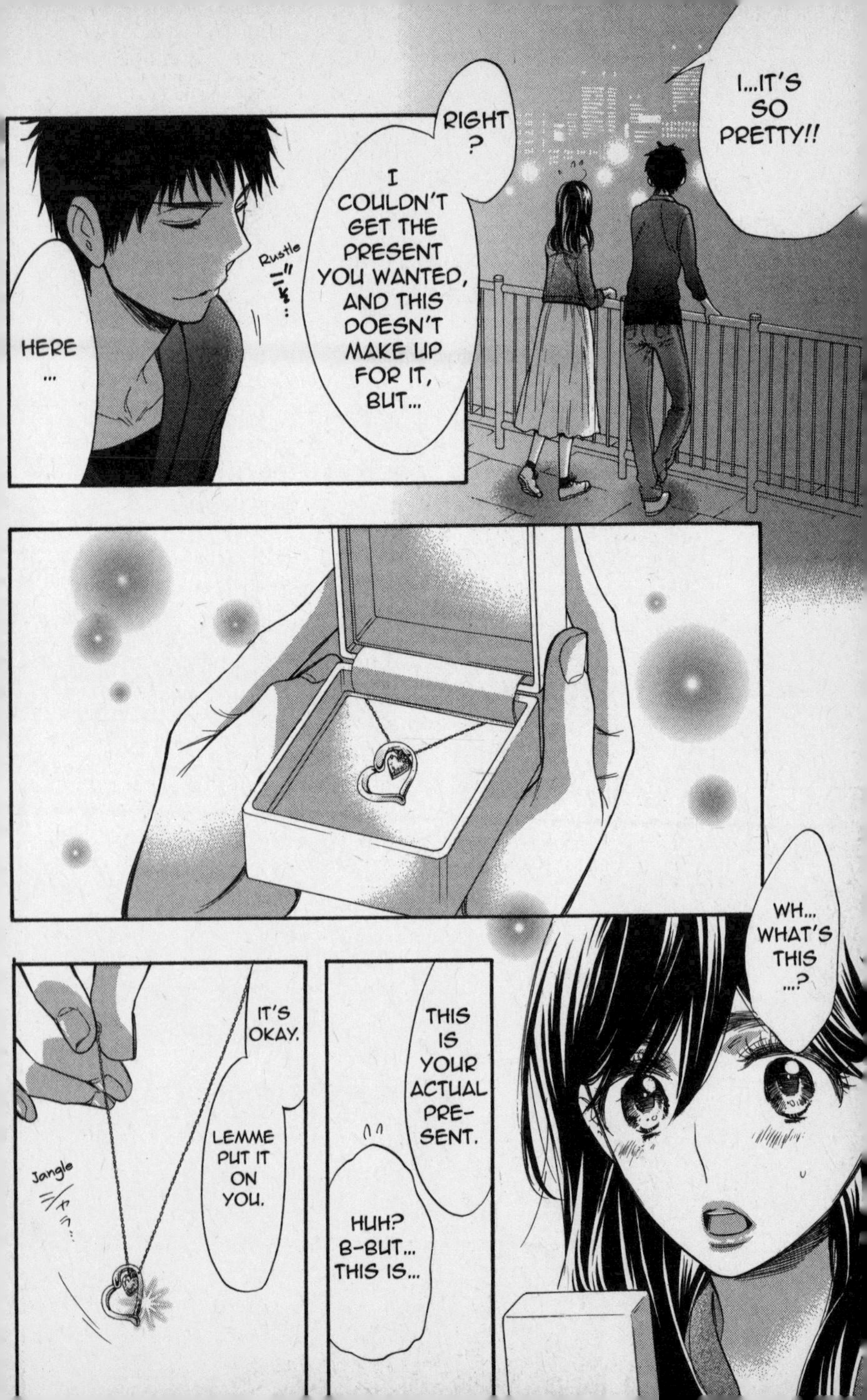
I...IT'S SO PRETTY!!
RIGHT?
I COULDN'T GET THE PRESENT YOU WANTED, AND THIS DOESN'T MAKE UP FOR IT, BUT...
Rustle
HERE...
WH... WHAT'S THIS ...?
THIS IS YOUR ACTUAL PRE-SENT.
HUH? B-BUT... THIS IS...
IT'S OKAY.
LEMME PUT IT ON YOU.
Jangle

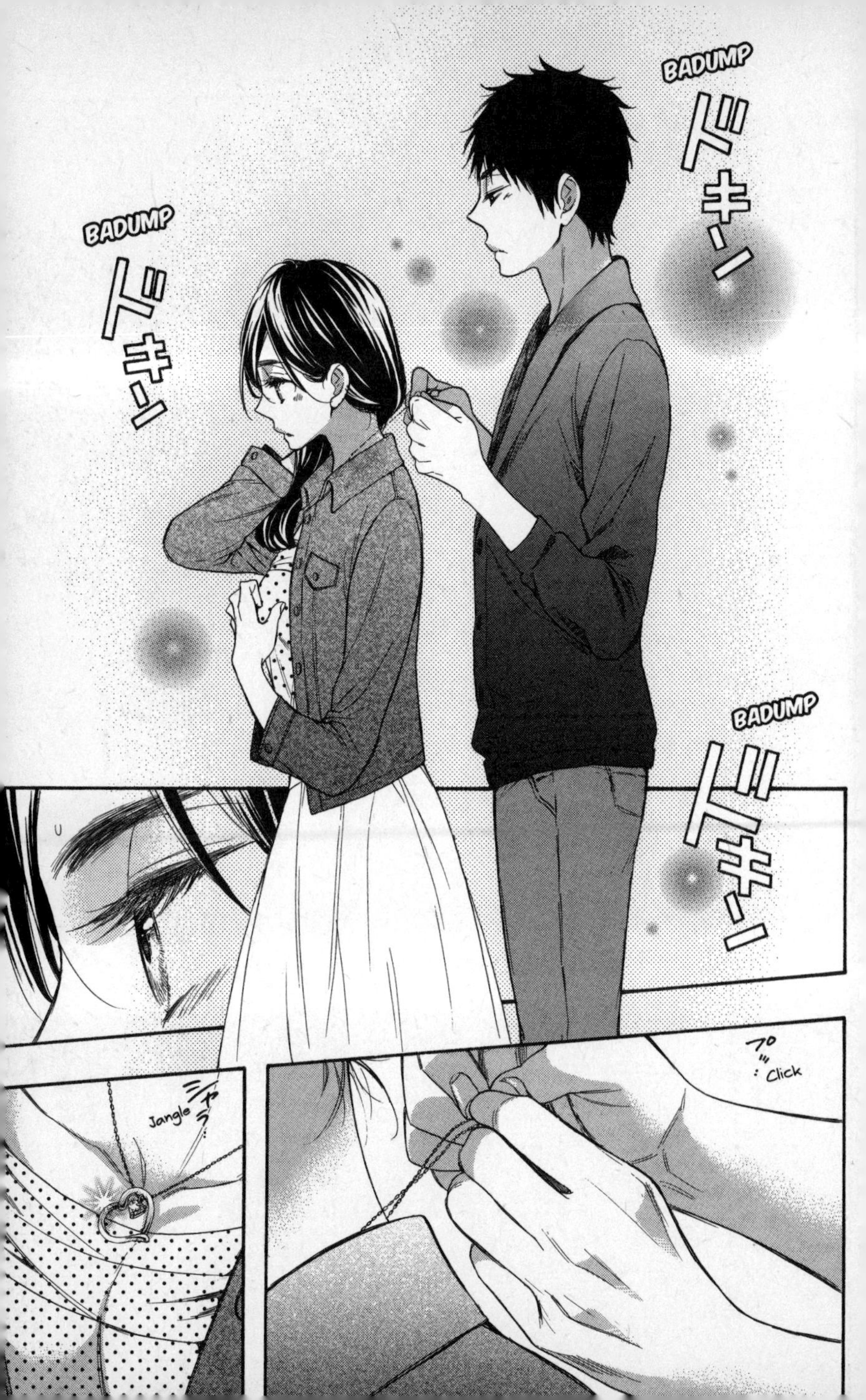
BADUMP
ドキーン
BADUMP
ドキーン
BADUMP
ドキーン
プ
Click
Jangle
シャラ

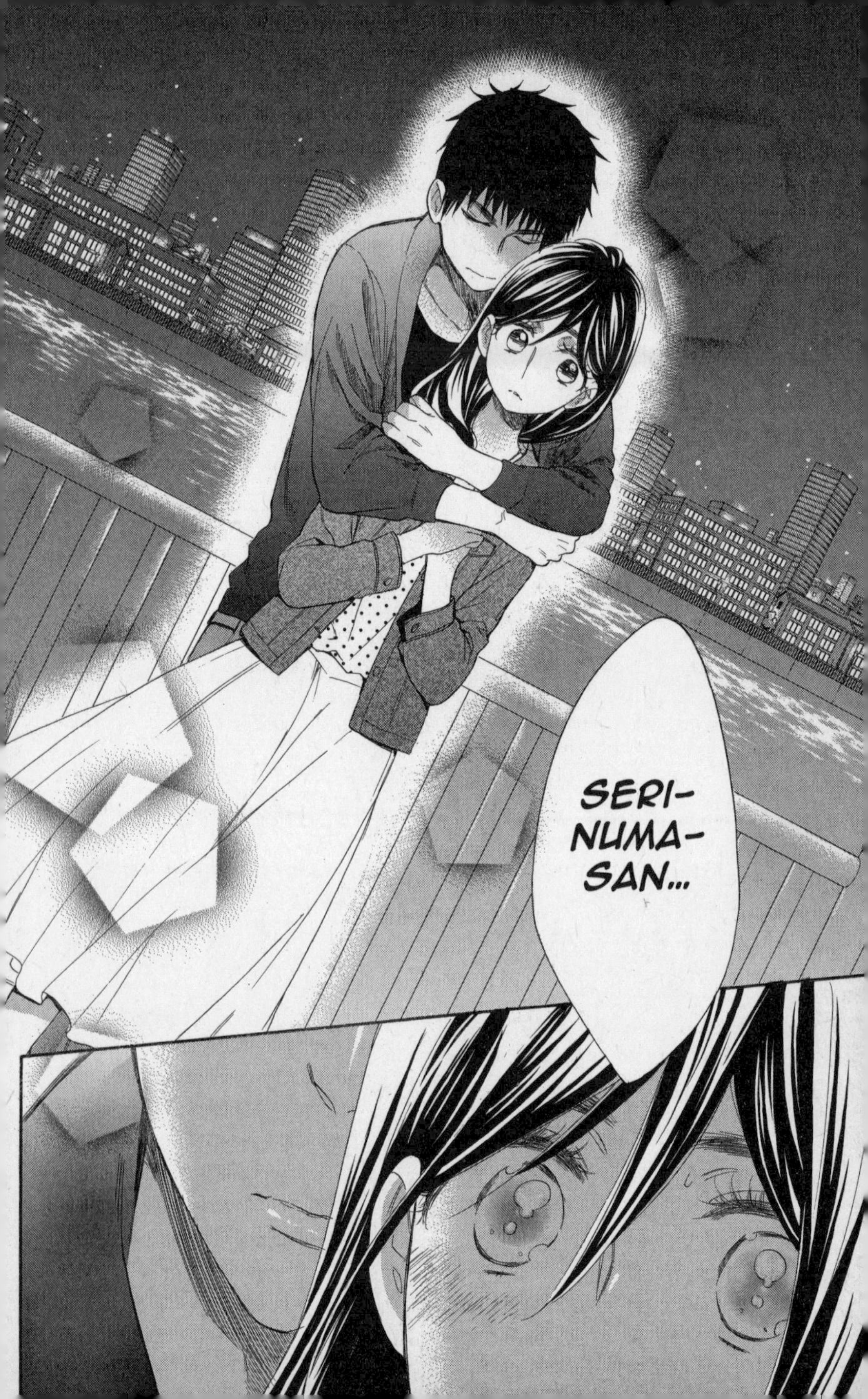
SERI-NUMA-SAN...

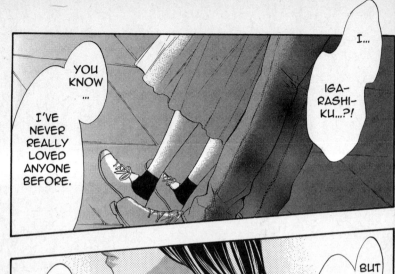

YOU KNOW ... I'VE NEVER REALLY LOVED ANYONE BEFORE.

I... IGA-RASHI-KU...?!

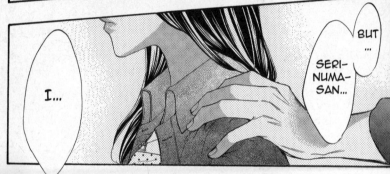

I...

BUT ... SERI-NUMA-SAN...

TRULY.

...LOVE YOU.

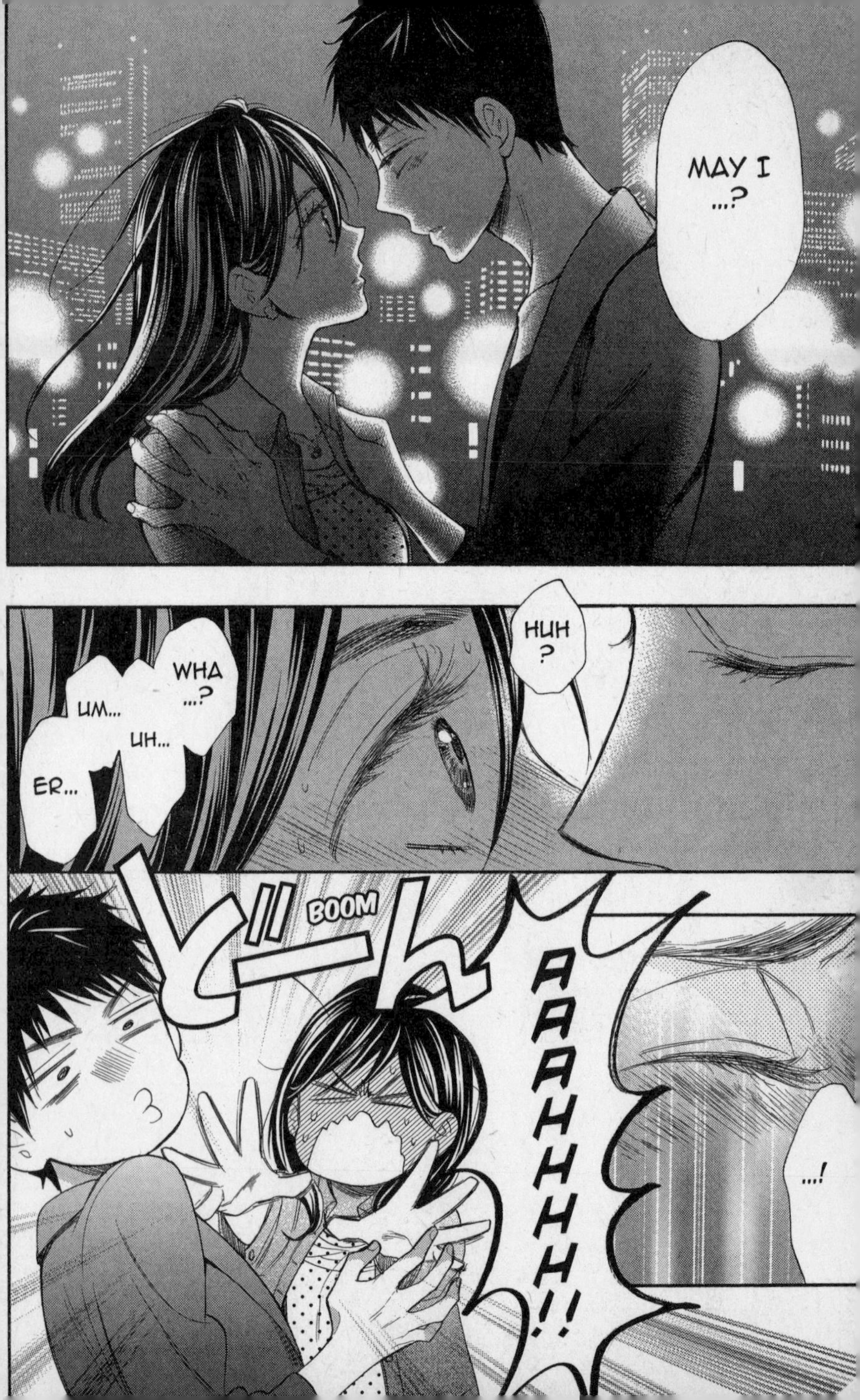
MAY I ...?
HUH ?
WHA ...?
UM...
UH...
ER...
BOOM
AAAHHHHH!!
...!

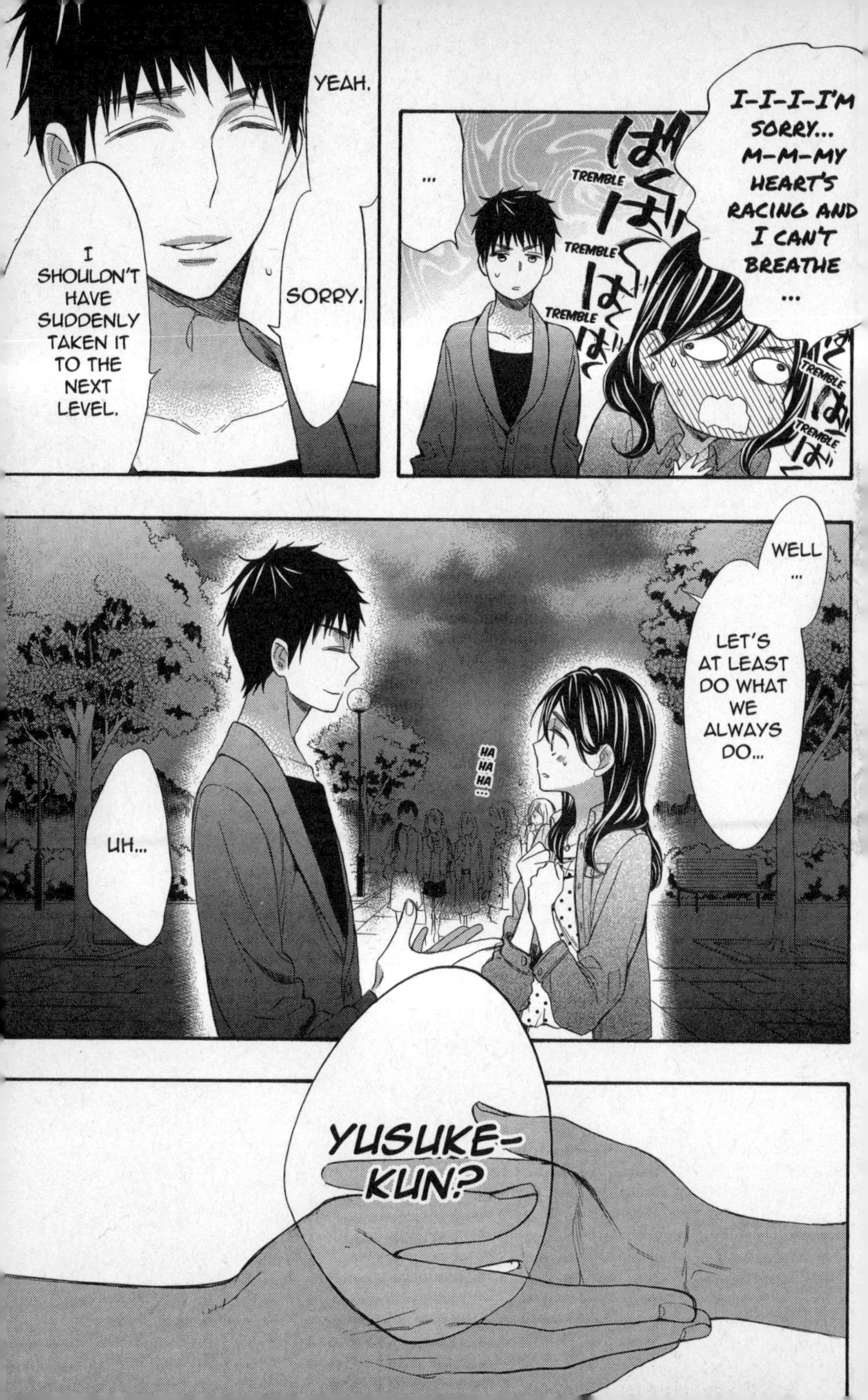
I-I-I-I'M SORRY... M-M-MY HEART'S RACING AND I CAN'T BREATHE ...
TREMBLE
TREMBLE
TREMBLE
TREMBLE
TREMBLE
...
YEAH.
SORRY.
I SHOULDN'T HAVE SUDDENLY TAKEN IT TO THE NEXT LEVEL.
WELL ...
LET'S AT LEAST DO WHAT WE ALWAYS DO...
HA HA HA...
UH...
YUSUKE-KUN?

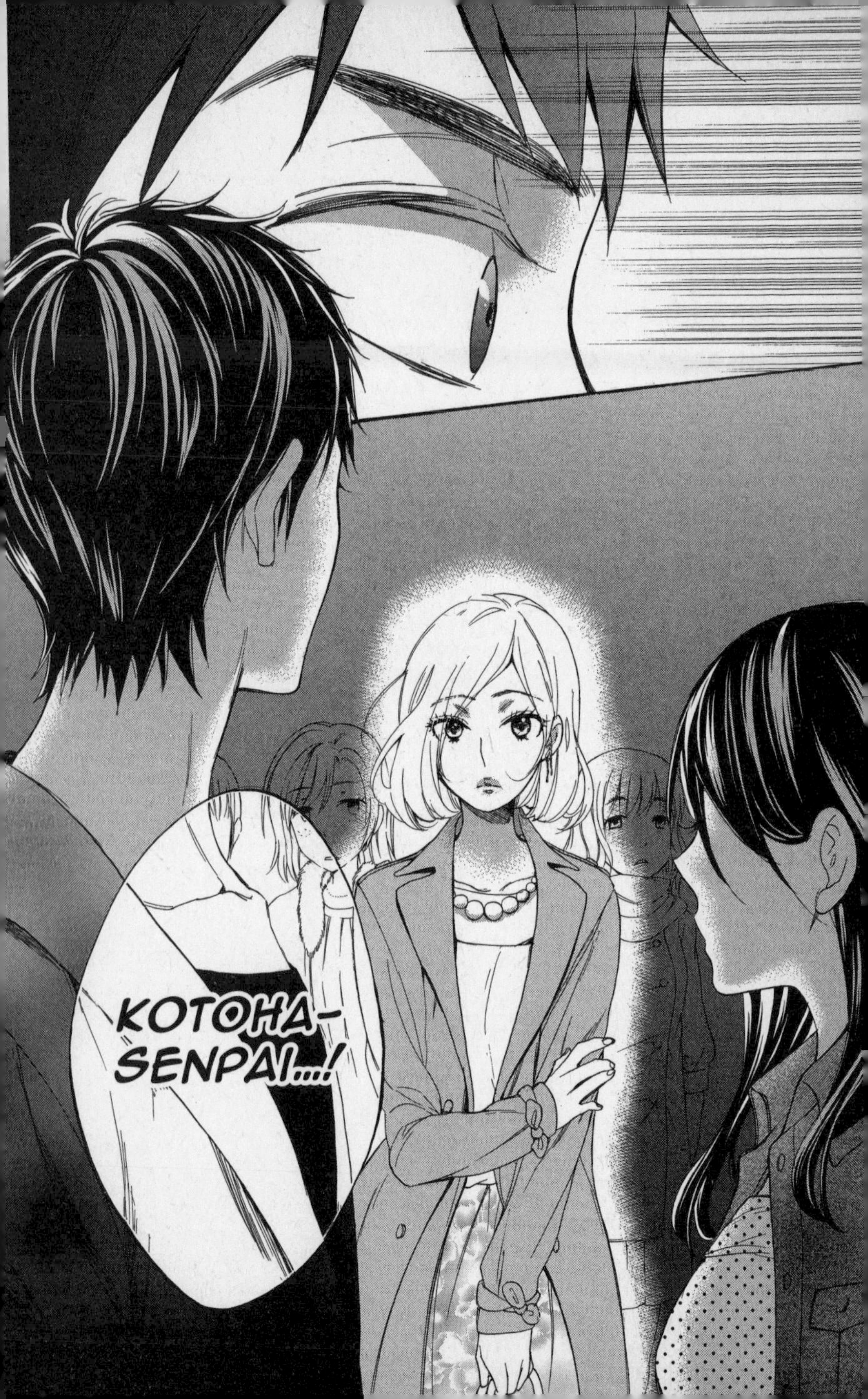
KOTOHA-SENPAI...!

#35 THE GIRL THAT I ACTUALLY LIKE

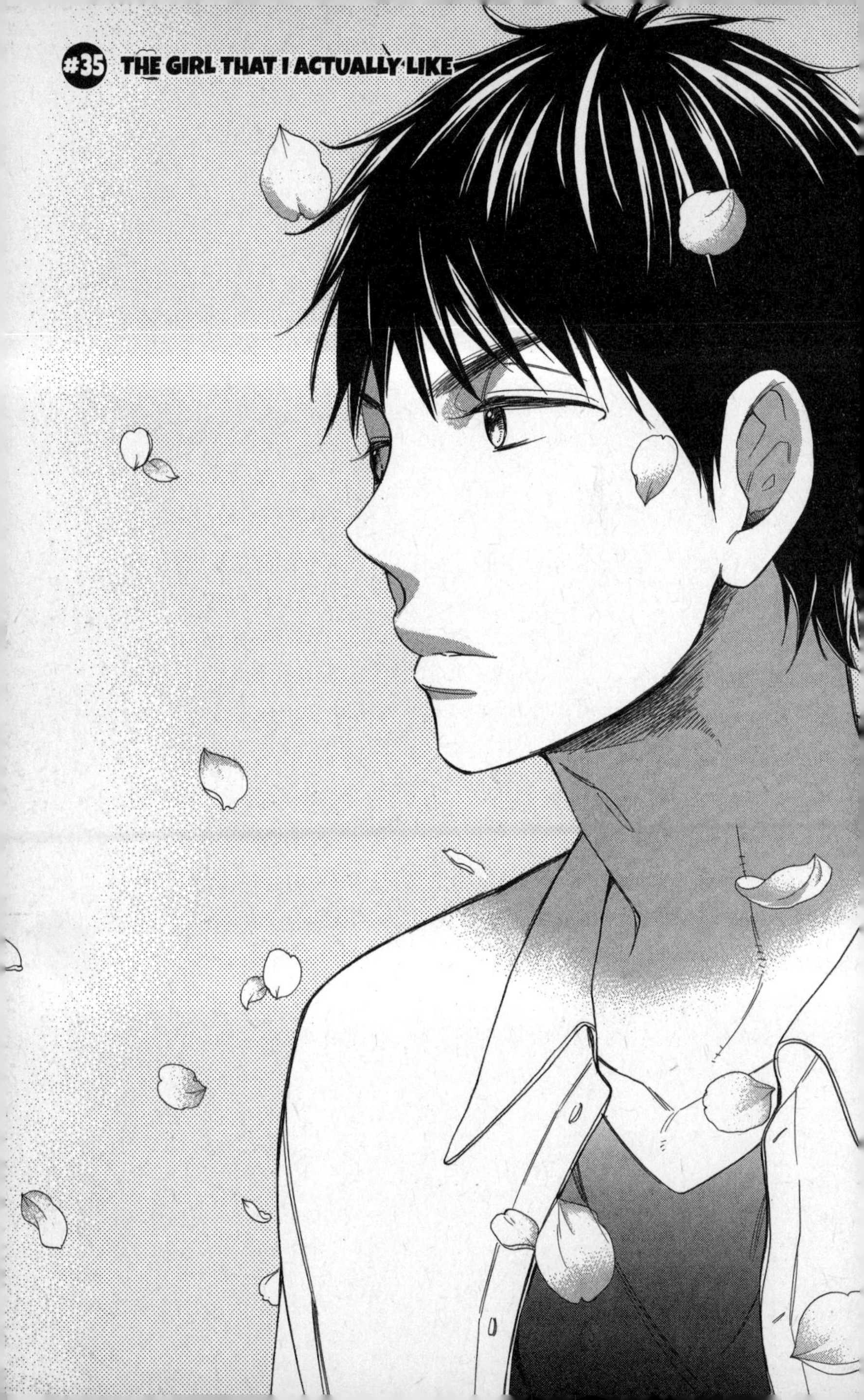

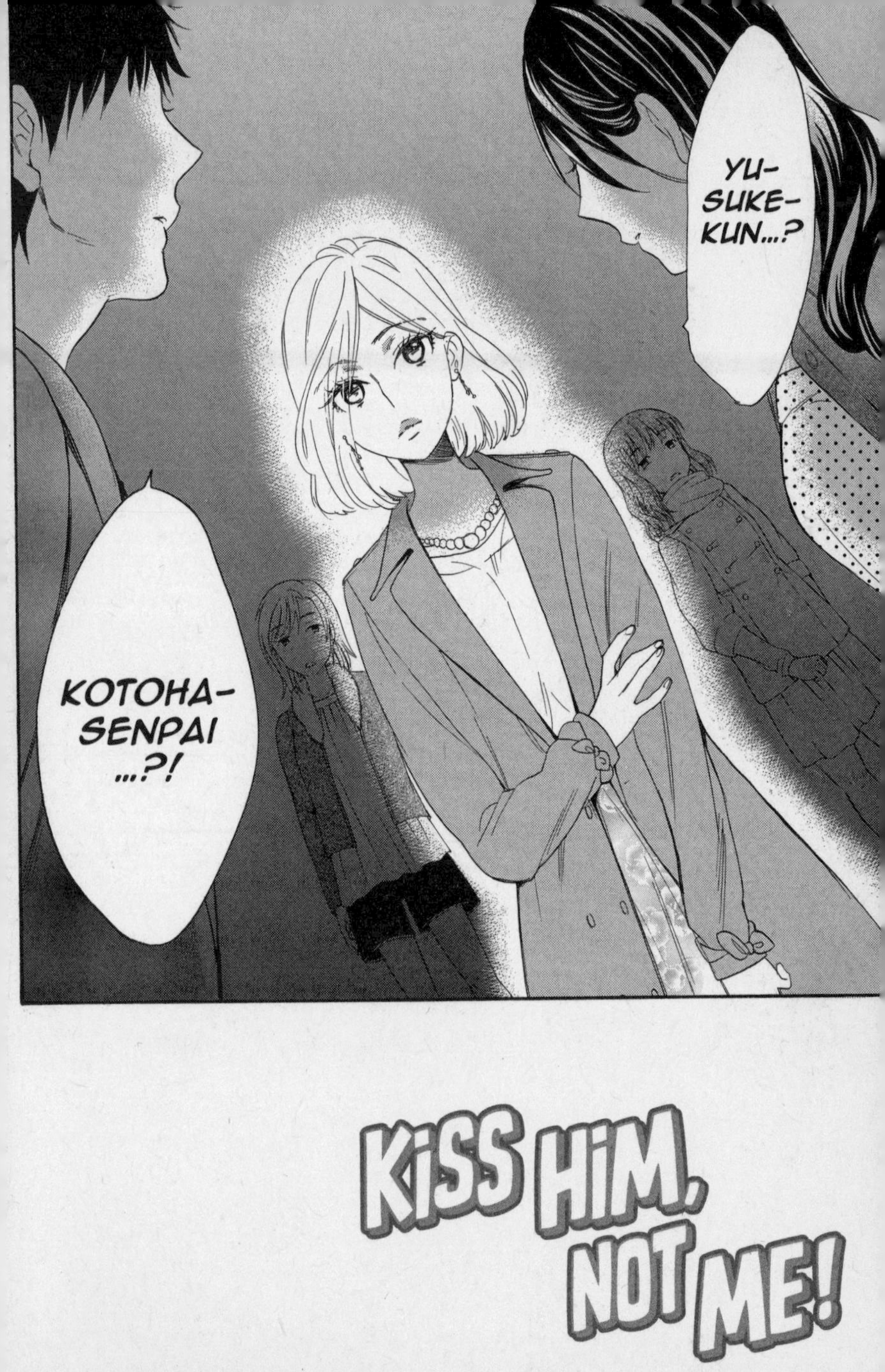
YU-SUKE-KUN...?
KOTOHA-SENPAI ...?!

KiSS HiM, NOT ME!

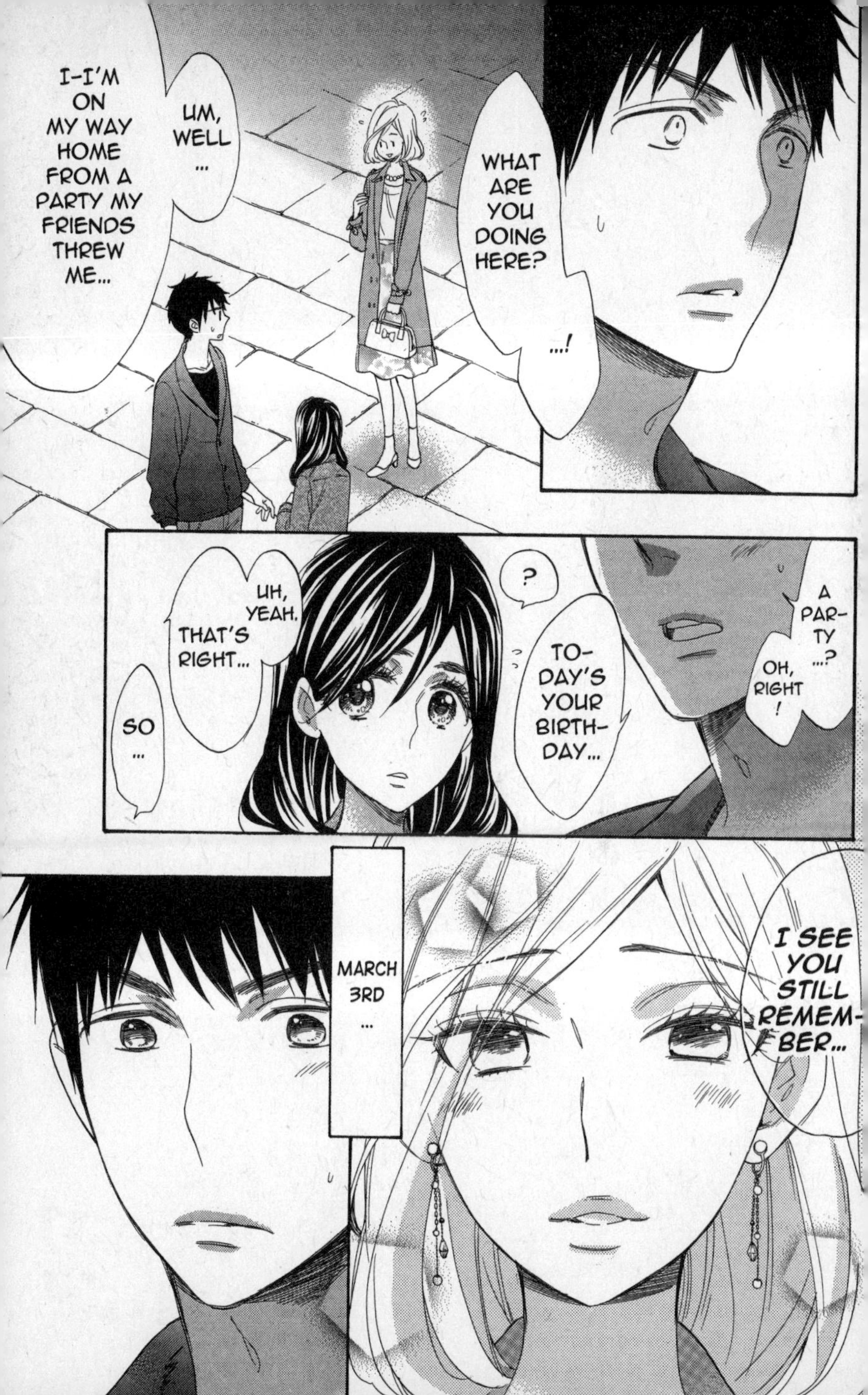
WHAT ARE YOU DOING HERE?
...!
UM, WELL ...
I-I'M ON MY WAY HOME FROM A PARTY MY FRIENDS THREW ME...
A PAR-TY ...?
OH, RIGHT!
?
TO-DAY'S YOUR BIRTH-DAY...
UH, YEAH. THAT'S RIGHT...
SO ...
I SEE YOU STILL REMEM-BER...
MARCH 3RD ...

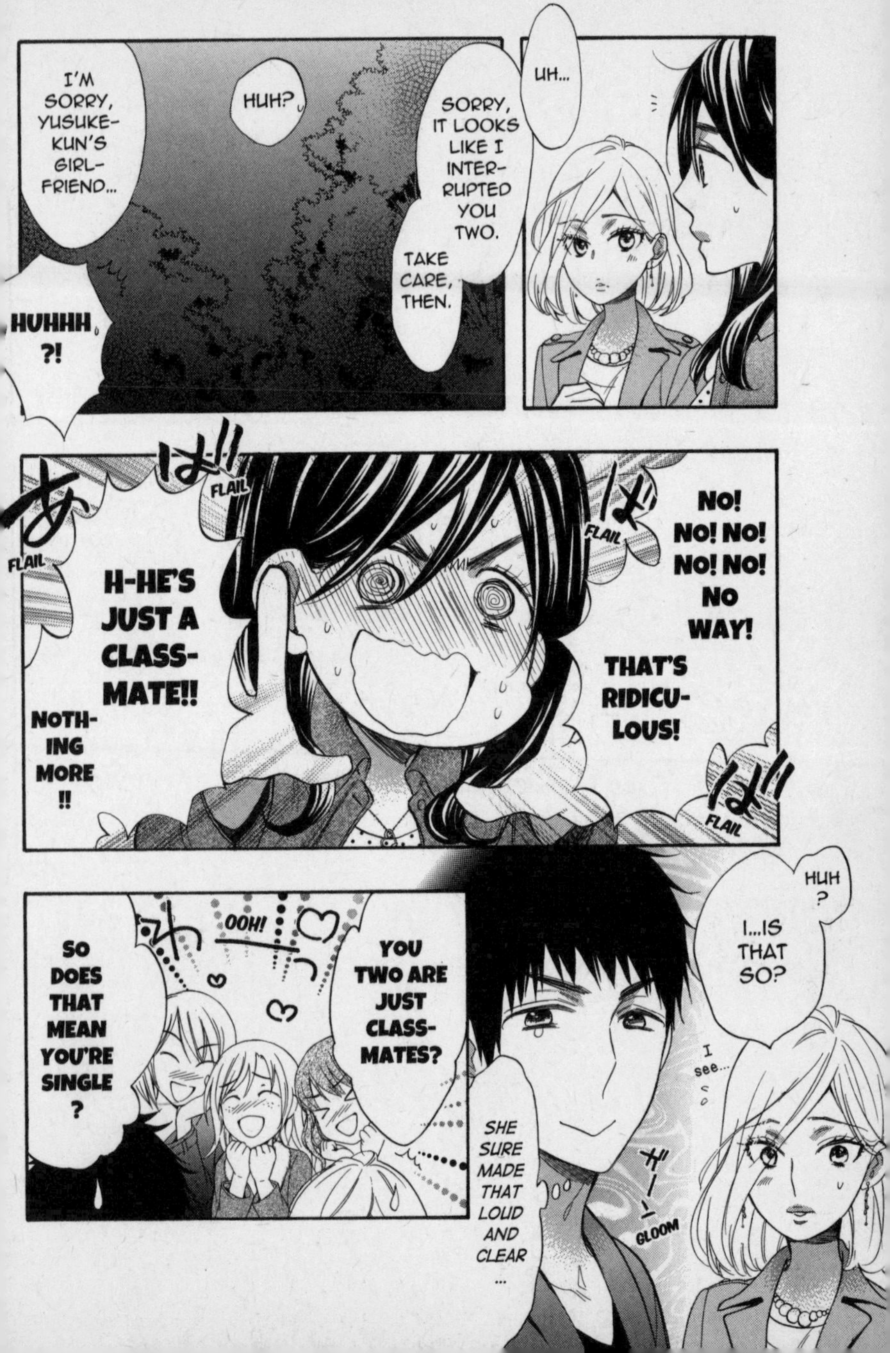
UH...
SORRY, IT LOOKS LIKE I INTERRUPTED YOU TWO.
TAKE CARE, THEN.
HUH?
I'M SORRY, YUSUKE-KUN'S GIRLFRIEND...
HUHHH?!
は!! FLAIL
は FLAIL
NO! NO! NO! NO! NO! NO WAY!
THAT'S RIDICULOUS!
は!! FLAIL
あ FLAIL
H-HE'S JUST A CLASSMATE!!
NOTHING MORE!!
HUH?
I...IS THAT SO?
I see...
GLOOM
SHE SURE MADE THAT LOUD AND CLEAR...
YOU TWO ARE JUST CLASSMATES?
OOH!
SO DOES THAT MEAN YOU'RE SINGLE?

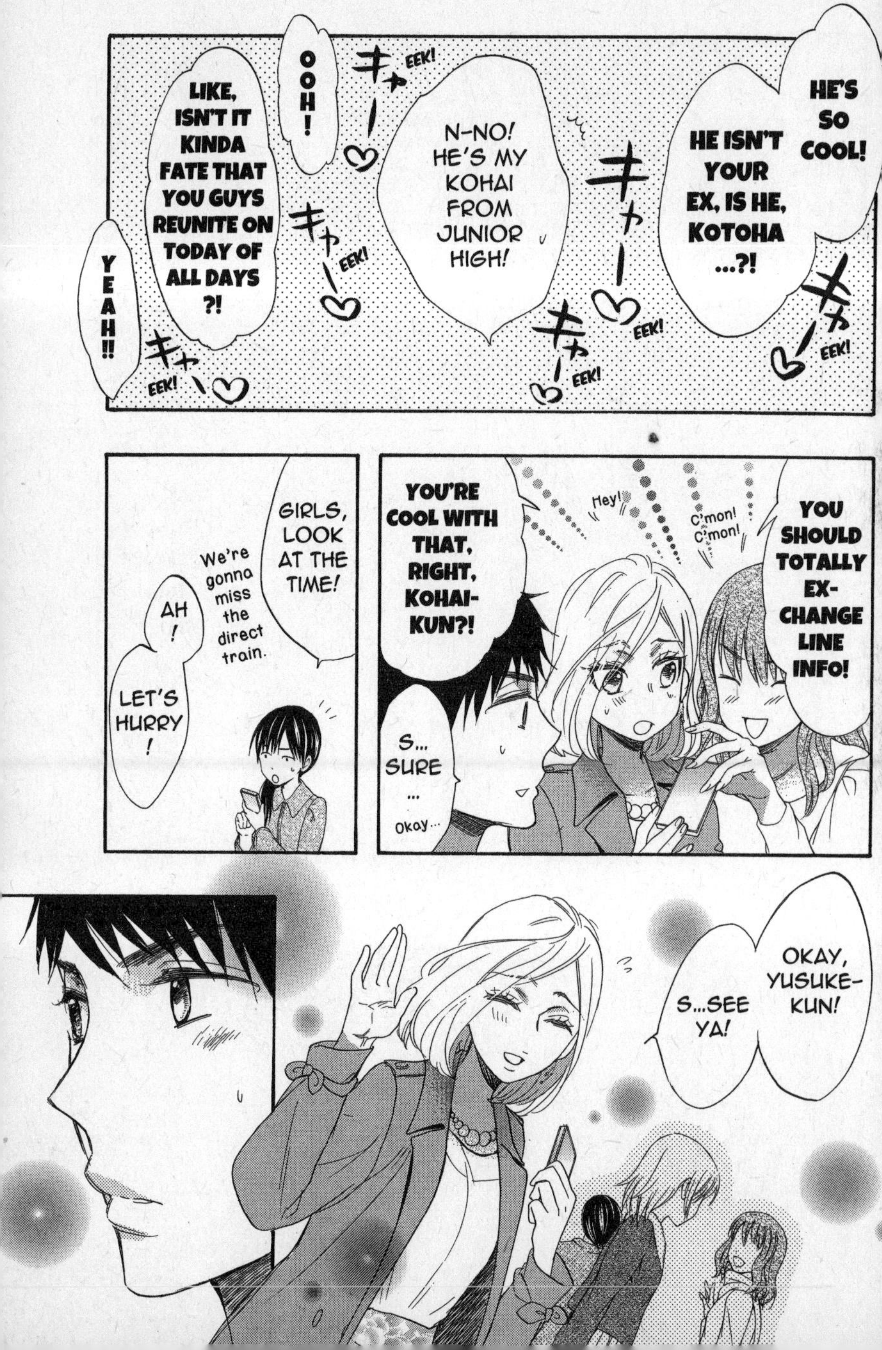
HE'S SO COOL!
HE ISN'T YOUR EX, IS HE, KOTOHA...?!
EEK!
EEK!
EEK!
N-NO! HE'S MY KOHAI FROM JUNIOR HIGH!
EEK!
OOH!
EEK!
LIKE, ISN'T IT KINDA FATE THAT YOU GUYS REUNITE ON TODAY OF ALL DAYS?!
YEAH!!
EEK!
YOU SHOULD TOTALLY EX-CHANGE LINE INFO!
C'mon! C'mon!
Hey!
YOU'RE COOL WITH THAT, RIGHT, KOHAI-KUN?!
S... SURE...
Okay...
GIRLS, LOOK AT THE TIME!
We're gonna miss the direct train.
AH!
LET'S HURRY!
OKAY, YUSUKE-KUN!
S...SEE YA!

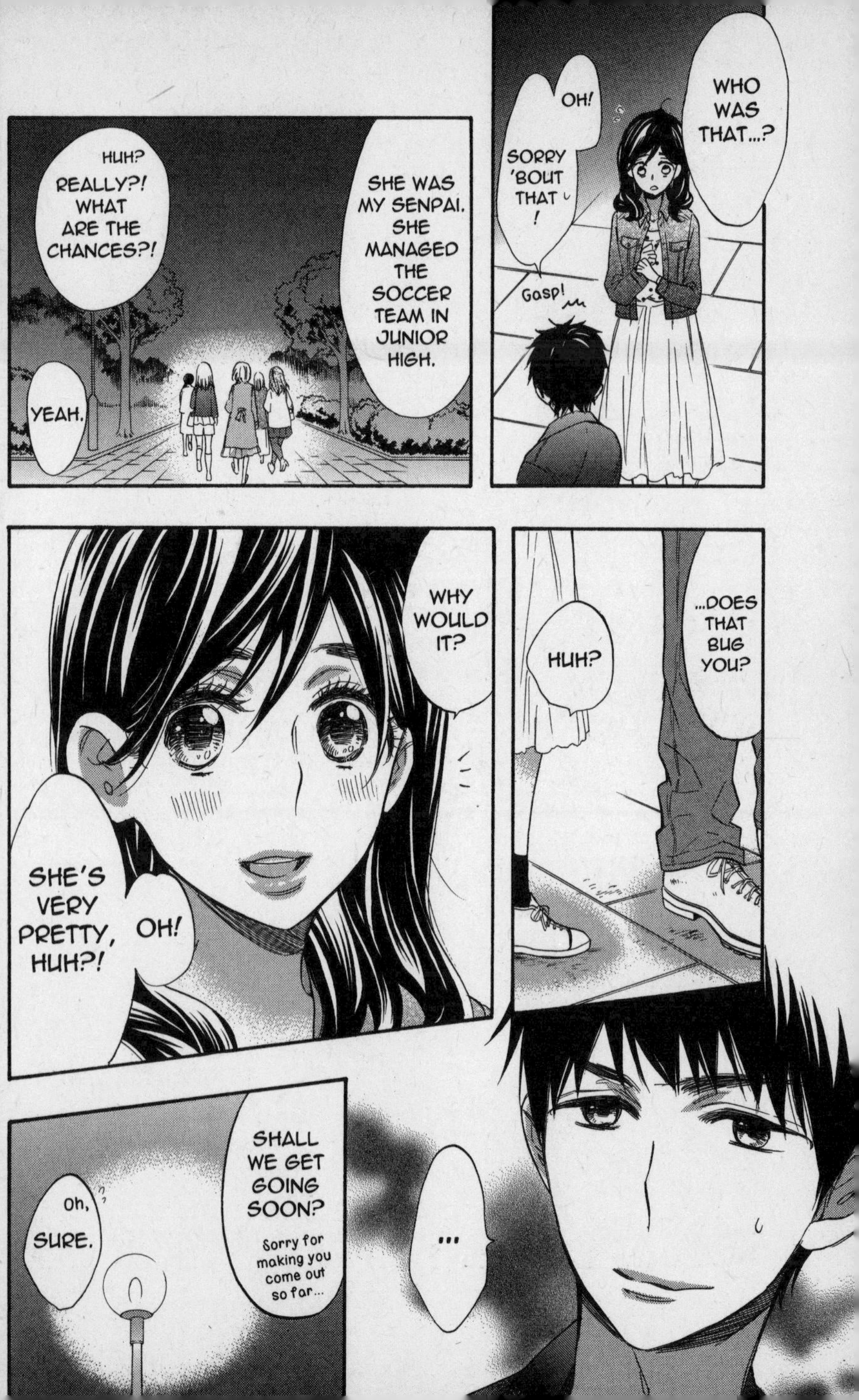
WHO WAS THAT...?
OH!
SORRY 'BOUT THAT!
Gasp!
SHE WAS MY SENPAI. SHE MANAGED THE SOCCER TEAM IN JUNIOR HIGH.
HUH? REALLY?! WHAT ARE THE CHANCES?!
YEAH.
...DOES THAT BUG YOU?
HUH?
WHY WOULD IT?
OH!
SHE'S VERY PRETTY, HUH?!
...
SHALL WE GET GOING SOON?
Sorry for making you come out so far...
Oh, SURE.

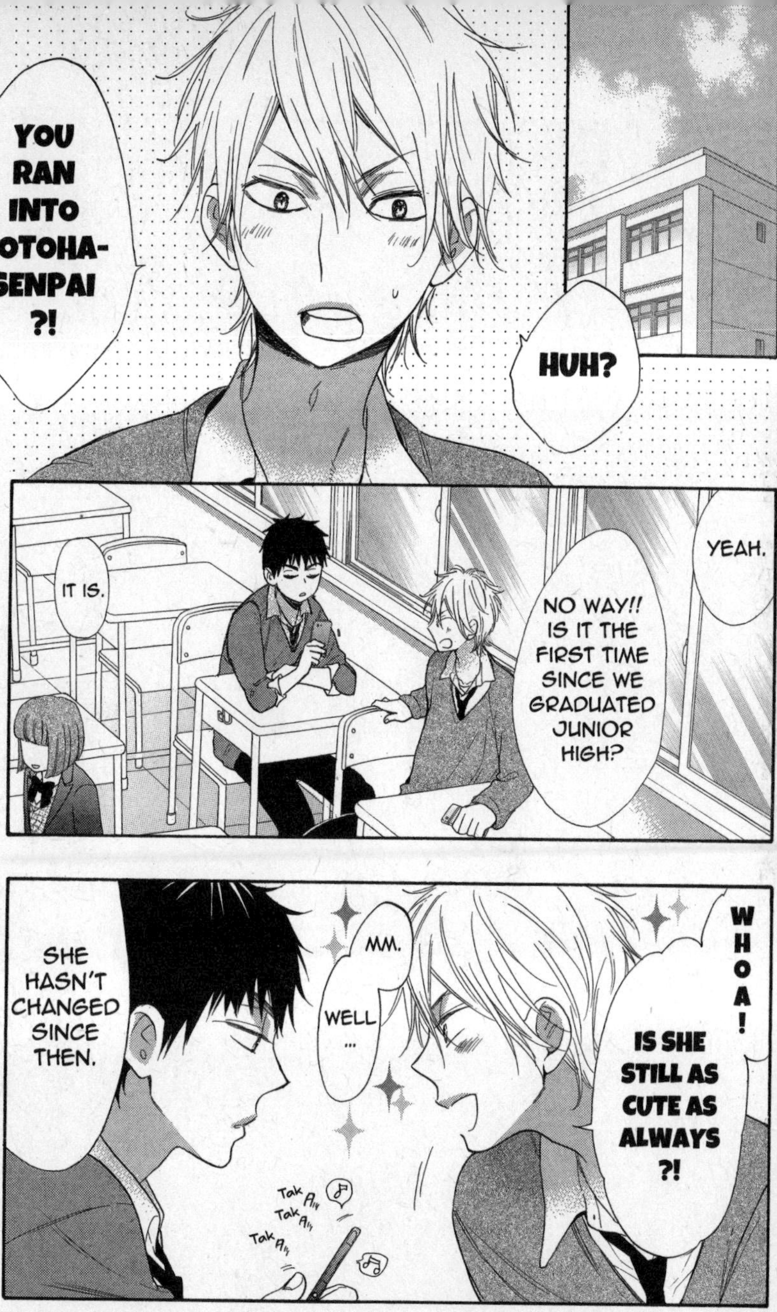
HUH?
YOU RAN INTO KOTOHA-SENPAI?!
YEAH.
NO WAY!! IS IT THE FIRST TIME SINCE WE GRADUATED JUNIOR HIGH?
IT IS.
WHOA!
IS SHE STILL AS CUTE AS ALWAYS?!
MM.
WELL...
SHE HASN'T CHANGED SINCE THEN.
Tak Tak Tak

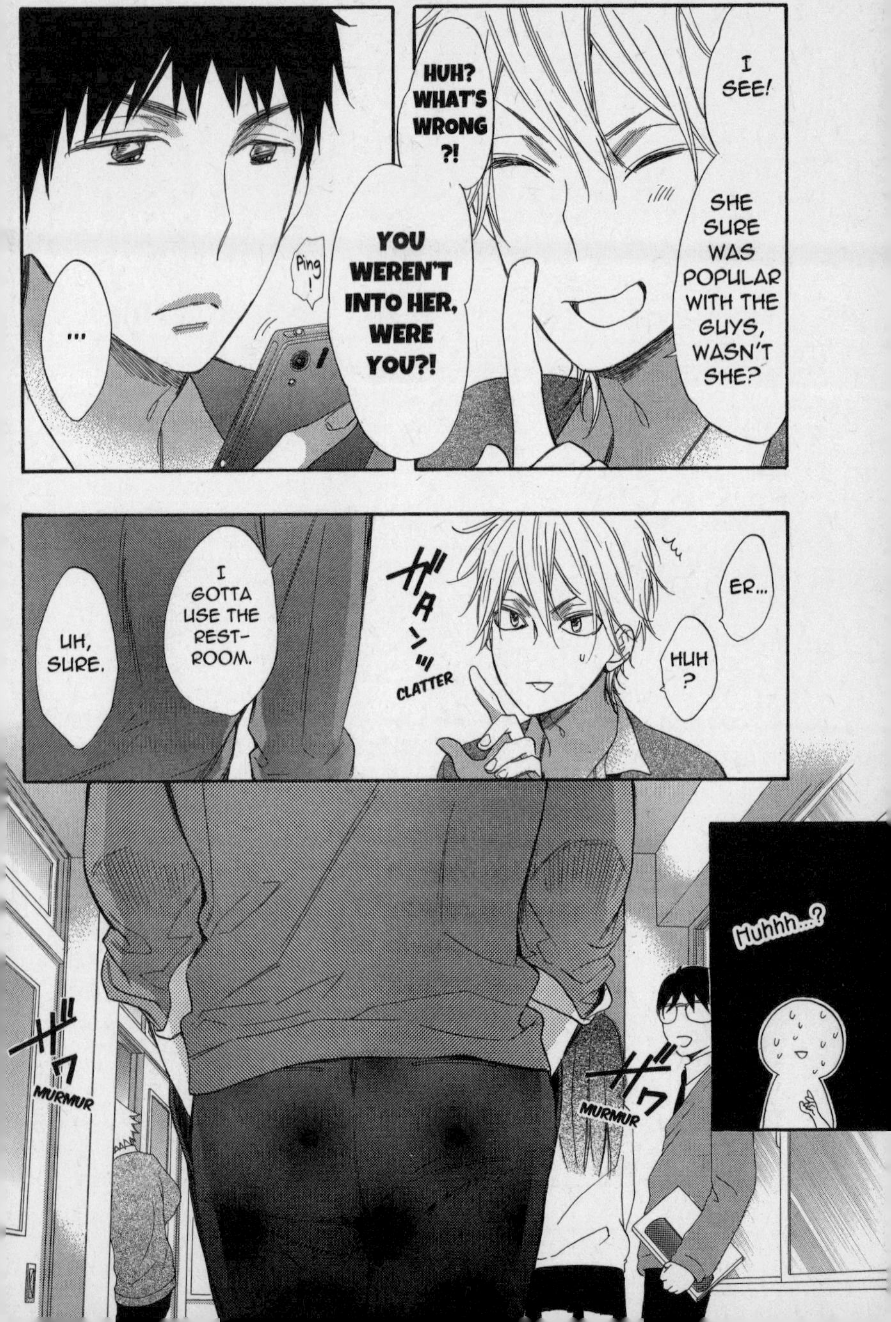
I SEE!
SHE SURE WAS POPULAR WITH THE GUYS, WASN'T SHE?
YOU WEREN'T INTO HER, WERE YOU?!
HUH? WHAT'S WRONG ?!
Ping !
...
ER...
HUH ?
CLATTER
I GOTTA USE THE REST-ROOM.
UH, SURE.
Huhhh...?
MURMUR
MURMUR

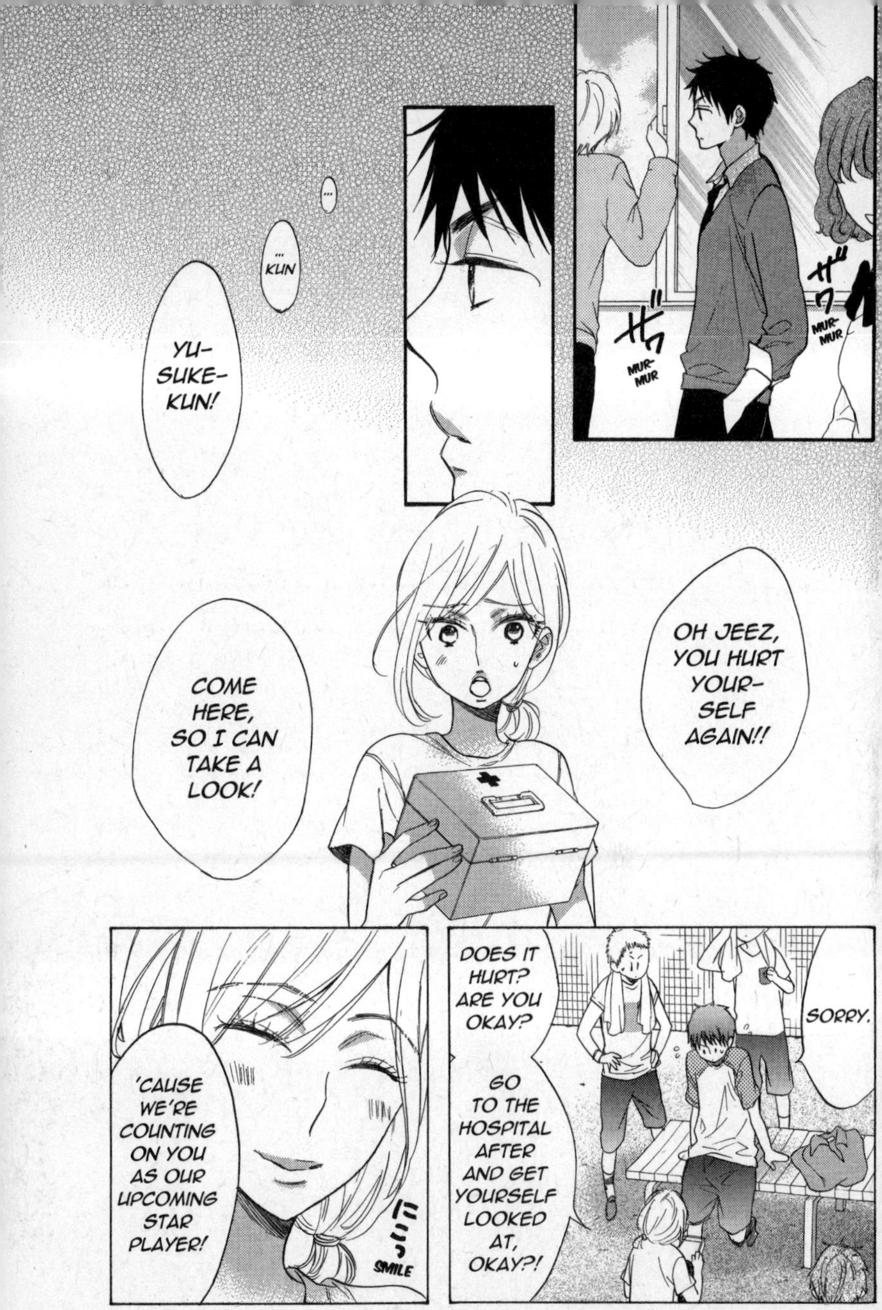
ザワ
MUR-MUR
ザワ
MUR-MUR
...
...KUN
YU-SUKE-KUN!
OH JEEZ, YOU HURT YOURSELF AGAIN!!
COME HERE, SO I CAN TAKE A LOOK!
SORRY.
DOES IT HURT? ARE YOU OKAY?
GO TO THE HOSPITAL AFTER AND GET YOURSELF LOOKED AT, OKAY?!
'CAUSE WE'RE COUNTING ON YOU AS OUR UPCOMING STAR PLAYER!
にこっ
SMILE

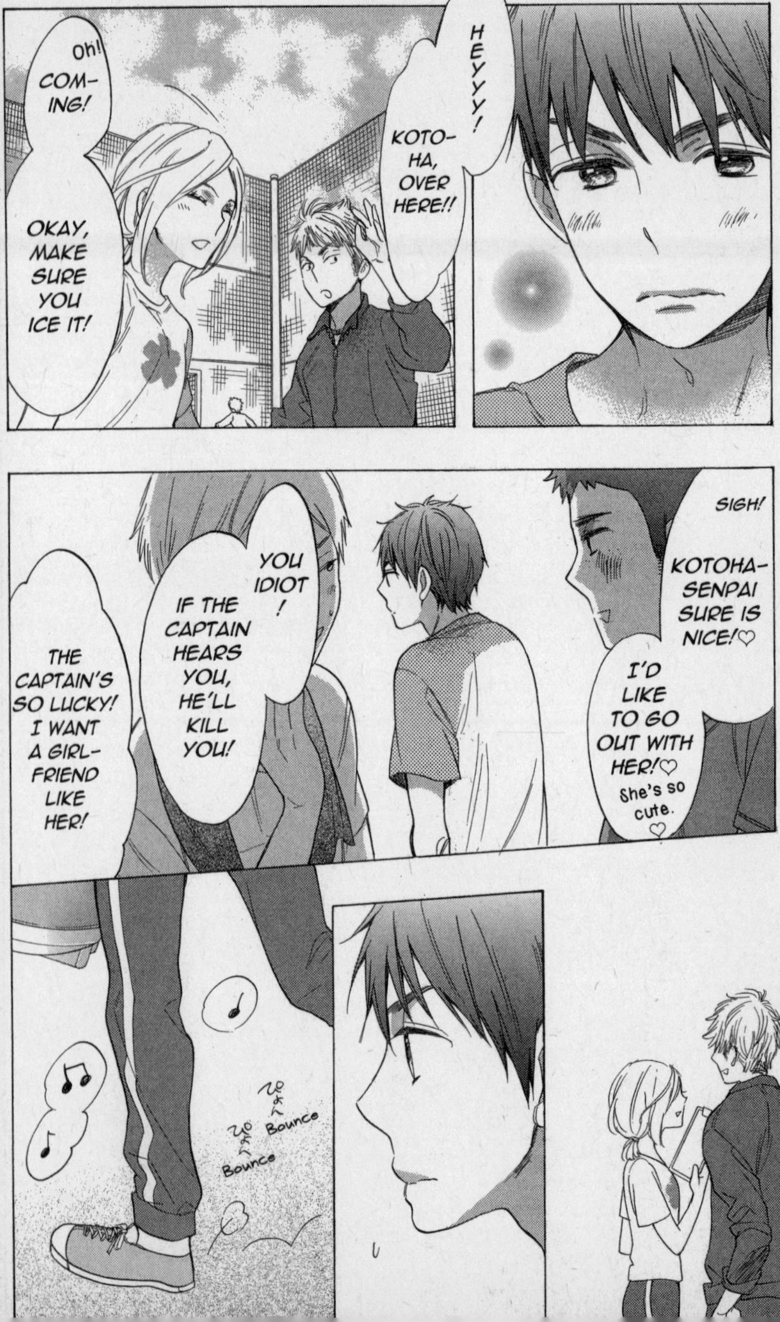
HEYYY!
KOTO-HA, OVER HERE!!
Oh! COMING!
OKAY, MAKE SURE YOU ICE IT!
SIGH!
KOTOHA-SENPAI SURE IS NICE!♡
I'D LIKE TO GO OUT WITH HER!♡
She's so cute. ♡
YOU IDIOT!
IF THE CAPTAIN HEARS YOU, HE'LL KILL YOU!
THE CAPTAIN'S SO LUCKY! I WANT A GIRL-FRIEND LIKE HER!
ぴょん Bounce
ぴょん Bounce

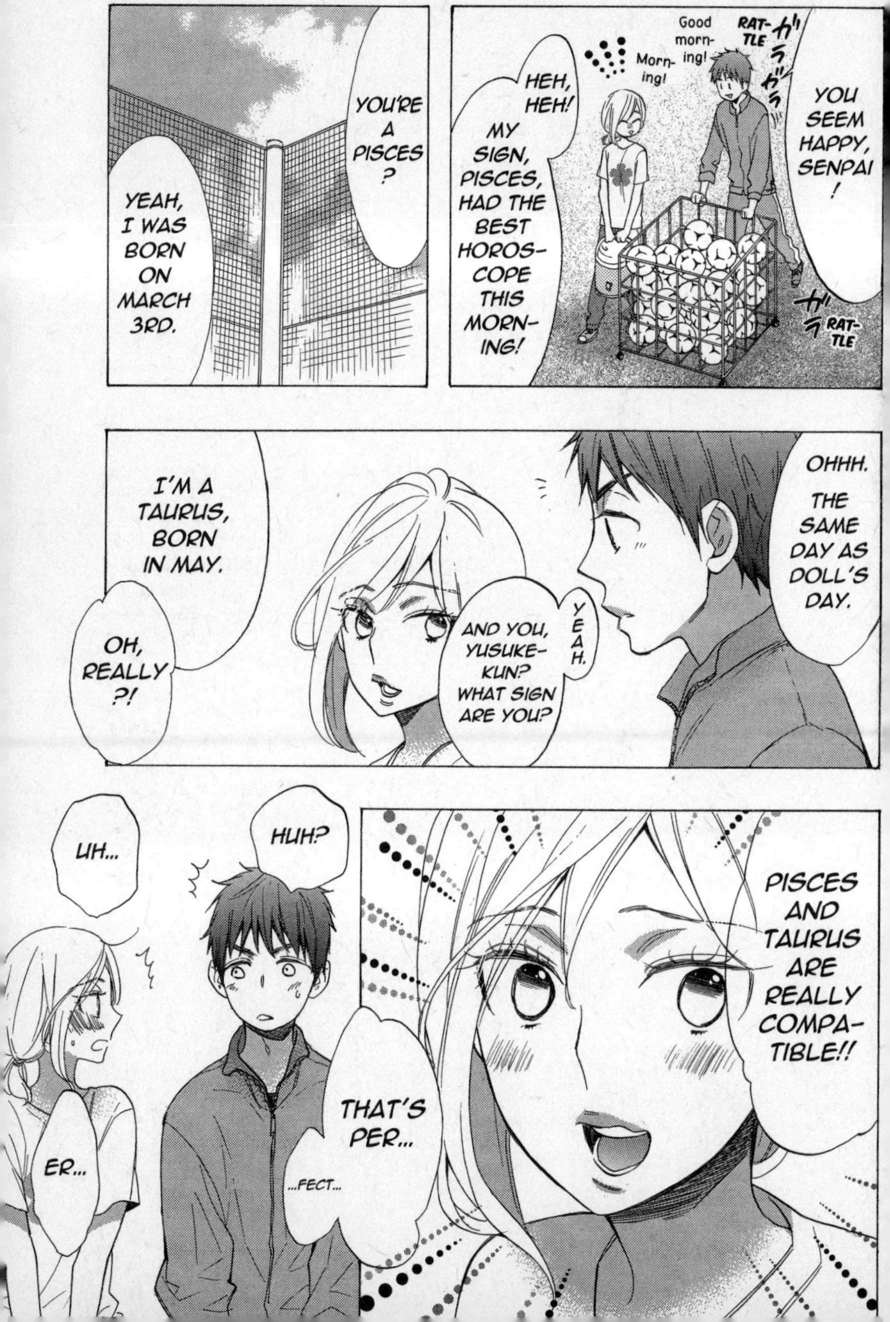
RATTLE
YOU SEEM HAPPY, SENPAI!
Good morning!
Morning!
RATTLE
HEH, HEH! MY SIGN, PISCES, HAD THE BEST HOROSCOPE THIS MORNING!
YOU'RE A PISCES?
YEAH, I WAS BORN ON MARCH 3RD.
OHHH. THE SAME DAY AS DOLL'S DAY.
YEAH.
AND YOU, YUSUKE-KUN? WHAT SIGN ARE YOU?
I'M A TAURUS, BORN IN MAY.
OH, REALLY?!
PISCES AND TAURUS ARE REALLY COMPATIBLE!!
THAT'S PER...
...FECT...
HUH?
UH...
ER...

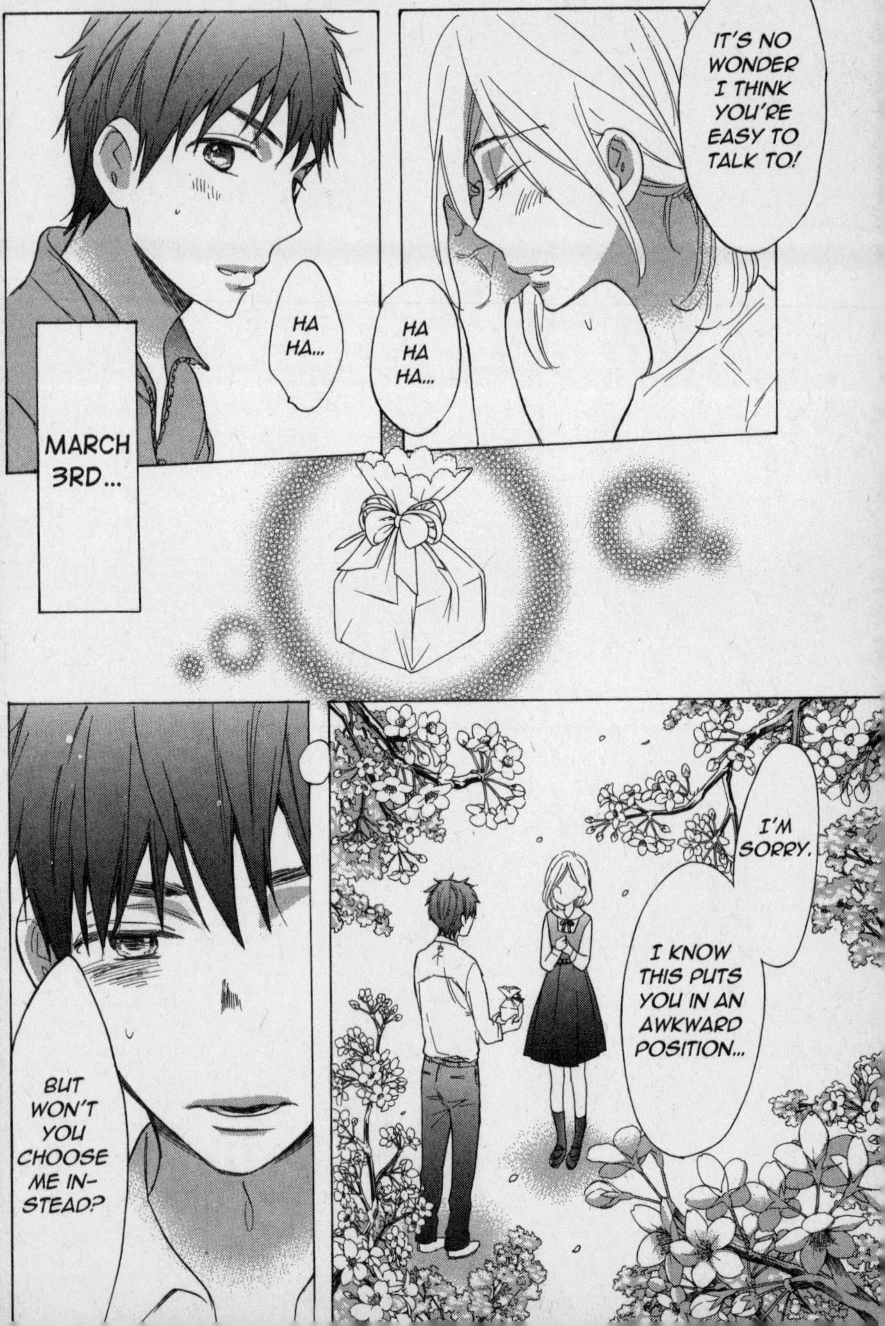
IT'S NO WONDER I THINK YOU'RE EASY TO TALK TO!
HA HA HA...
HA HA...
MARCH 3RD...
I'M SORRY.
I KNOW THIS PUTS YOU IN AN AWKWARD POSITION...
BUT WON'T YOU CHOOSE ME IN-STEAD?

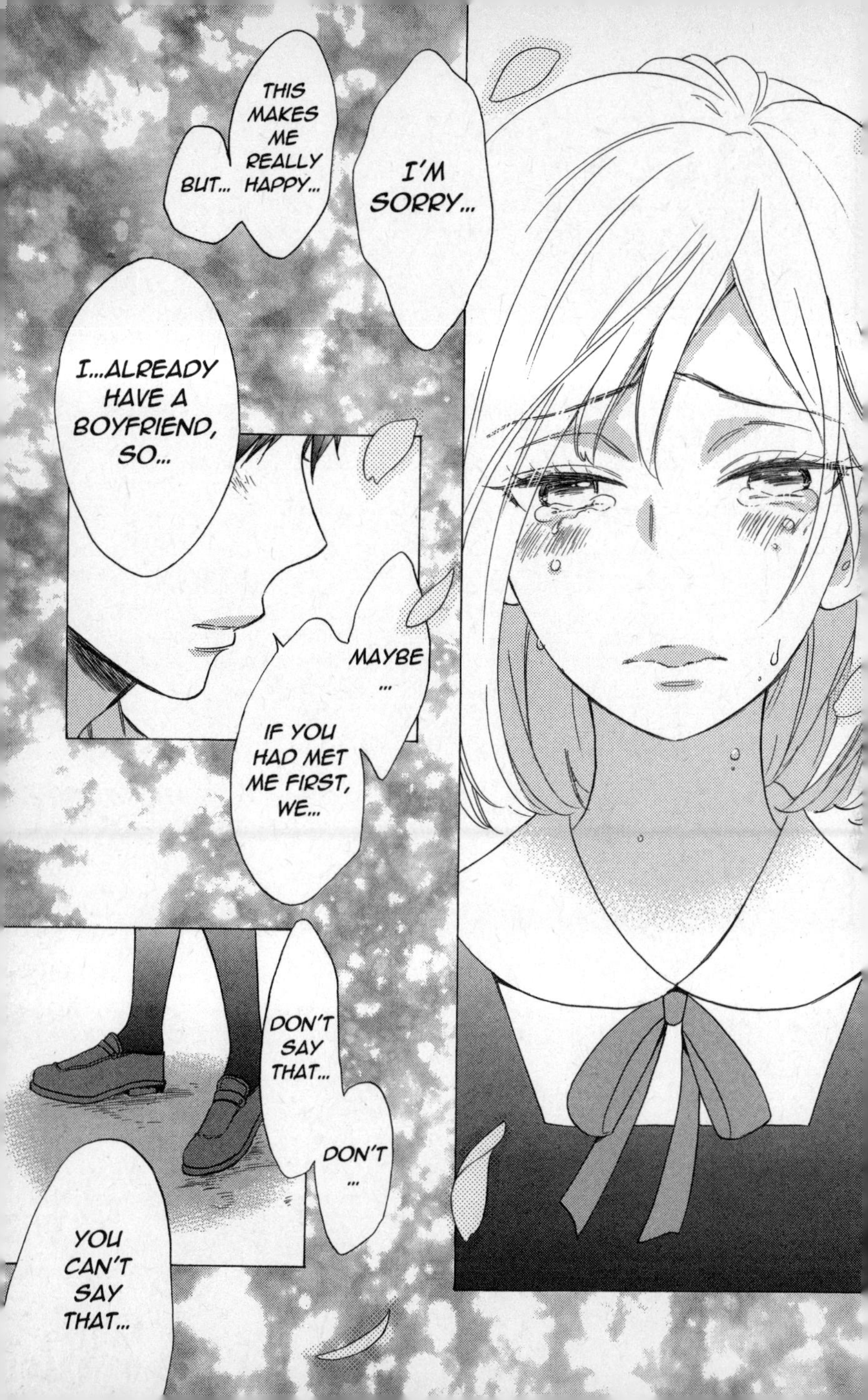
I'M SORRY...
THIS MAKES ME REALLY HAPPY...
BUT...
I...ALREADY HAVE A BOYFRIEND, SO...
MAYBE ...
IF YOU HAD MET ME FIRST, WE...
DON'T SAY THAT...
DON'T ...
YOU CAN'T SAY THAT...

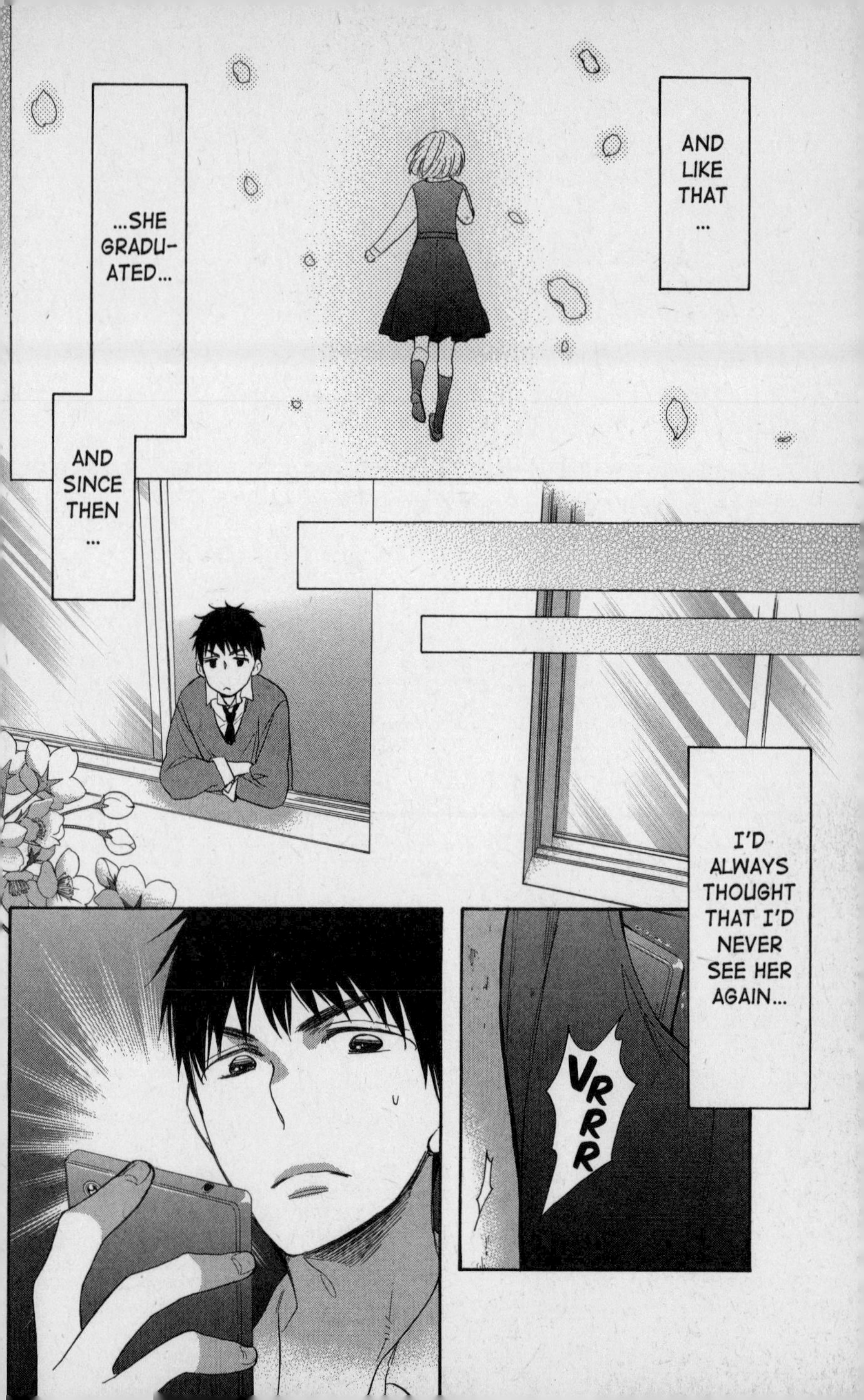
AND LIKE THAT ...
...SHE GRADUATED...
AND SINCE THEN ...
I'D ALWAYS THOUGHT THAT I'D NEVER SEE HER AGAIN...
VRRR

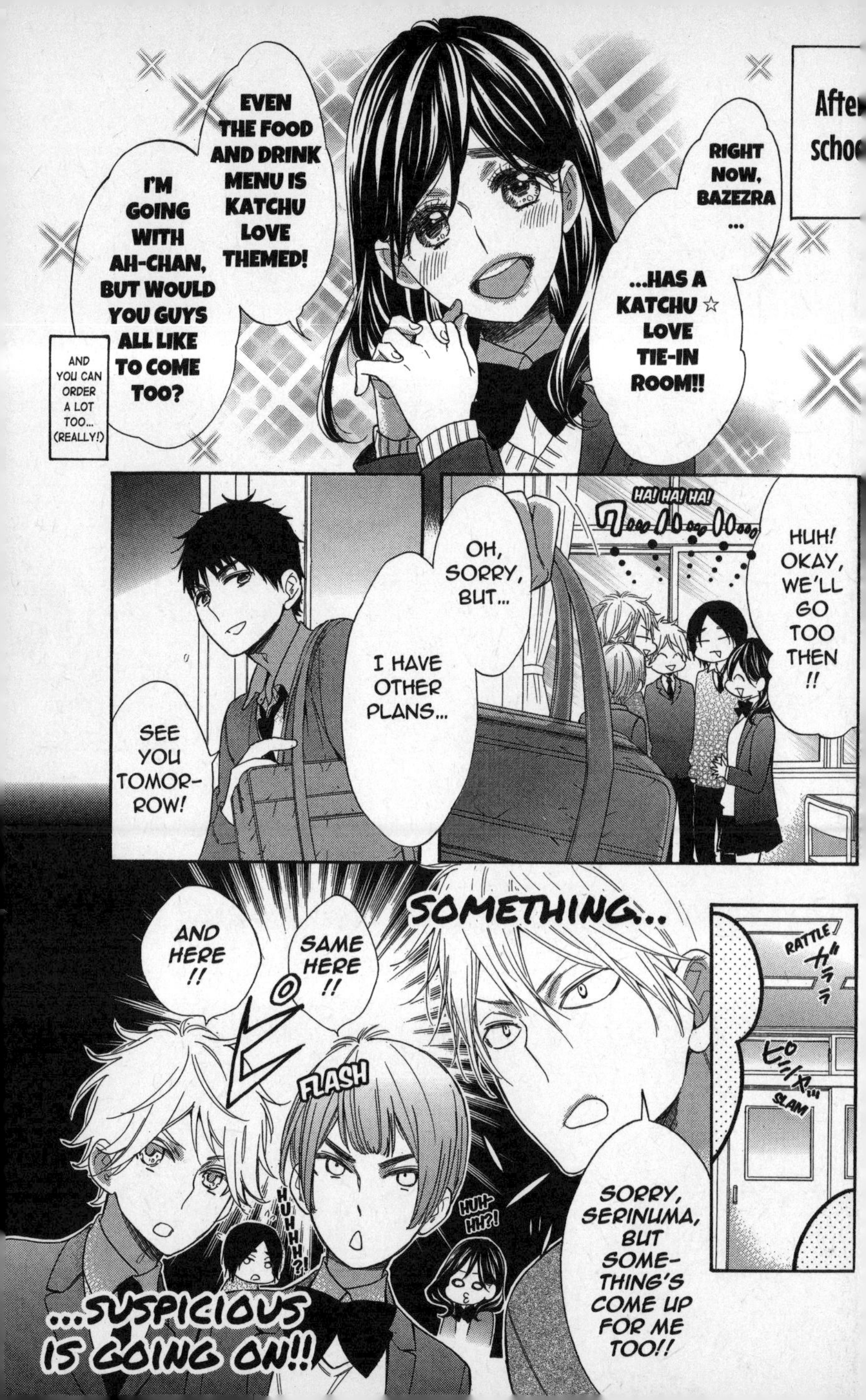
Afte
schoo
RIGHT NOW, BAZEZRA ...
...HAS A KATCHU ☆ LOVE TIE-IN ROOM!!
EVEN THE FOOD AND DRINK MENU IS KATCHU LOVE THEMED!
I'M GOING WITH AH-CHAN, BUT WOULD YOU GUYS ALL LIKE TO COME TOO?
AND YOU CAN ORDER A LOT TOO... (REALLY!)
HA! HA! HA!
HUH! OKAY, WE'LL GO TOO THEN!!
OH, SORRY, BUT...
I HAVE OTHER PLANS...
SEE YOU TOMORROW!
RATTLE
SLAM
SOMETHING...
SORRY, SERINUMA, BUT SOME-THING'S COME UP FOR ME TOO!!
SAME HERE!!
AND HERE!!
FLASH
HUH-HH?!
HUHHH?!
...SUSPICIOUS IS GOING ON!!

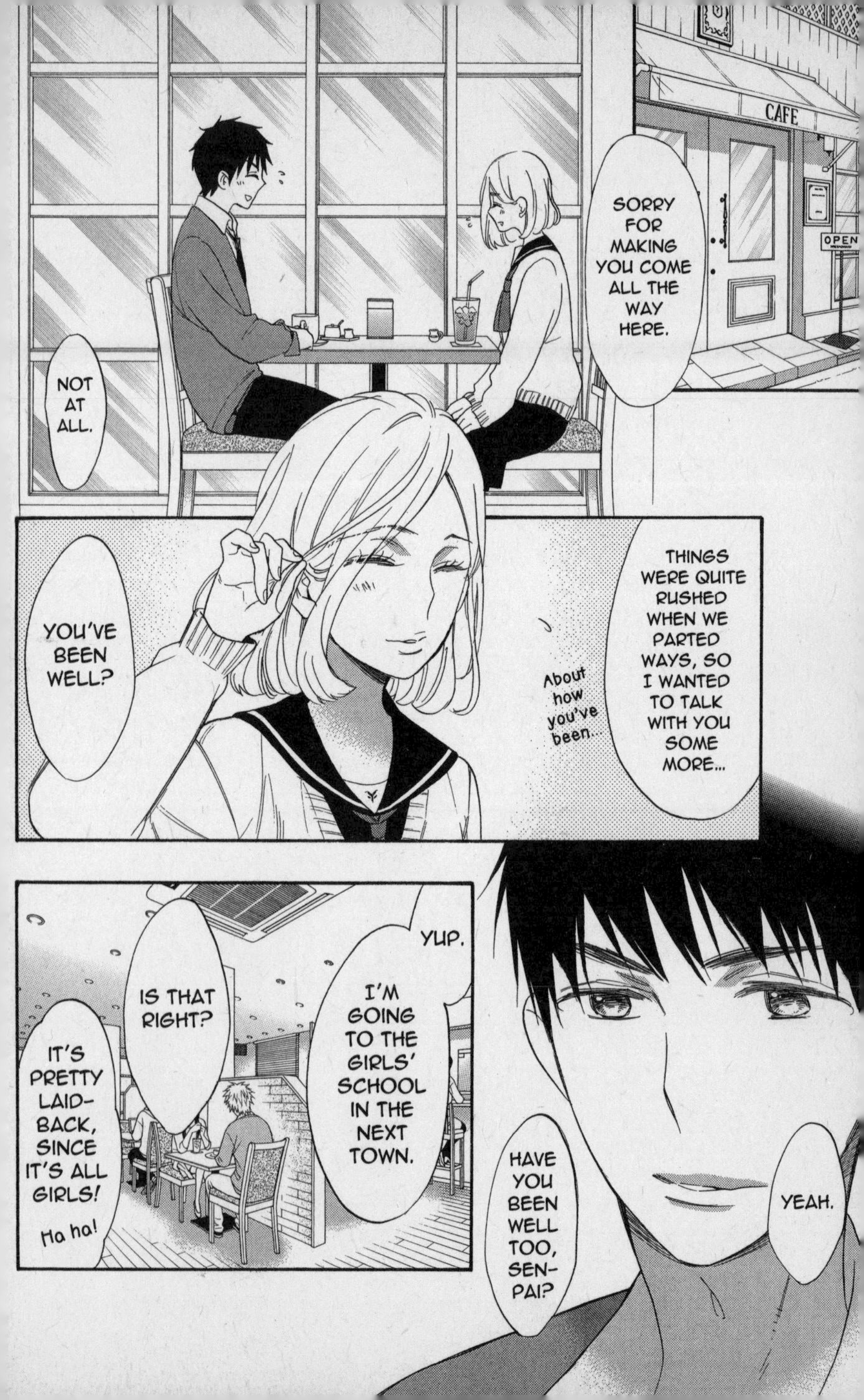

CAFE
OPEN
SORRY FOR MAKING YOU COME ALL THE WAY HERE.
NOT AT ALL.
THINGS WERE QUITE RUSHED WHEN WE PARTED WAYS, SO I WANTED TO TALK WITH YOU SOME MORE...
About how you've been...
YOU'VE BEEN WELL?
YUP.
I'M GOING TO THE GIRLS' SCHOOL IN THE NEXT TOWN.
IS THAT RIGHT?
IT'S PRETTY LAID-BACK, SINCE IT'S ALL GIRLS!
Ha ha!
HAVE YOU BEEN WELL TOO, SEN-PAI?
YEAH.

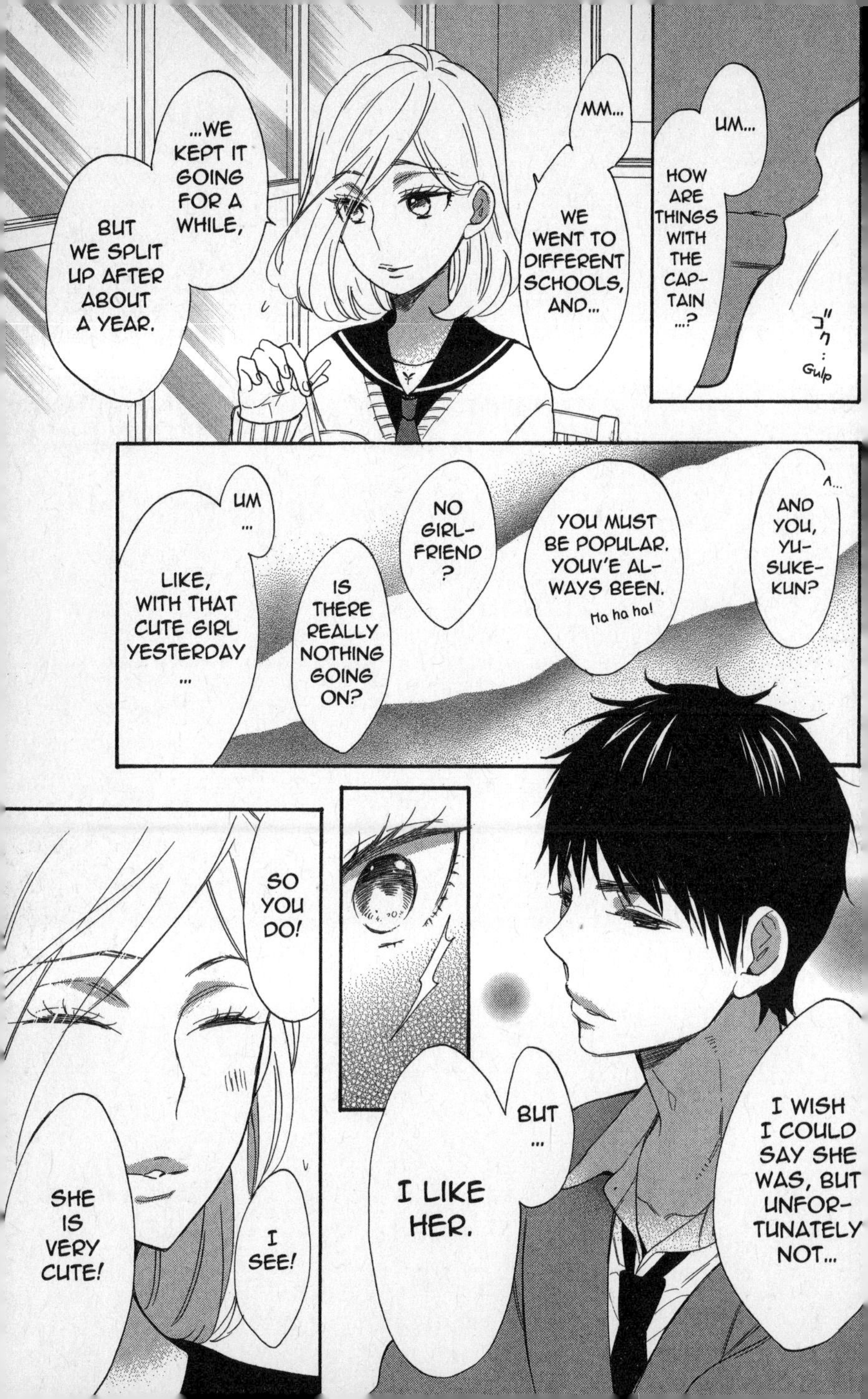
UM... HOW ARE THINGS WITH THE CAPTAIN...?
Gulp
MM... WE WENT TO DIFFERENT SCHOOLS, AND...
...WE KEPT IT GOING FOR A WHILE,
BUT WE SPLIT UP AFTER ABOUT A YEAR.
AND YOU, YUSUKE-KUN?
YOU MUST BE POPULAR. YOUV'E ALWAYS BEEN.
Ha ha ha!
NO GIRLFRIEND?
IS THERE REALLY NOTHING GOING ON?
UM... LIKE, WITH THAT CUTE GIRL YESTERDAY...
I WISH I COULD SAY SHE WAS, BUT UNFORTUNATELY NOT...
BUT...
I LIKE HER.
SO YOU DO!
I SEE!
SHE IS VERY CUTE!

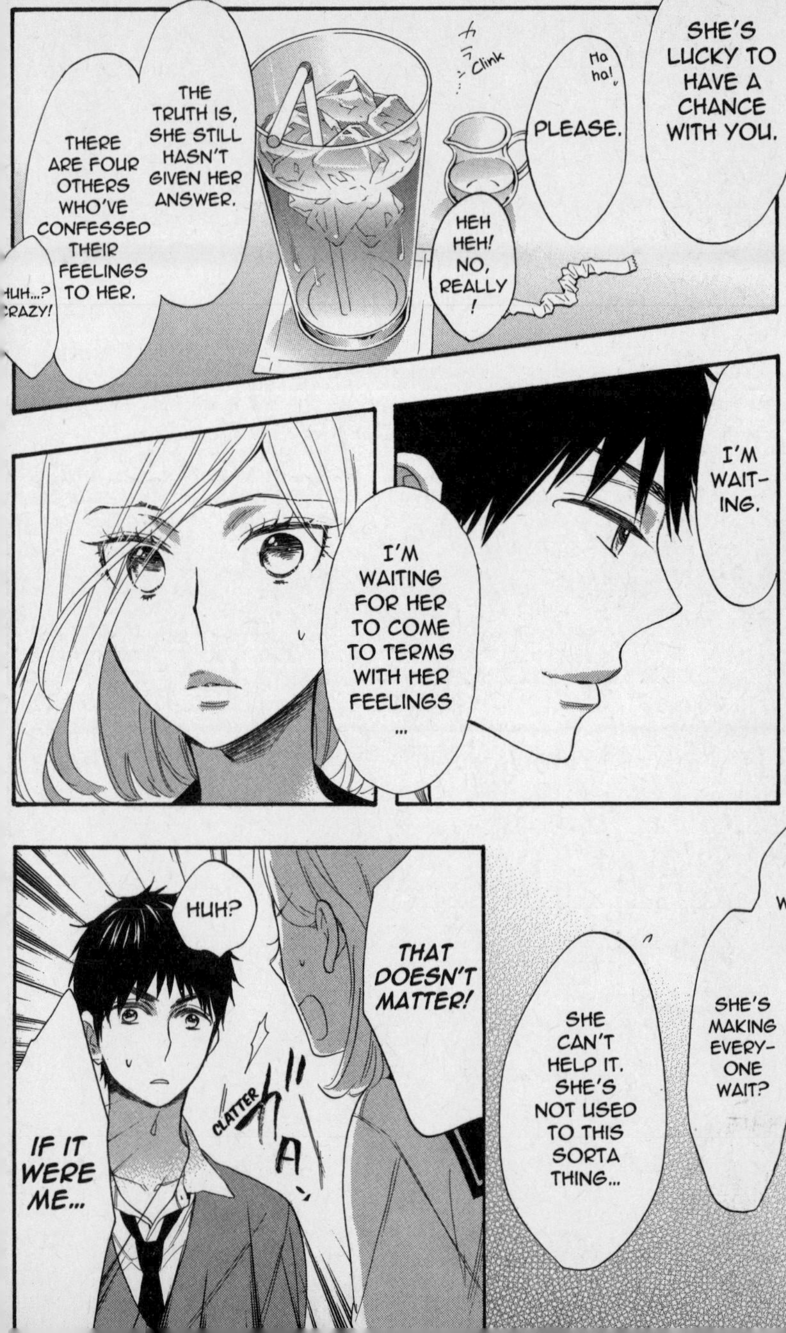
SHE'S LUCKY TO HAVE A CHANCE WITH YOU.
Ha ha!
PLEASE.
Clink
HEH HEH! NO, REALLY!
THE TRUTH IS, SHE STILL HASN'T GIVEN HER ANSWER.
THERE ARE FOUR OTHERS WHO'VE CONFESSED THEIR FEELINGS TO HER.
UH...? RAZY!
I'M WAIT-ING.
I'M WAITING FOR HER TO COME TO TERMS WITH HER FEELINGS ...
WHAT ...?
SHE'S MAKING EVERY-ONE WAIT?
SHE CAN'T HELP IT. SHE'S NOT USED TO THIS SORTA THING...
THAT DOESN'T MATTER!
CLATTER
HUH?
IF IT WERE ME...

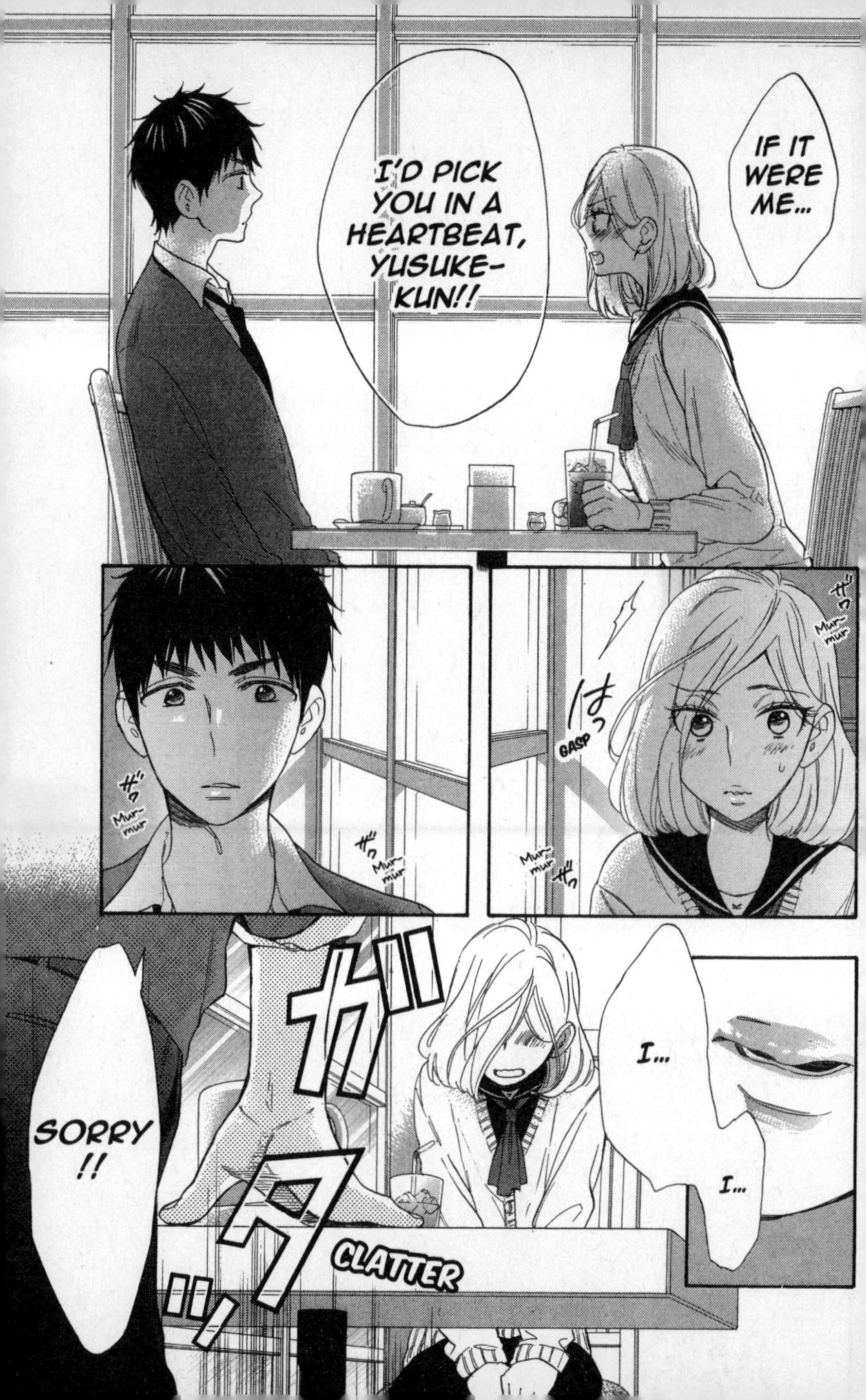
IF IT WERE ME...
I'D PICK YOU IN A HEARTBEAT, YUSUKE-KUN!!
ザワ
Mur-mur
はっ
GASP
Mur-mur
ザワ
ザワ
Mur-mur
ザワ
Mur-mur
I...
I...
CLATTER
SORRY!!

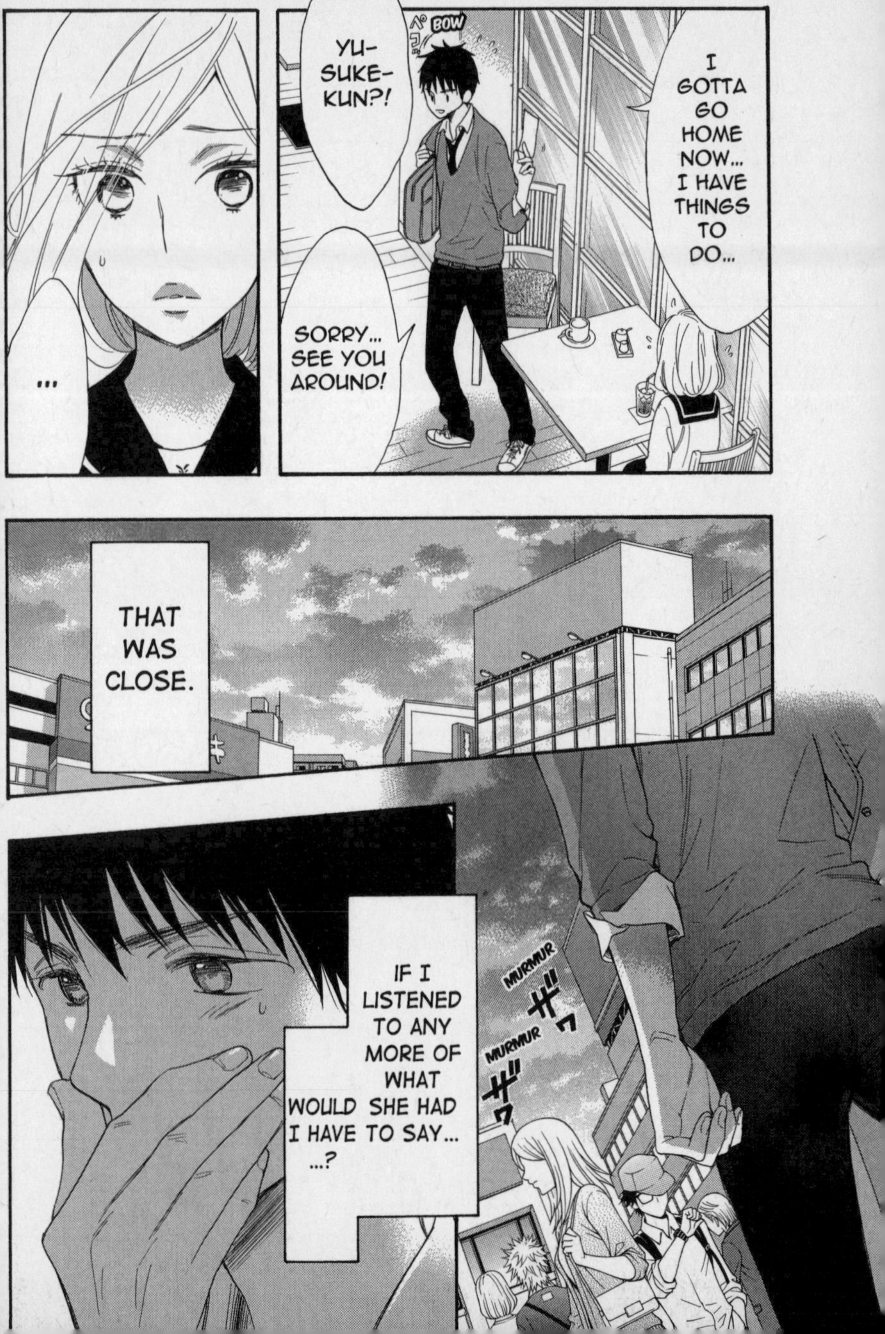
I GOTTA GO HOME NOW... I HAVE THINGS TO DO...
BOW
YU-SUKE-KUN?!
SORRY... SEE YOU AROUND!
...
THAT WAS CLOSE.
IF I LISTENED TO ANY MORE OF WHAT SHE HAD TO SAY...
WOULD I HAVE ...?
MURMUR
MURMUR

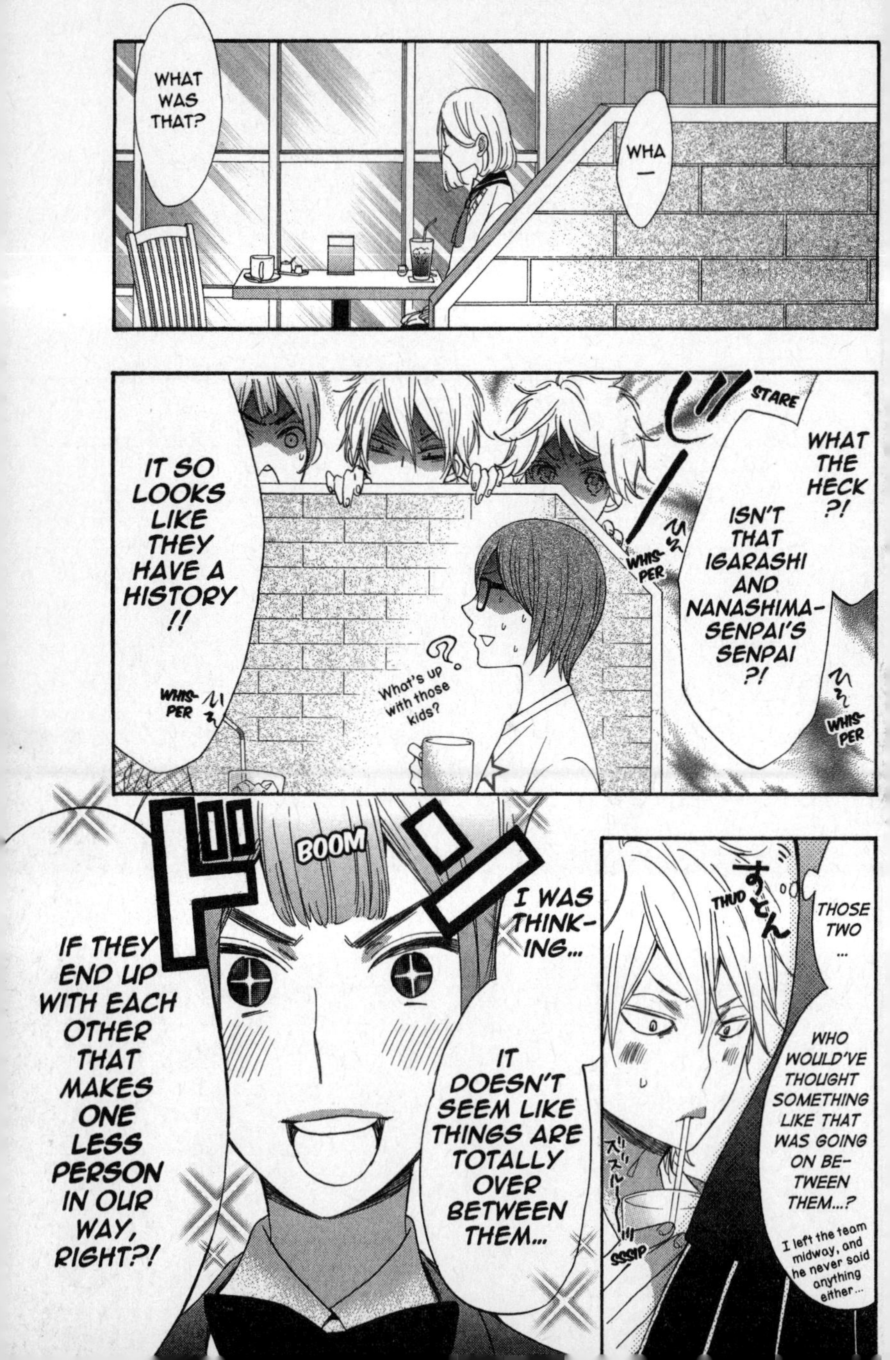
WHA —
WHAT WAS THAT?
STARE
WHAT THE HECK?!
ISN'T THAT IGARASHI AND NANASHIMA-SENPAI'S SENPAI?!
WHISPER
WHISPER
What's up with those kids?
IT SO LOOKS LIKE THEY HAVE A HISTORY!!
WHISPER
すとん
THUD
THOSE TWO...
WHO WOULD'VE THOUGHT SOMETHING LIKE THAT WAS GOING ON BETWEEN THEM...?
I left the team midway, and he never said anything either...
SSSIP
BOOM
I WAS THINKING...
IT DOESN'T SEEM LIKE THINGS ARE TOTALLY OVER BETWEEN THEM...
IF THEY END UP WITH EACH OTHER THAT MAKES ONE LESS PERSON IN OUR WAY, RIGHT?!

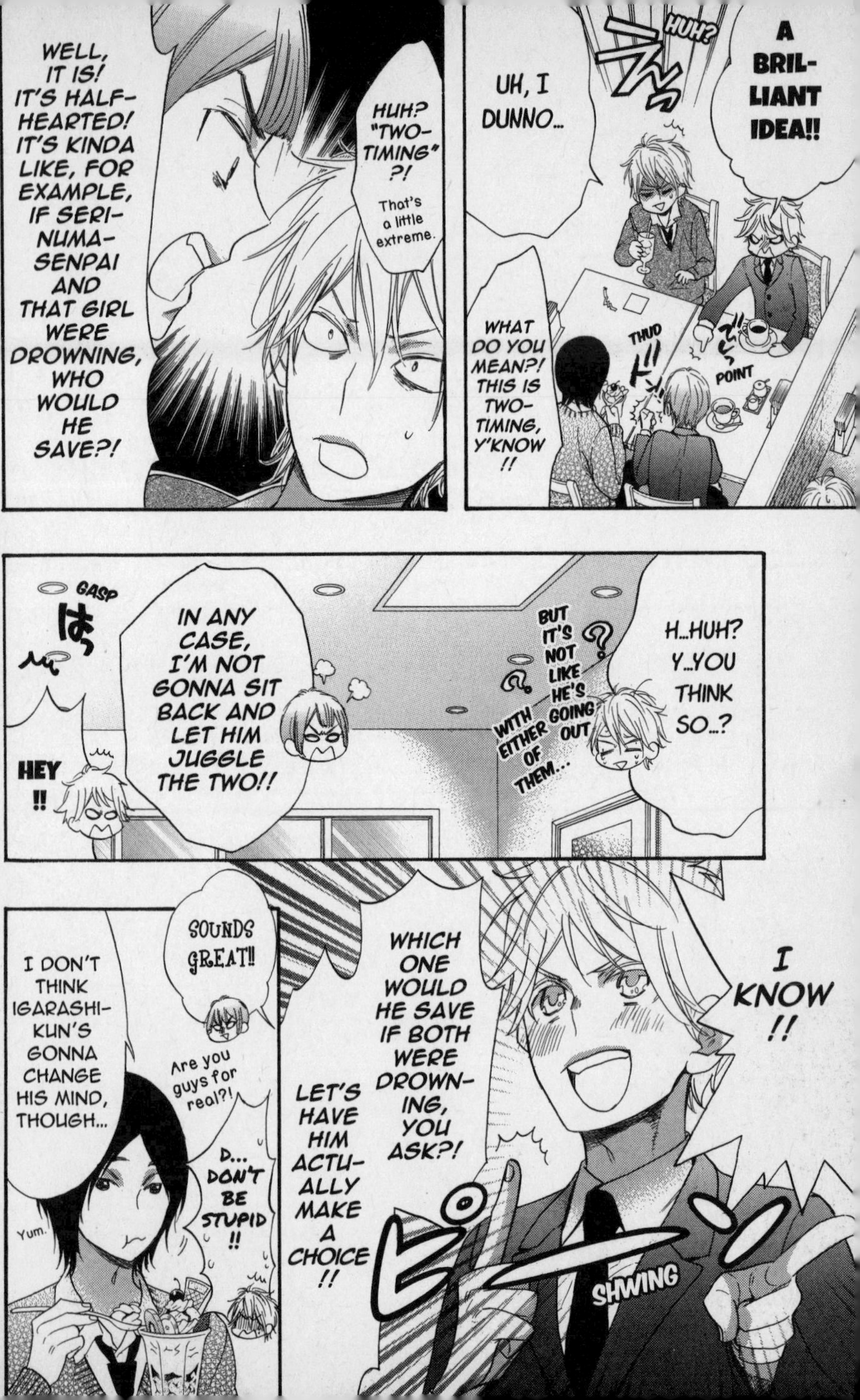

A BRILLIANT IDEA!!
HUH?
UH, I DUNNO...
POINT
THUD
WHAT DO YOU MEAN?! THIS IS TWO-TIMING, Y'KNOW!!
HUH? "TWO-TIMING"?!
That's a little extreme.
WELL, IT IS! IT'S HALF-HEARTED! IT'S KINDA LIKE, FOR EXAMPLE, IF SERINUMA-SENPAI AND THAT GIRL WERE DROWNING, WHO WOULD HE SAVE?!
H...HUH? Y...YOU THINK SO..?
BUT IT'S NOT LIKE HE'S GOING OUT WITH EITHER OF THEM...
IN ANY CASE, I'M NOT GONNA SIT BACK AND LET HIM JUGGLE THE TWO!!
GASP
HEY!!
I KNOW!!
WHICH ONE WOULD HE SAVE IF BOTH WERE DROWNING, YOU ASK?!
LET'S HAVE HIM ACTUALLY MAKE A CHOICE!!
SHWING
SOUNDS GREAT!!
I DON'T THINK IGARASHI-KUN'S GONNA CHANGE HIS MIND, THOUGH...
Are you guys for real?!
D... DON'T BE STUPID!!
Yum.

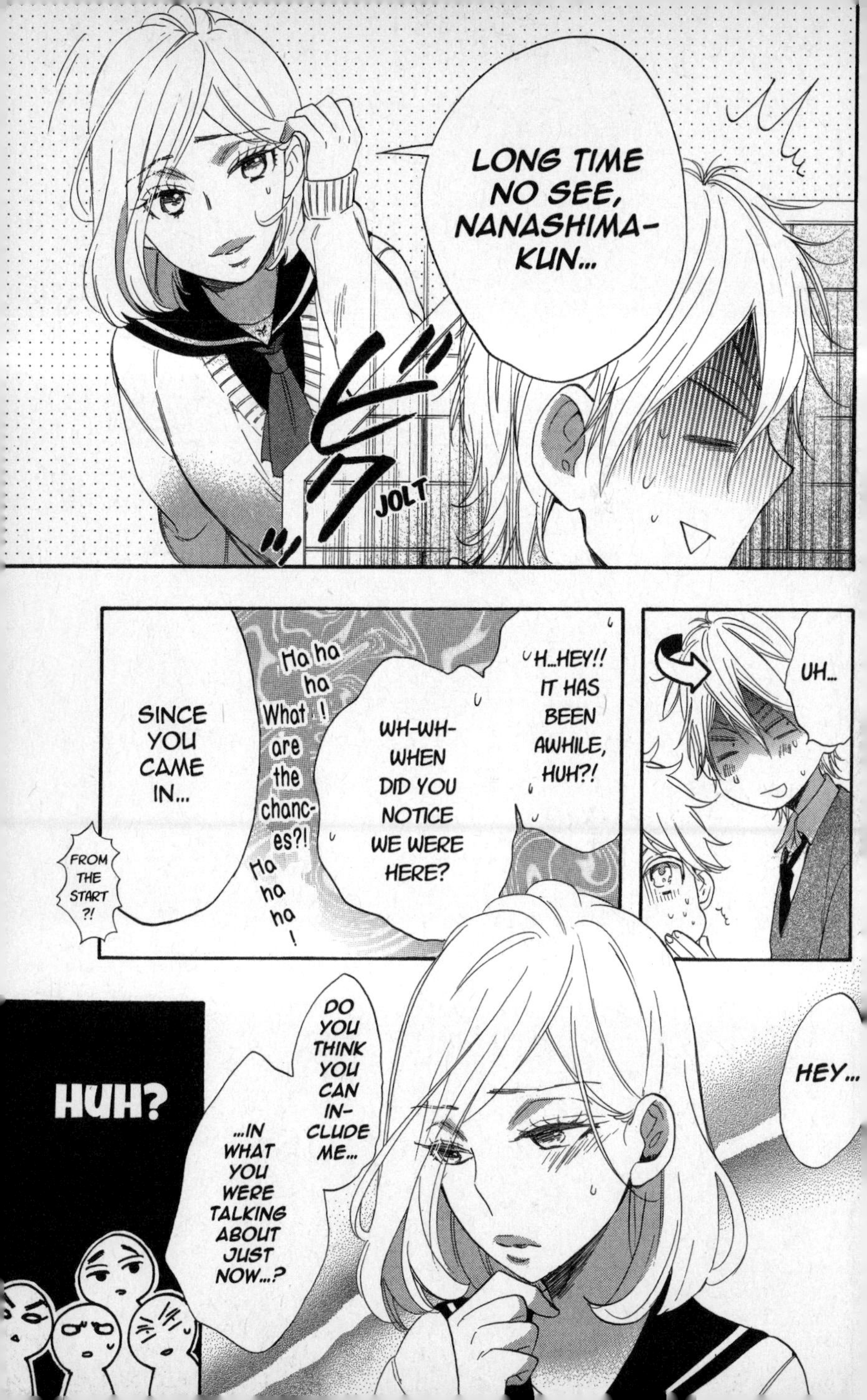
LONG TIME NO SEE, NANASHIMA-KUN...
JOLT
UH...
H...HEY!! IT HAS BEEN AWHILE, HUH?!
WH-WH-WHEN DID YOU NOTICE WE WERE HERE?
Ha ha ha What are the chances?! Ha ha ha!
SINCE YOU CAME IN...
FROM THE START?!
HEY...
DO YOU THINK YOU CAN IN-CLUDE ME...
...IN WHAT YOU WERE TALKING ABOUT JUST NOW...?
HUH?

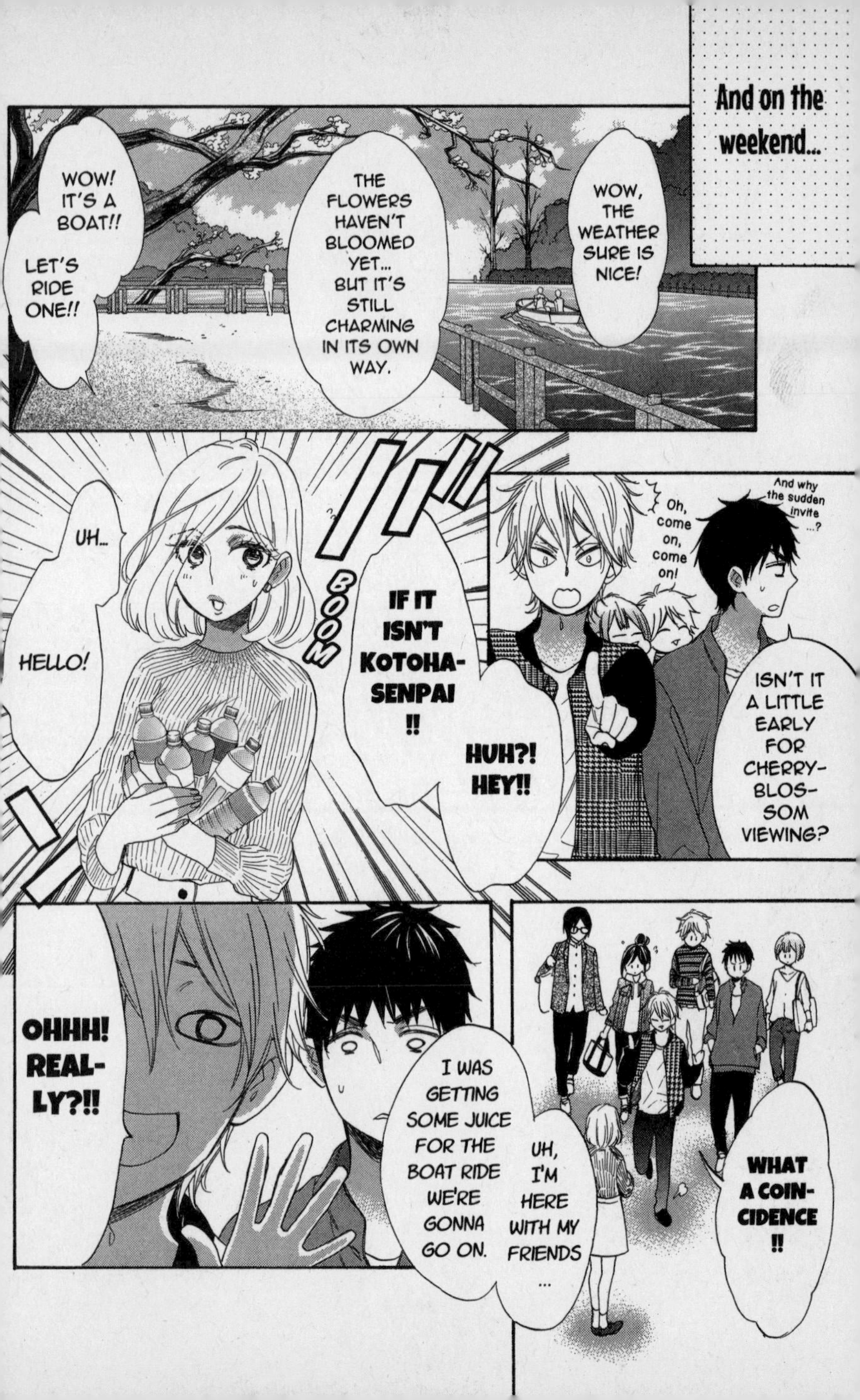
And on the weekend...
WOW, THE WEATHER SURE IS NICE!
THE FLOWERS HAVEN'T BLOOMED YET... BUT IT'S STILL CHARMING IN ITS OWN WAY.
WOW! IT'S A BOAT!! LET'S RIDE ONE!!
And why the sudden invite...?
Oh, come on, come on!
ISN'T IT A LITTLE EARLY FOR CHERRY-BLOSSOM VIEWING?
IF IT ISN'T KOTOHA-SENPAI!!
HUH?! HEY!!
BOOM
UH... HELLO!
WHAT A COINCIDENCE!!
UH, I'M HERE WITH MY FRIENDS...
I WAS GETTING SOME JUICE FOR THE BOAT RIDE WE'RE GONNA GO ON.
OHHH! REALLY?!!

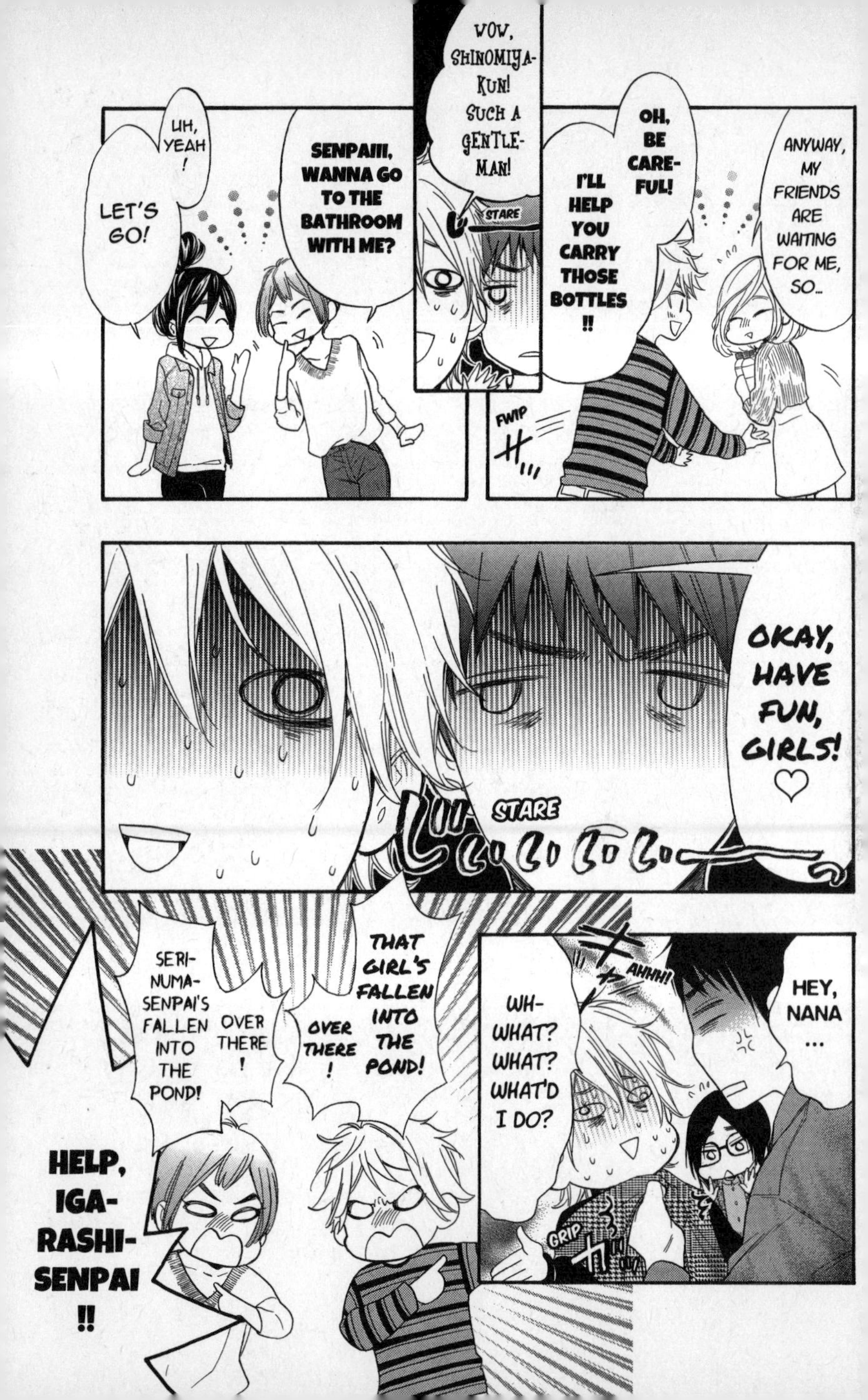
ANYWAY, MY FRIENDS ARE WAITING FOR ME, SO...
OH, BE CAREFUL!
I'LL HELP YOU CARRY THOSE BOTTLES!!
FWIP
WOW, SHINOMIYA-KUN! SUCH A GENTLEMAN!
STARE
SENPAIII, WANNA GO TO THE BATHROOM WITH ME?
UH, YEAH!
LET'S GO!
OKAY, HAVE FUN, GIRLS! ♡
STARE
HEY, NANA...
AHHH!
WH-WHAT? WHAT? WHAT'D I DO?
GRIP
THAT GIRL'S FALLEN INTO THE POND!
OVER THERE!
OVER THERE!
SERINUMA-SENPAI'S FALLEN INTO THE POND!
HELP, IGARASHI-SENPAI!!

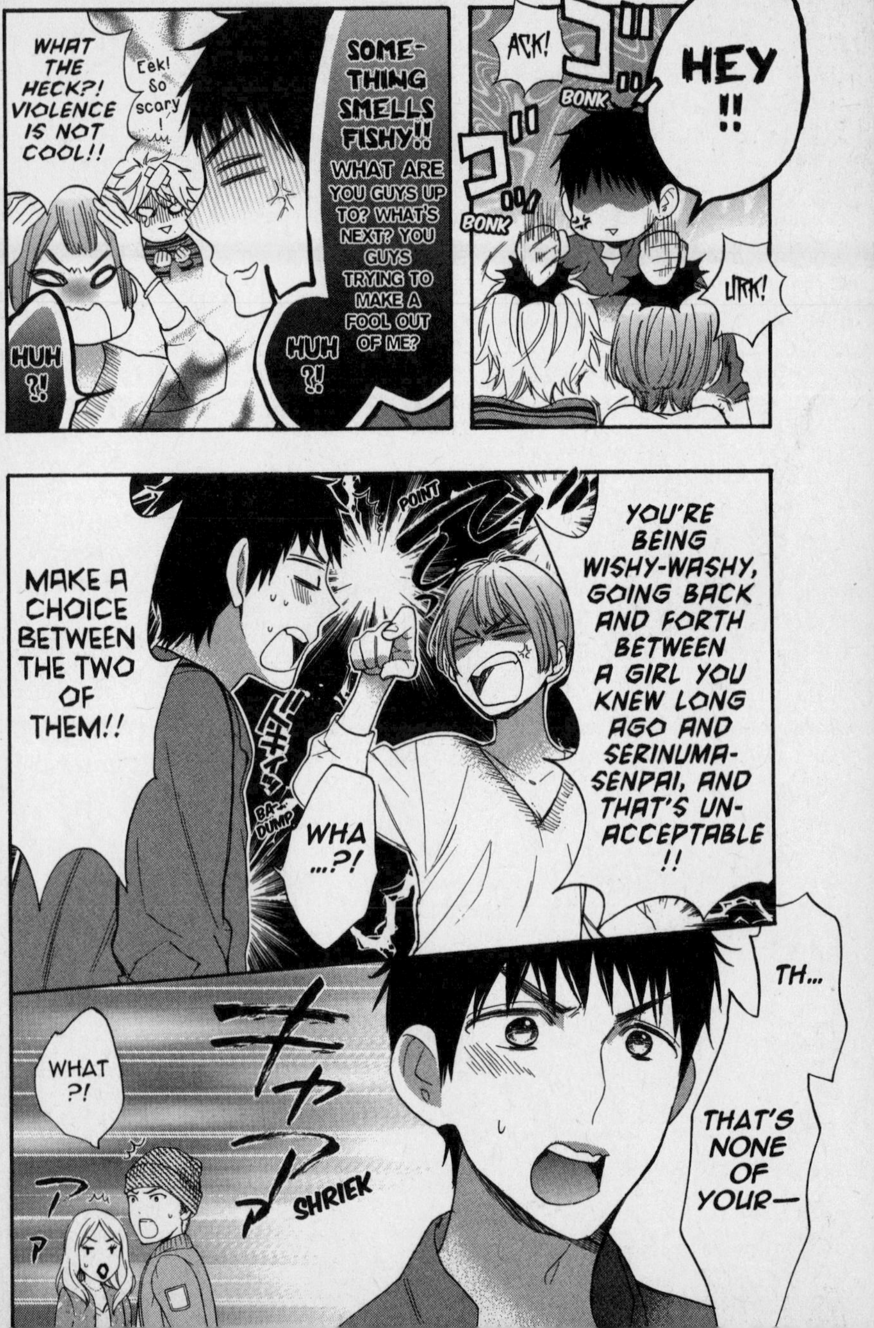
HEY!!
ACK!
BONK
BONK
URK!
SOME-THING SMELLS FISHY!!
WHAT ARE YOU GUYS UP TO? WHAT'S NEXT? YOU GUYS TRYING TO MAKE A FOOL OUT OF ME?
HUH?!
WHAT THE HECK?! VIOLENCE IS NOT COOL!!
Eek! So scary!
HUH?!
YOU'RE BEING WISHY-WASHY, GOING BACK AND FORTH BETWEEN A GIRL YOU KNEW LONG AGO AND SERINUMA-SENPAI, AND THAT'S UN-ACCEPTABLE!!
POINT
BA-DUMP
WHA...?!
MAKE A CHOICE BETWEEN THE TWO OF THEM!!
TH...
THAT'S NONE OF YOUR—
SHRIEK
WHAT?!

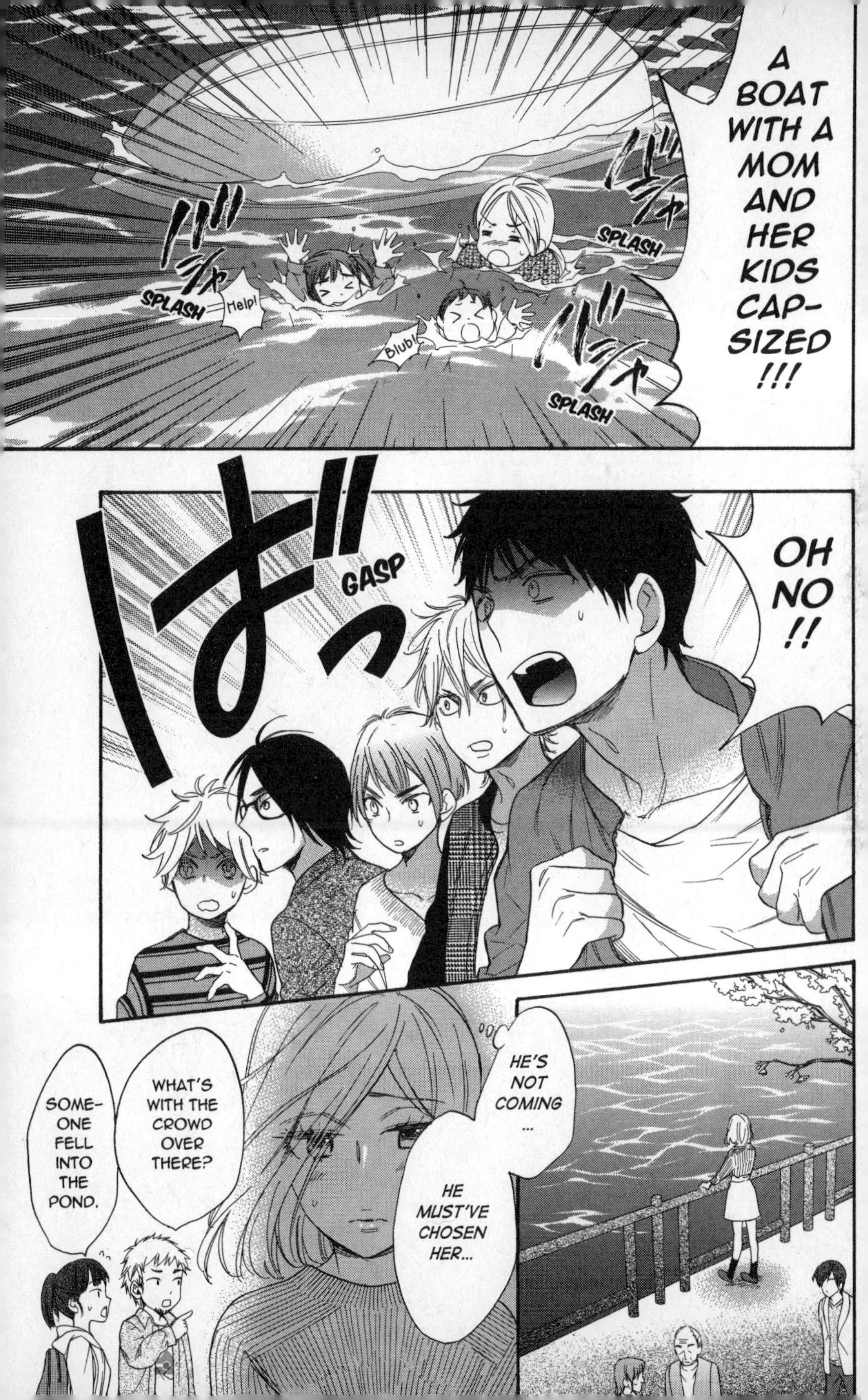
A BOAT WITH A MOM AND HER KIDS CAP-SIZED!!!
SPLASH
SPLASH
Help!
Blub!
SPLASH
OH NO!!
GASP
HE'S NOT COMING...
HE MUST'VE CHOSEN HER...
WHAT'S WITH THE CROWD OVER THERE?
SOME-ONE FELL INTO THE POND.

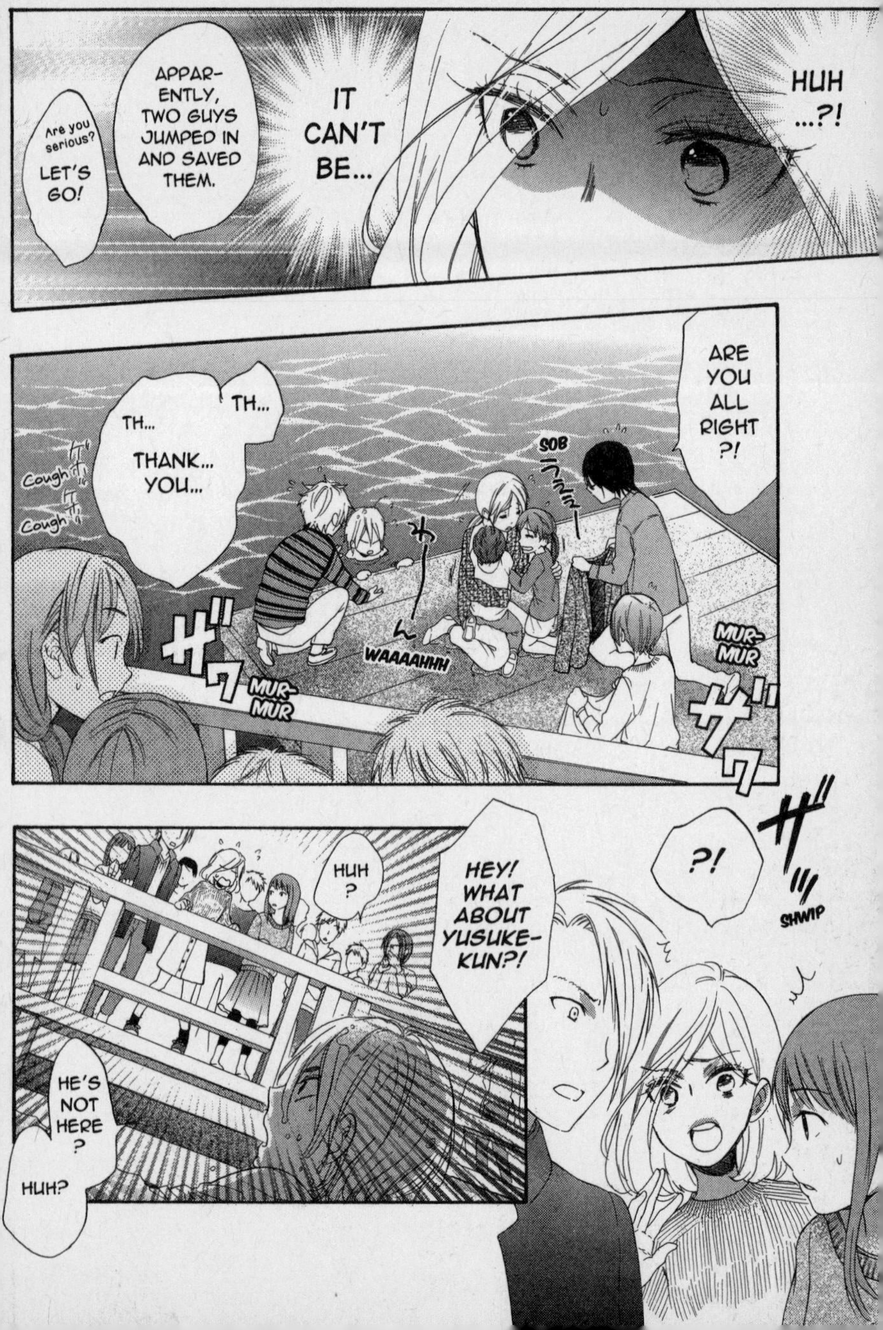
HUH ...?!
IT CAN'T BE...
APPARENTLY, TWO GUYS JUMPED IN AND SAVED THEM.
Are you serious?
LET'S GO!
ARE YOU ALL RIGHT?!
MUR-MUR
SOB
WAAAAHHH
TH...
TH...
THANK... YOU...
Cough
Cough
MUR-MUR
?!
SHWIP
HEY! WHAT ABOUT YUSUKE-KUN?!
HUH?
HE'S NOT HERE?
HUH?

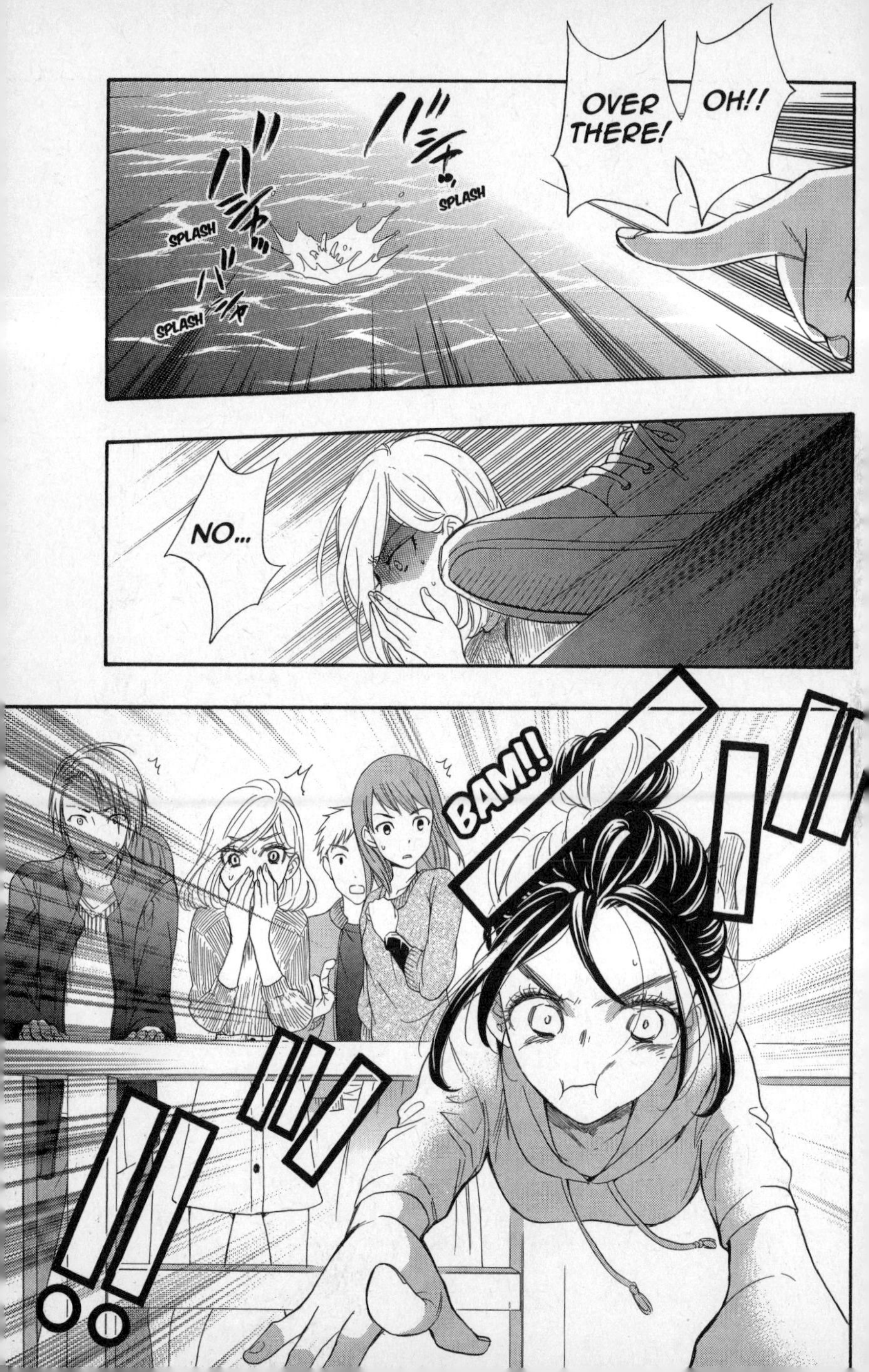
OH!!
OVER THERE!
SPLASH
SPLASH
SPLASH
NO...
BAM!!

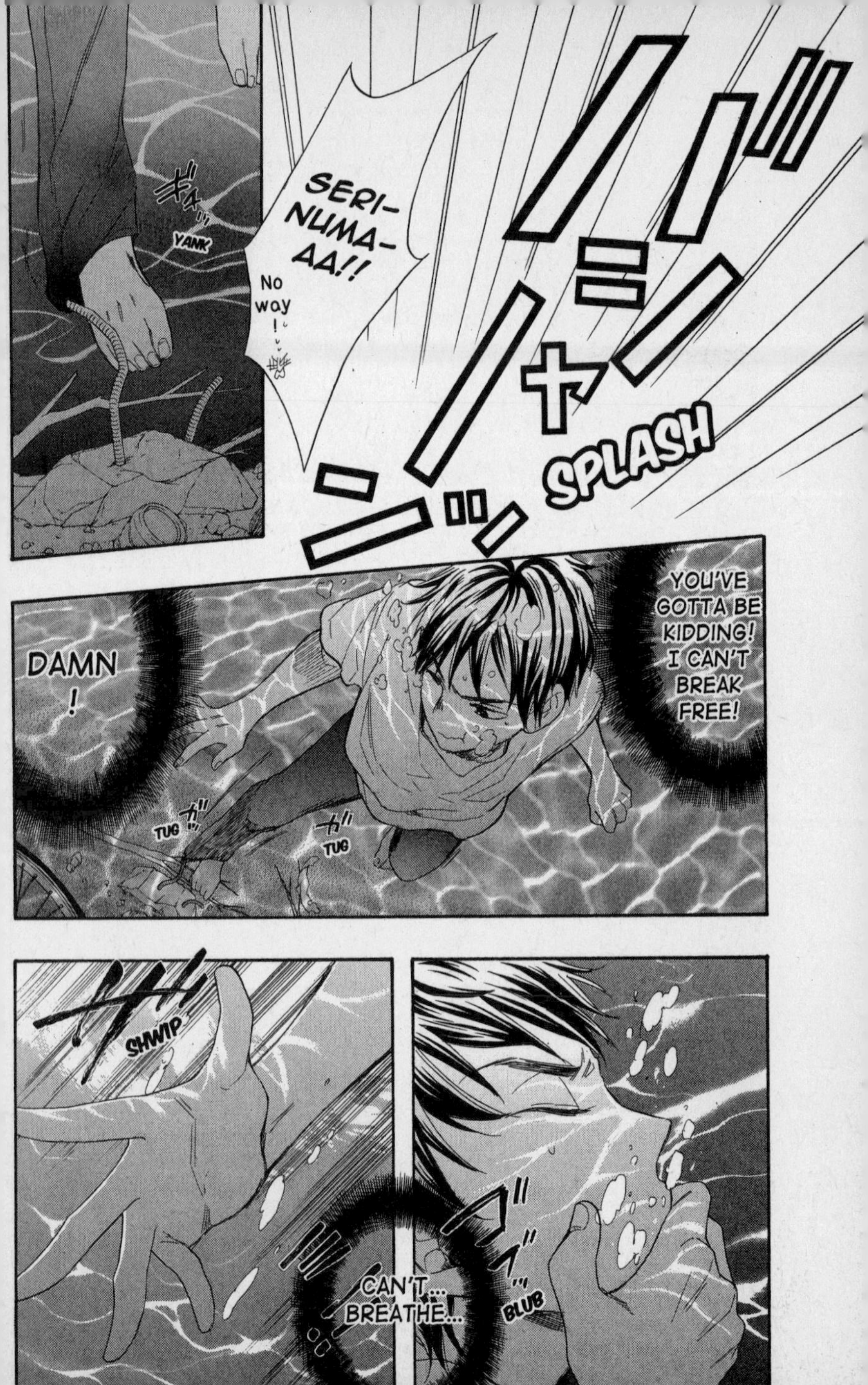
SERI-NUMA-AA!!
SPLASH
YANK
No way!
YOU'VE GOTTA BE KIDDING! I CAN'T BREAK FREE!
DAMN!
TUG
TUG
BLUB
CAN'T... BREATHE...
SHWIP

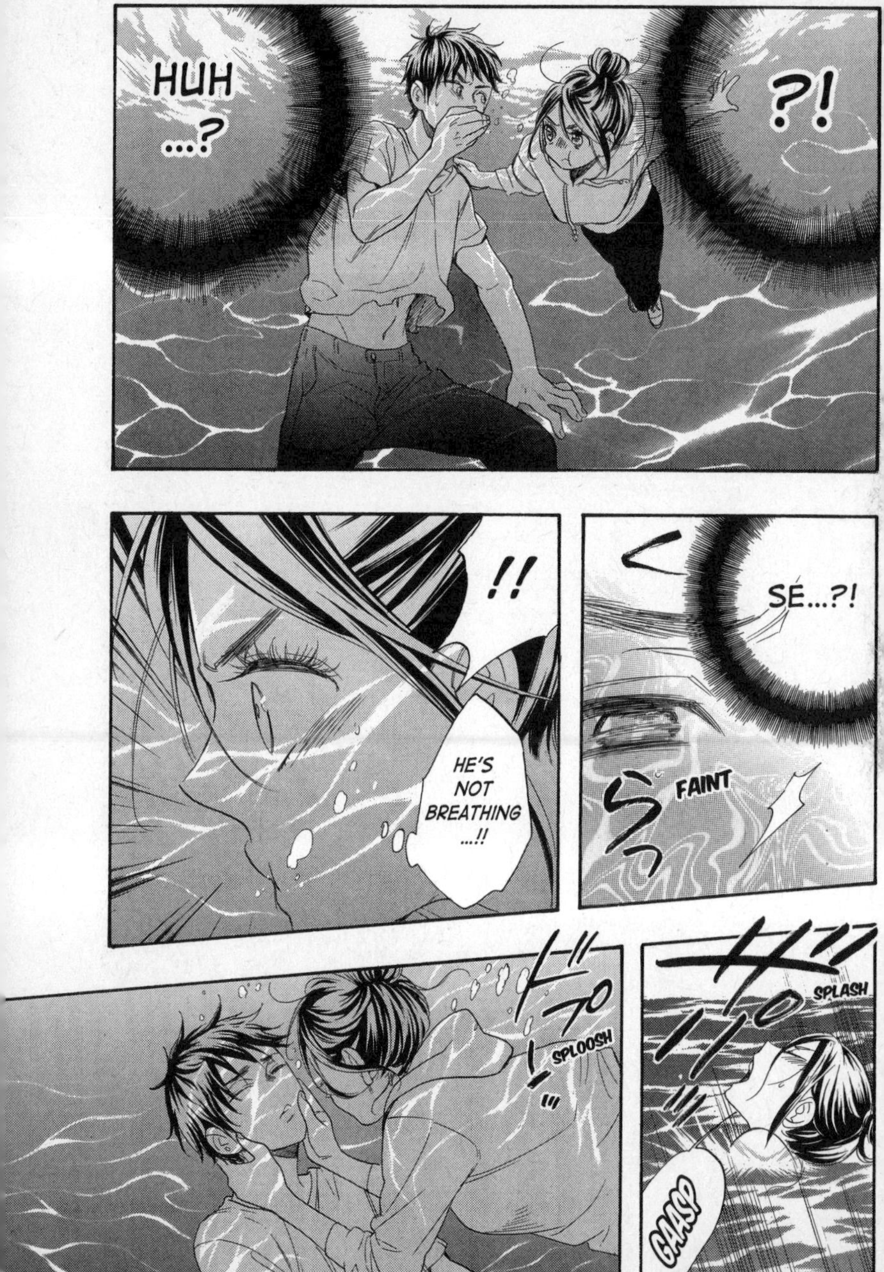
?!
HUH ...?
SE...?!
FAINT
!!
HE'S NOT BREATHING ...!!
SPLASH
GAASP
SPLOOSH

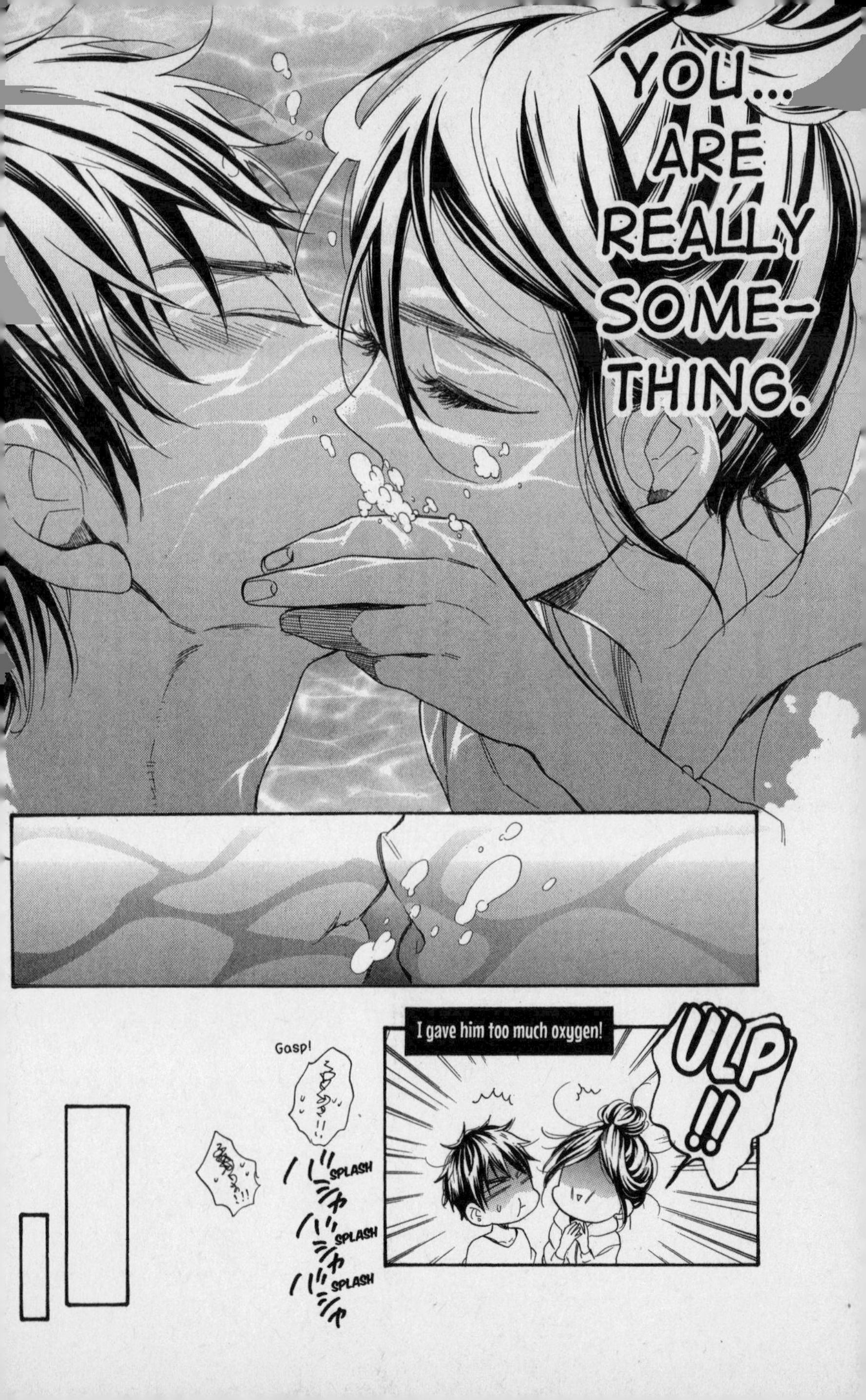
YOU... ARE REALLY SOME-THING.
I gave him too much oxygen!
ULP!!
Gasp!
SPLASH
SPLASH
SPLASH

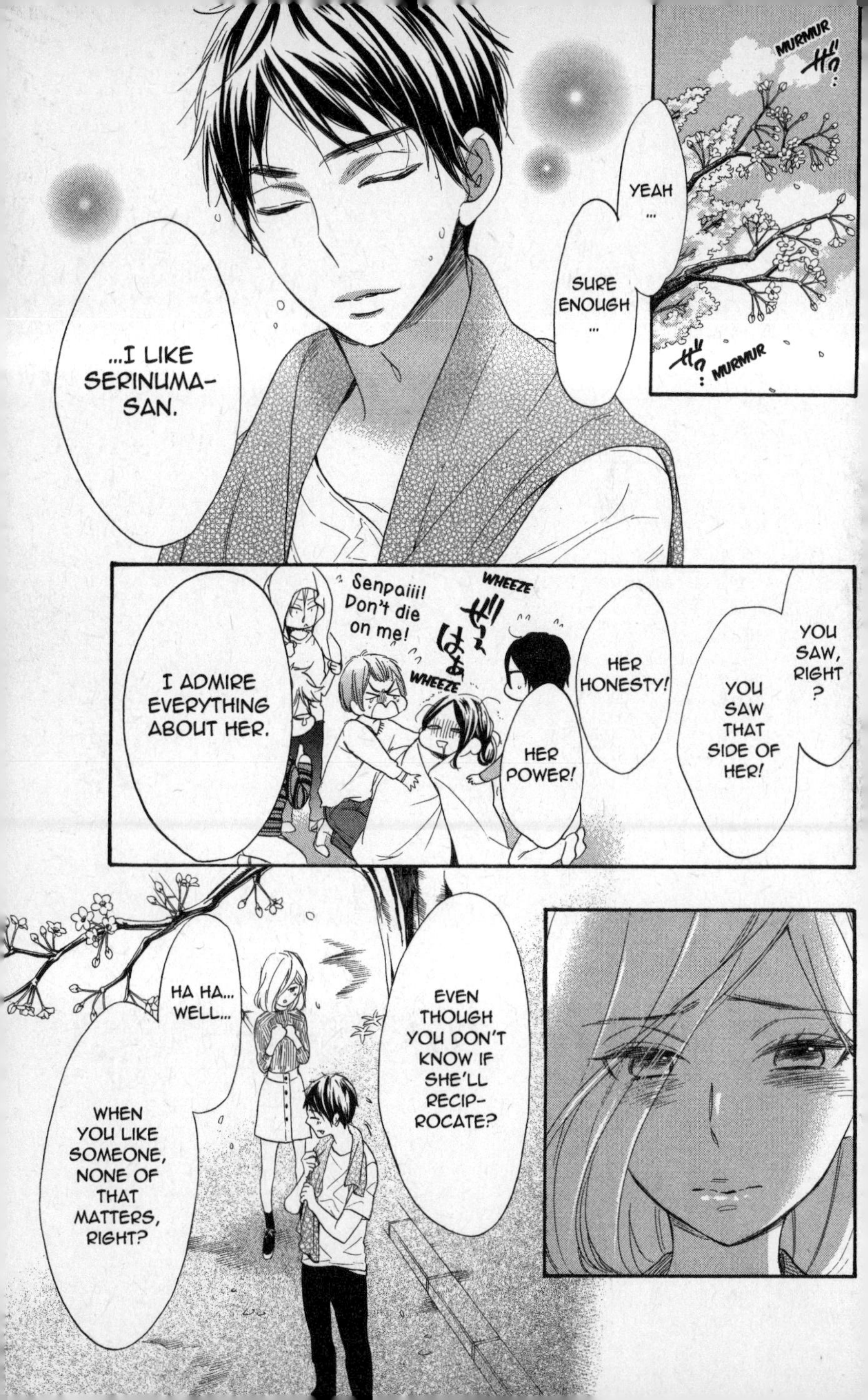
MURMUR
MURMUR
YEAH ... SURE ENOUGH ...
...I LIKE SERINUMA-SAN.
YOU SAW, RIGHT?
YOU SAW THAT SIDE OF HER!
HER HONESTY!
HER POWER!
WHEEZE
WHEEZE
Senpaiii! Don't die on me!
I ADMIRE EVERYTHING ABOUT HER.
EVEN THOUGH YOU DON'T KNOW IF SHE'LL RECIP-ROCATE?
HA HA... WELL...
WHEN YOU LIKE SOMEONE, NONE OF THAT MATTERS, RIGHT?

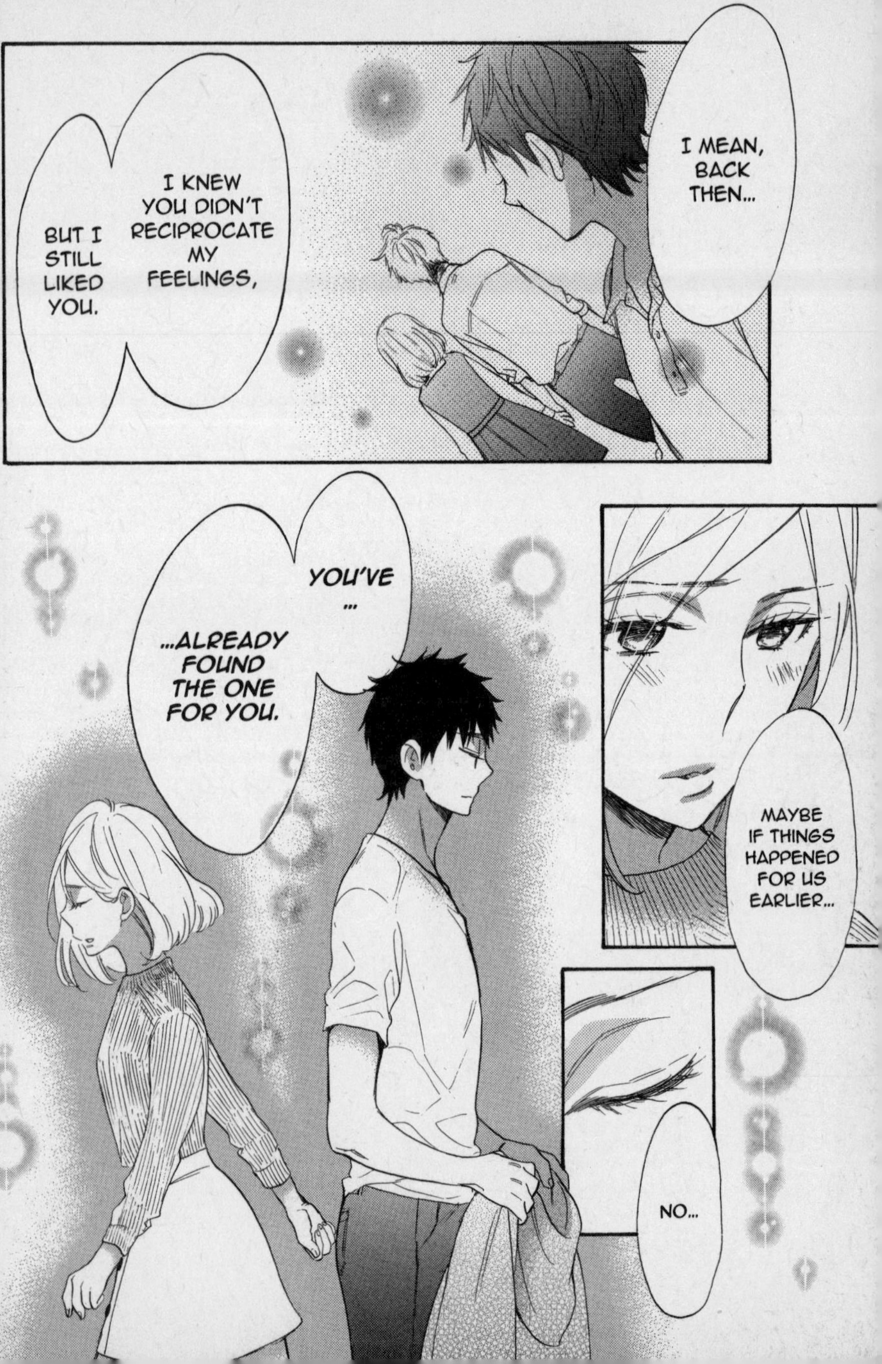
I MEAN, BACK THEN...
I KNEW YOU DIDN'T RECIPROCATE MY FEELINGS,
BUT I STILL LIKED YOU.
MAYBE IF THINGS HAPPENED FOR US EARLIER...
NO...
YOU'VE ...
...ALREADY FOUND THE ONE FOR YOU.

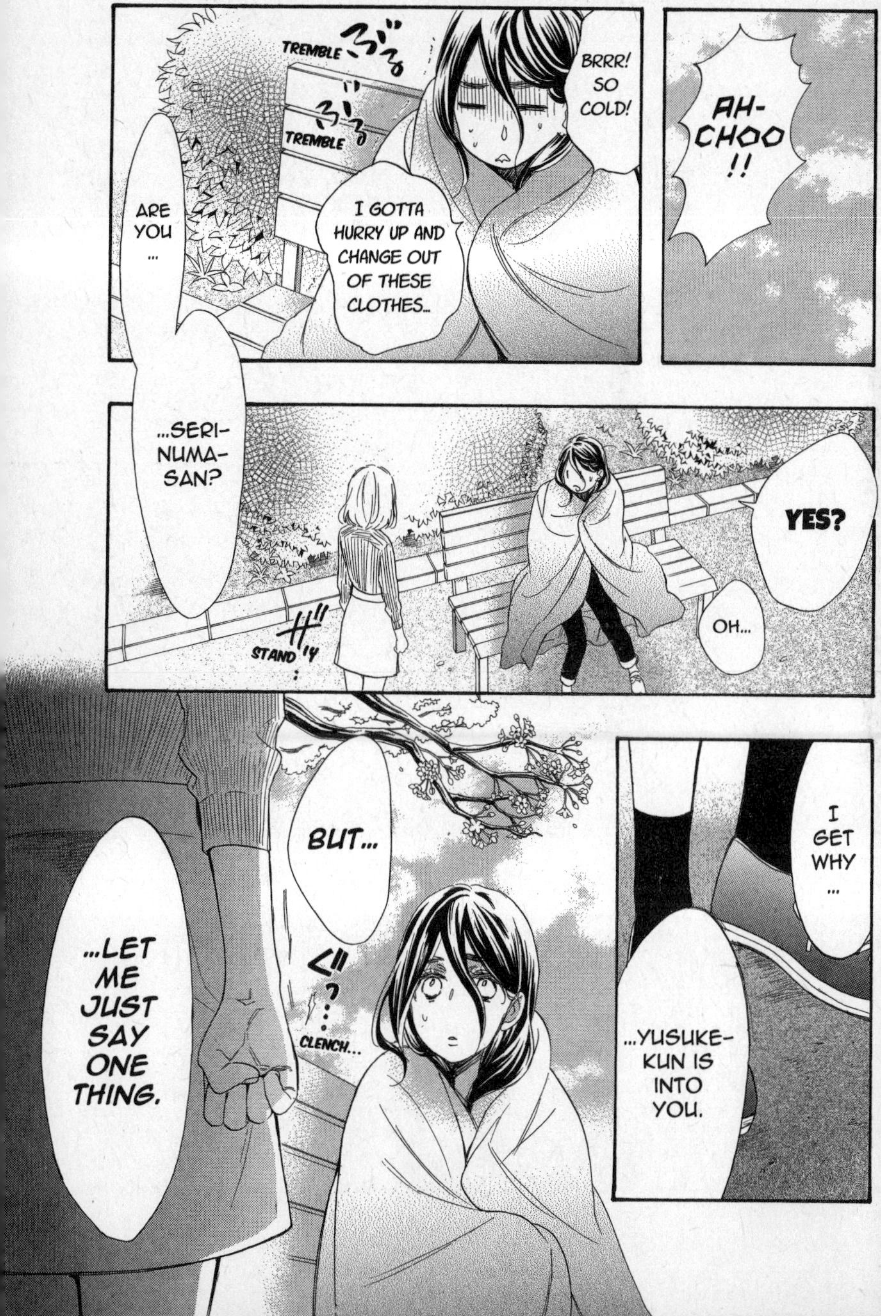
AH-CHOO!!
BRRR! SO COLD!
TREMBLE
TREMBLE
I GOTTA HURRY UP AND CHANGE OUT OF THESE CLOTHES...
ARE YOU ...
...SERI-NUMA-SAN?
YES?
OH...
STAND
I GET WHY ...
...YUSUKE-KUN IS INTO YOU.
BUT...
CLENCH...
...LET ME JUST SAY ONE THING.

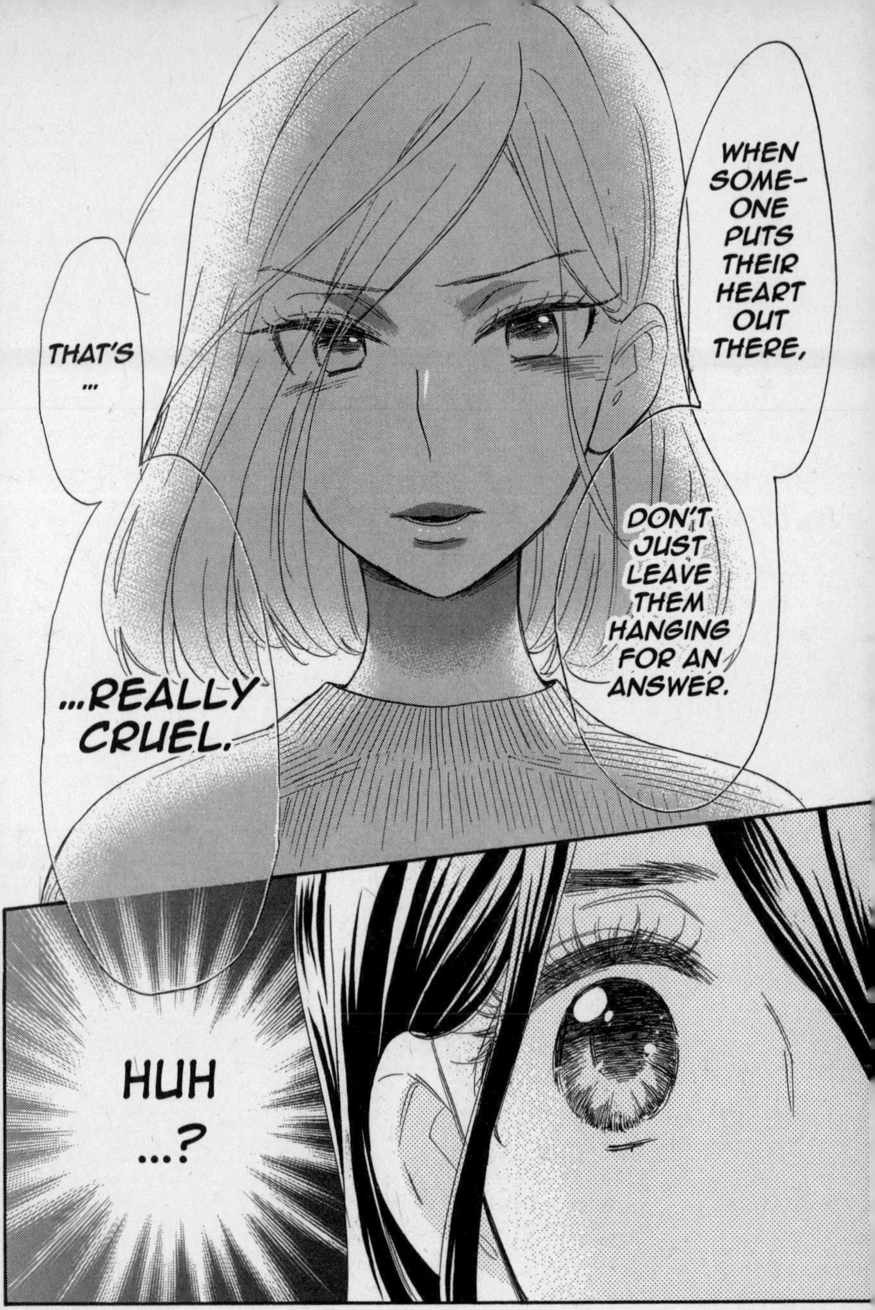
WHEN SOMEONE PUTS THEIR HEART OUT THERE,
DON'T JUST LEAVE THEM HANGING FOR AN ANSWER.
THAT'S ...
...REALLY CRUEL.
HUH ...?

#36 DECISION TIME

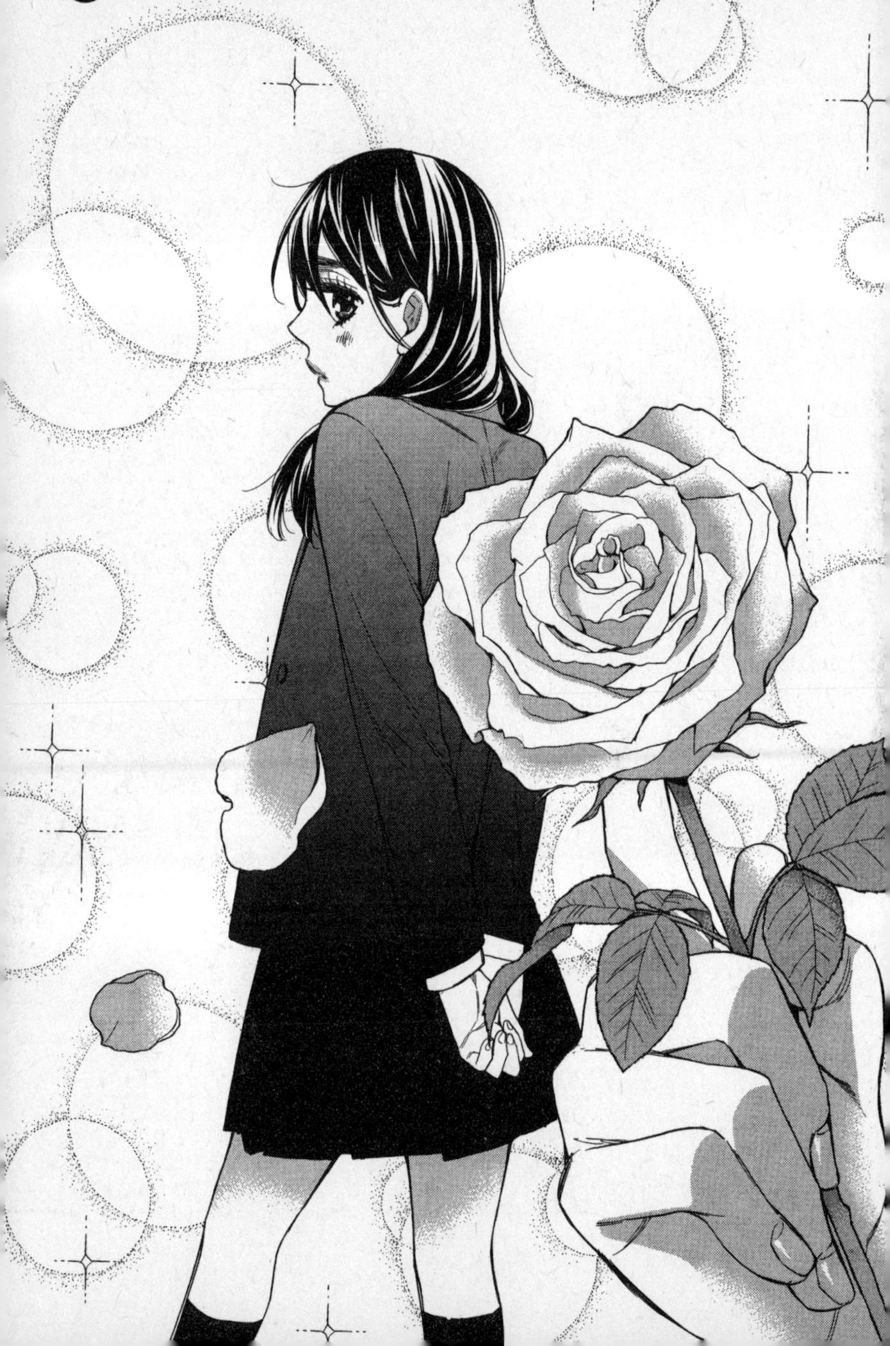

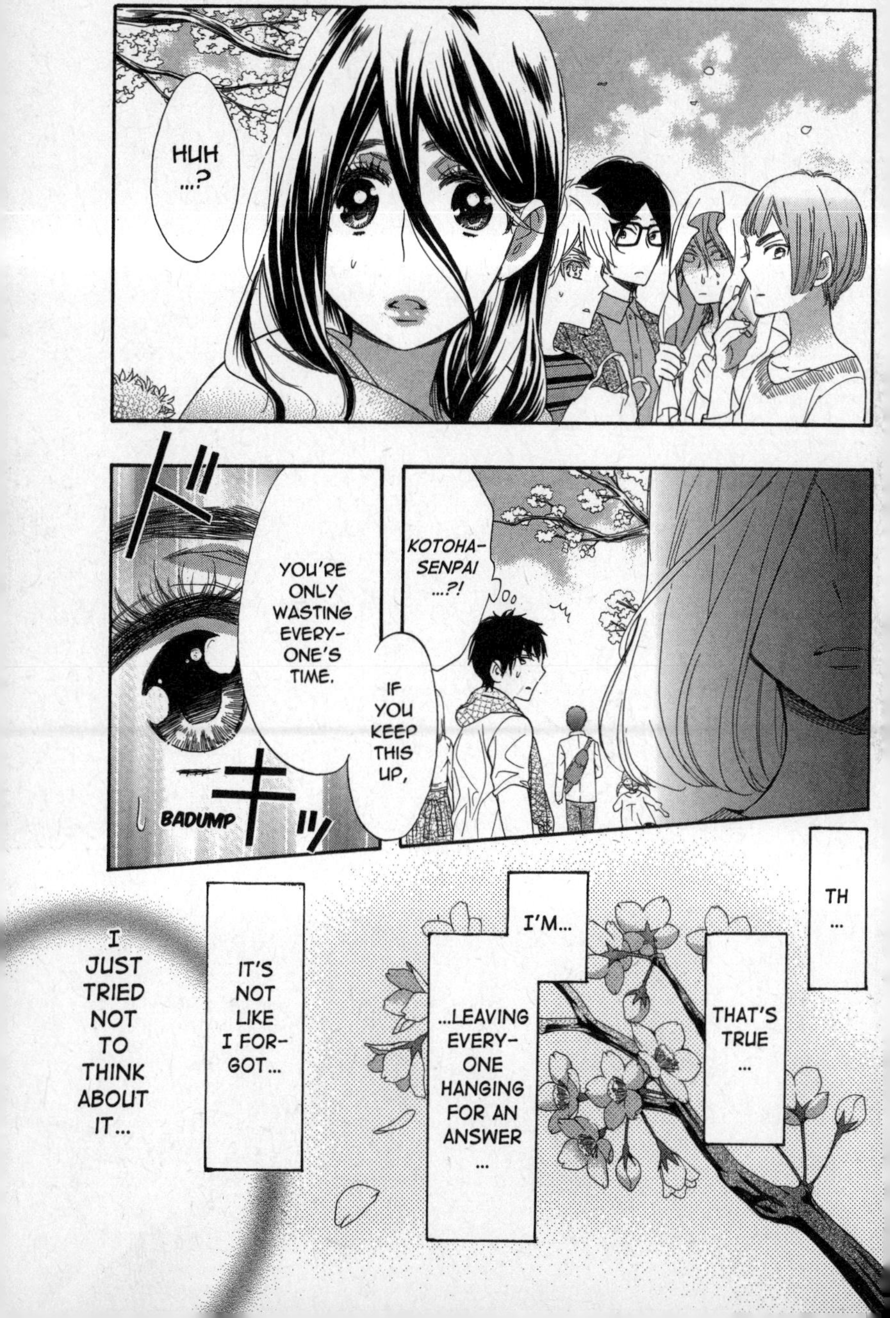
HUH ...?
KOTOHA-SENPAI ...?!
IF YOU KEEP THIS UP,
YOU'RE ONLY WASTING EVERY-ONE'S TIME.
BADUMP
TH ...
THAT'S TRUE ...
I'M...
...LEAVING EVERY-ONE HANGING FOR AN ANSWER ...
IT'S NOT LIKE I FOR-GOT...
I JUST TRIED NOT TO THINK ABOUT IT...

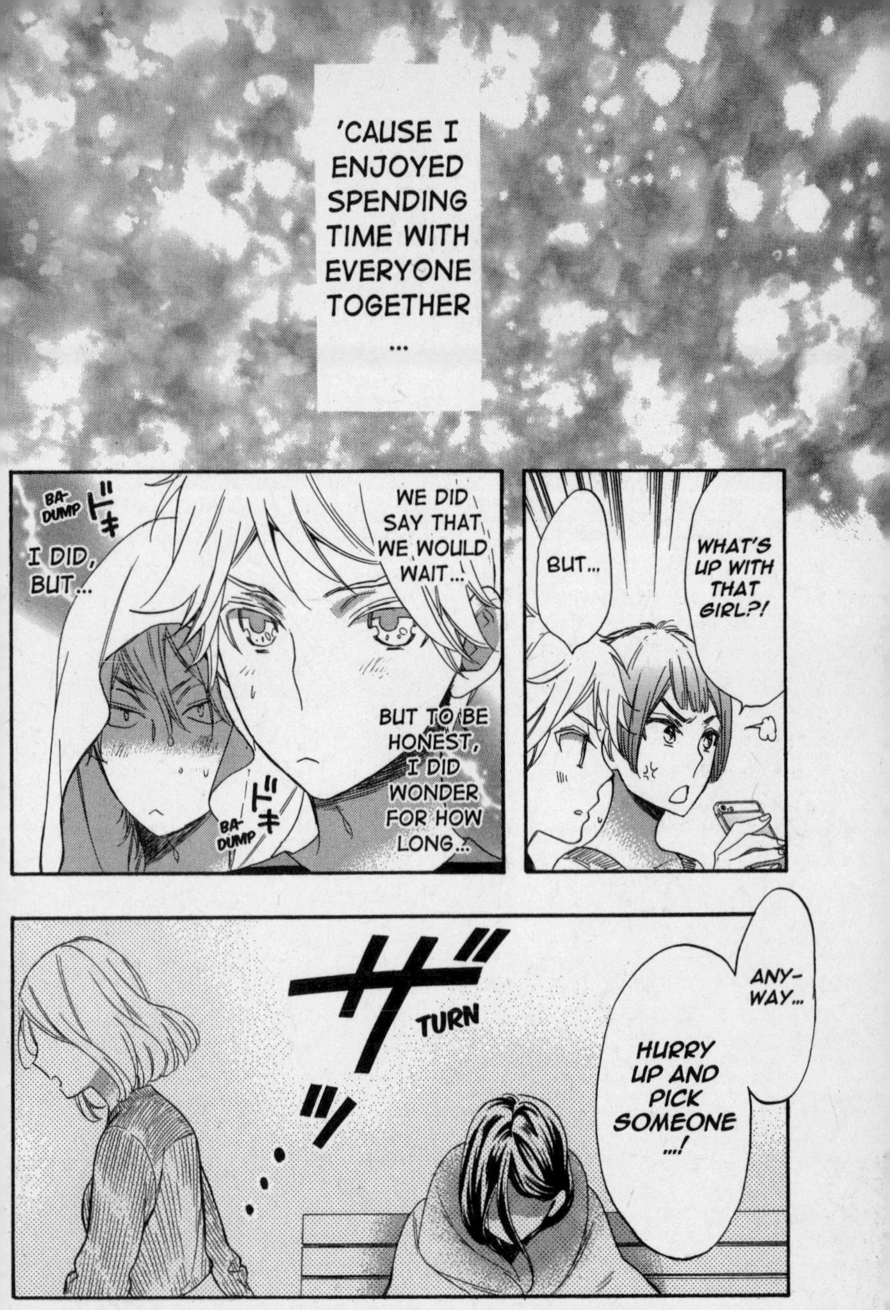
'CAUSE I ENJOYED SPENDING TIME WITH EVERYONE TOGETHER ...
WHAT'S UP WITH THAT GIRL?!
BUT...
WE DID SAY THAT WE WOULD WAIT...
BA-DUMP ドキ
I DID, BUT...
BUT TO BE HONEST, I DID WONDER FOR HOW LONG...
BA-DUMP ドキ
ANY-WAY...
HURRY UP AND PICK SOMEONE ...!
ザッ
TURN

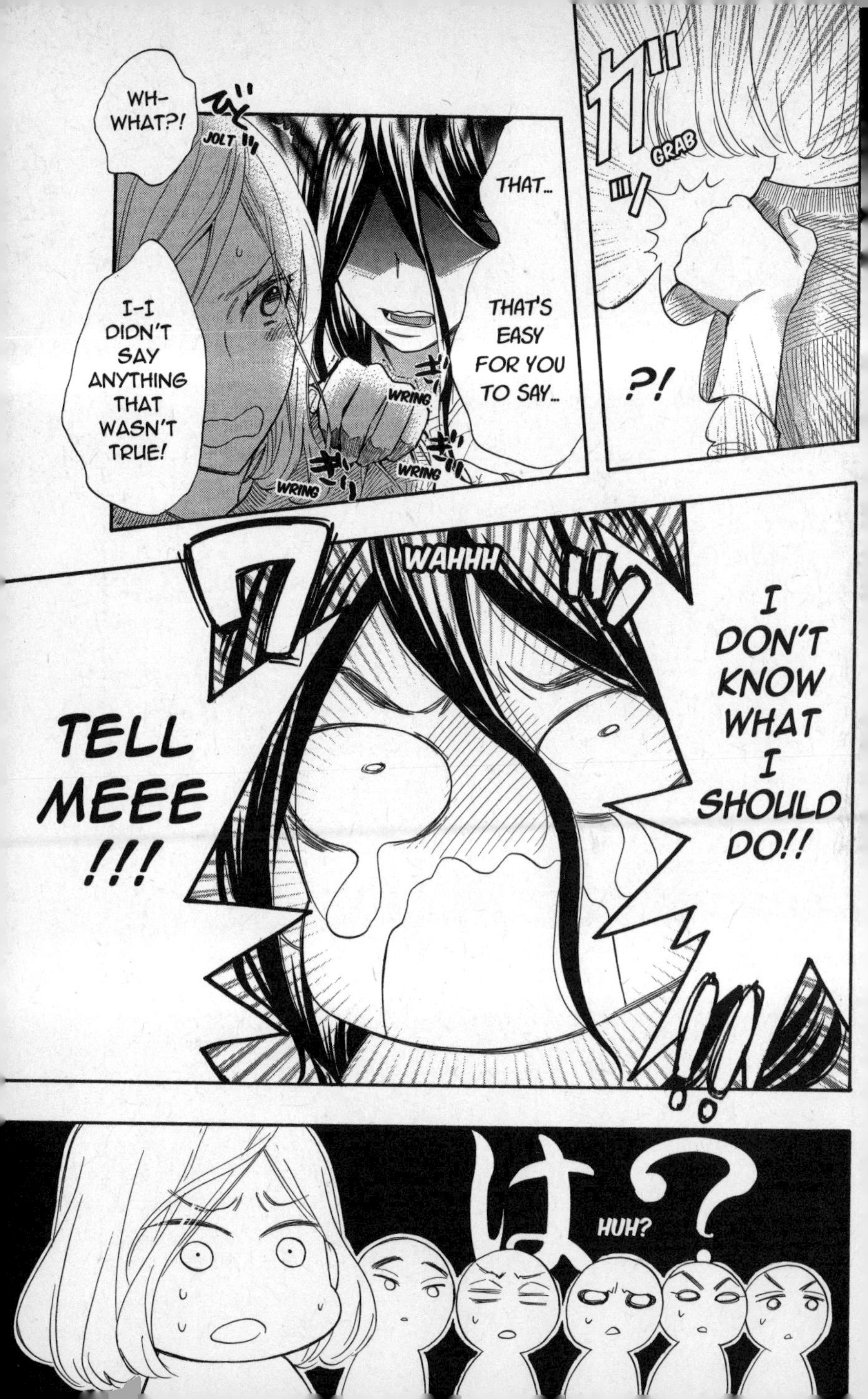
GRAB
?!
THAT...
THAT'S EASY FOR YOU TO SAY...
WRING
WRING
WRING
WH-WHAT?!
JOLT
I-I DIDN'T SAY ANYTHING THAT WASN'T TRUE!
I DON'T KNOW WHAT I SHOULD DO!!
WAHHH
TELL MEEE!!!
は?
HUH?

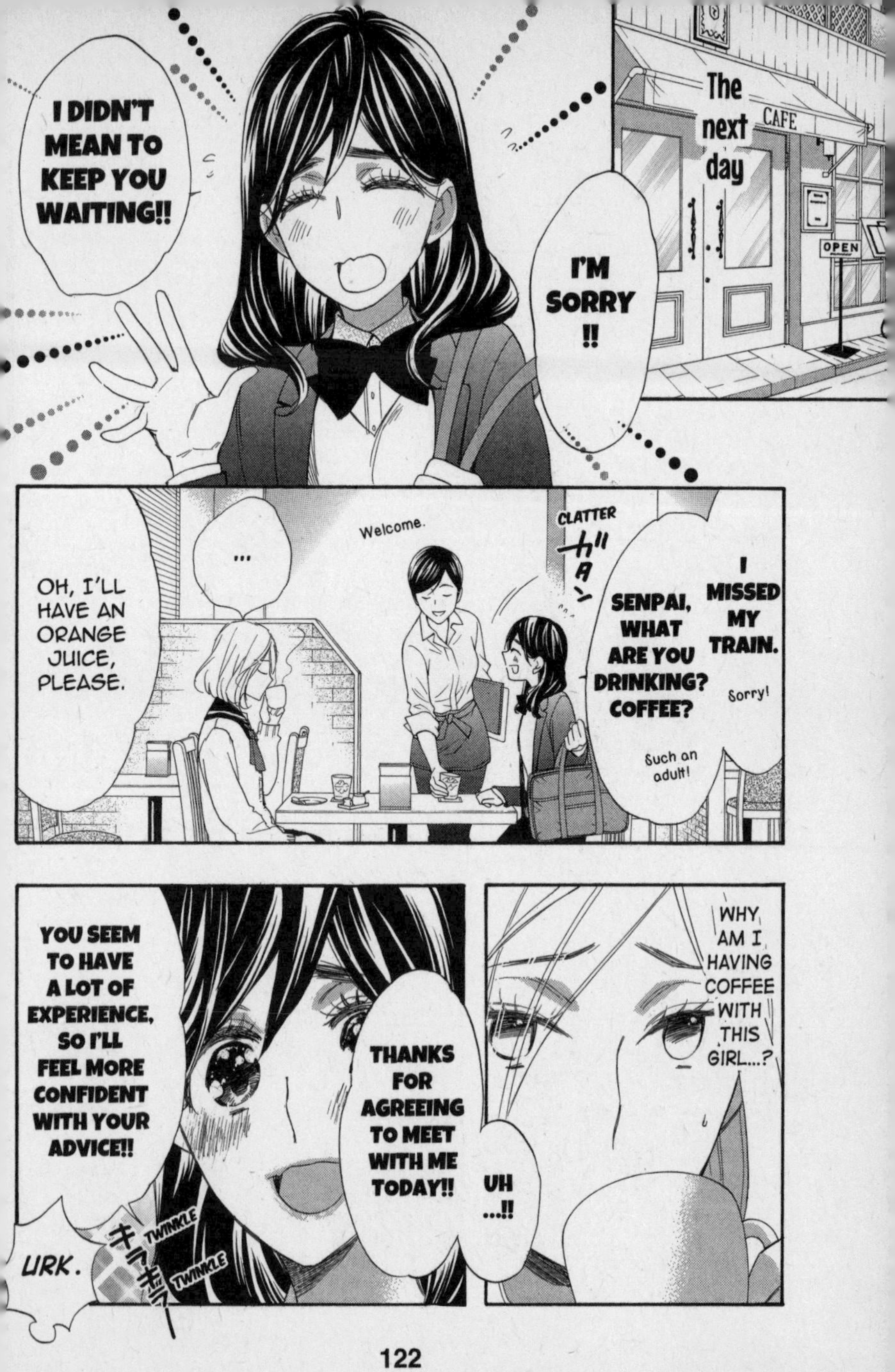
The next day
CAFE
OPEN
I'M SORRY!!
I DIDN'T MEAN TO KEEP YOU WAITING!!
I MISSED MY TRAIN.
Sorry!
SENPAI, WHAT ARE YOU DRINKING? COFFEE?
Such an adult!
CLATTER
Welcome.
...
OH, I'LL HAVE AN ORANGE JUICE, PLEASE.
WHY AM I HAVING COFFEE WITH THIS GIRL...?
UH ...!!
THANKS FOR AGREEING TO MEET WITH ME TODAY!!
YOU SEEM TO HAVE A LOT OF EXPERIENCE, SO I'LL FEEL MORE CONFIDENT WITH YOUR ADVICE!!
TWINKLE
TWINKLE
URK.

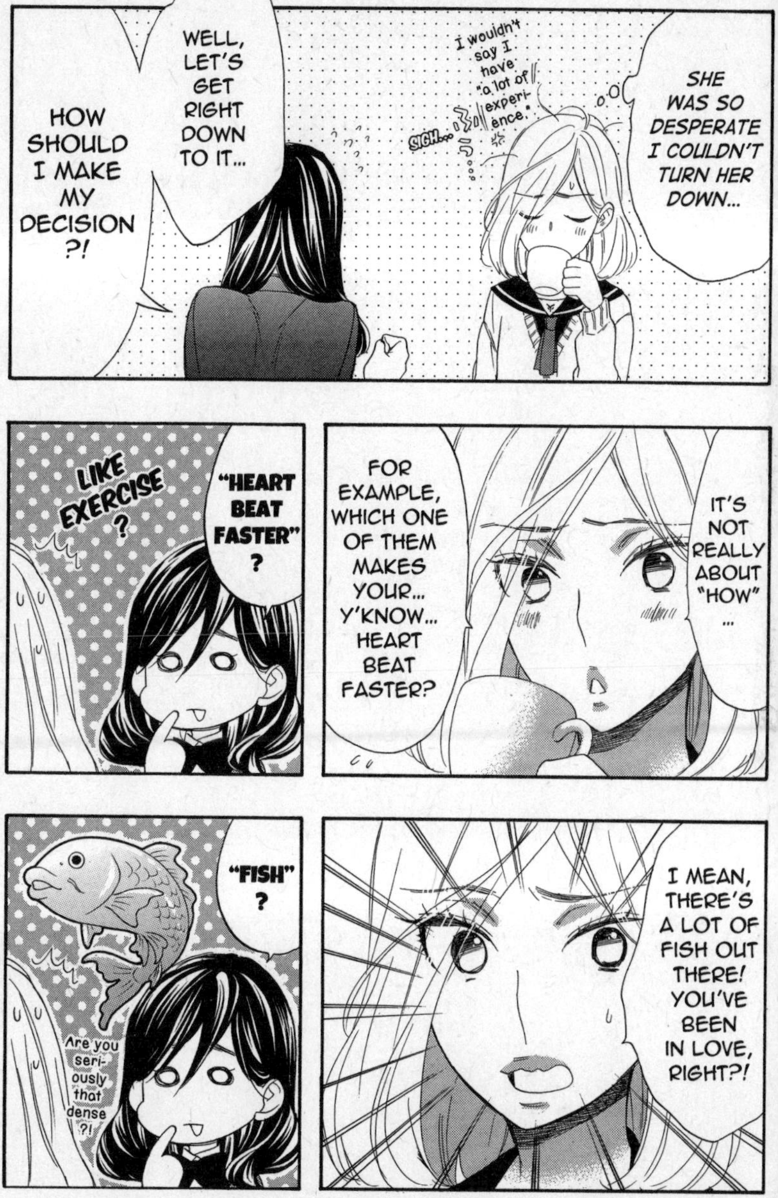
SHE WAS SO DESPERATE I COULDN'T TURN HER DOWN...
I wouldn't say I have "a lot of experience."
SIGH...
WELL, LET'S GET RIGHT DOWN TO IT...
HOW SHOULD I MAKE MY DECISION?!
IT'S NOT REALLY ABOUT "HOW"...
FOR EXAMPLE, WHICH ONE OF THEM MAKES YOUR... Y'KNOW... HEART BEAT FASTER?
"HEART BEAT FASTER"?
LIKE EXERCISE?
I MEAN, THERE'S A LOT OF FISH OUT THERE! YOU'VE BEEN IN LOVE, RIGHT?!
"FISH"?
Are you seriously that dense?!

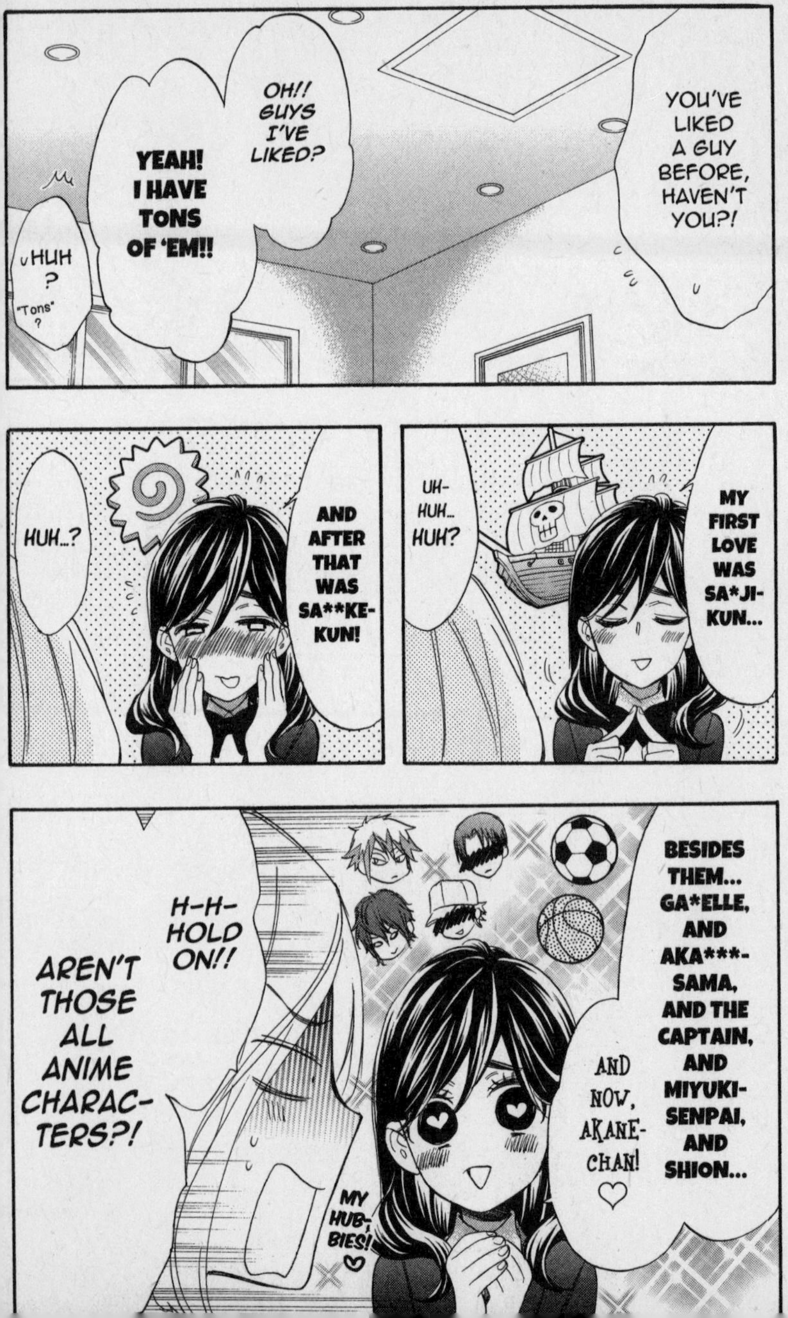
YOU'VE LIKED A GUY BEFORE, HAVEN'T YOU?!
OH!! GUYS I'VE LIKED?
YEAH! I HAVE TONS OF 'EM!!
HUH?
"Tons"?
MY FIRST LOVE WAS SA*JI-KUN...
UH-HUH... HUH?
AND AFTER THAT WAS SA**KE-KUN!
HUH...?
BESIDES THEM... GA*ELLE, AND AKA***-SAMA, AND THE CAPTAIN, AND MIYUKI-SENPAI, AND SHION...
AND NOW, AKANE-CHAN! ♡
MY HUBBIES! ♡
H-H-HOLD ON!!
AREN'T THOSE ALL ANIME CHARACTERS?!

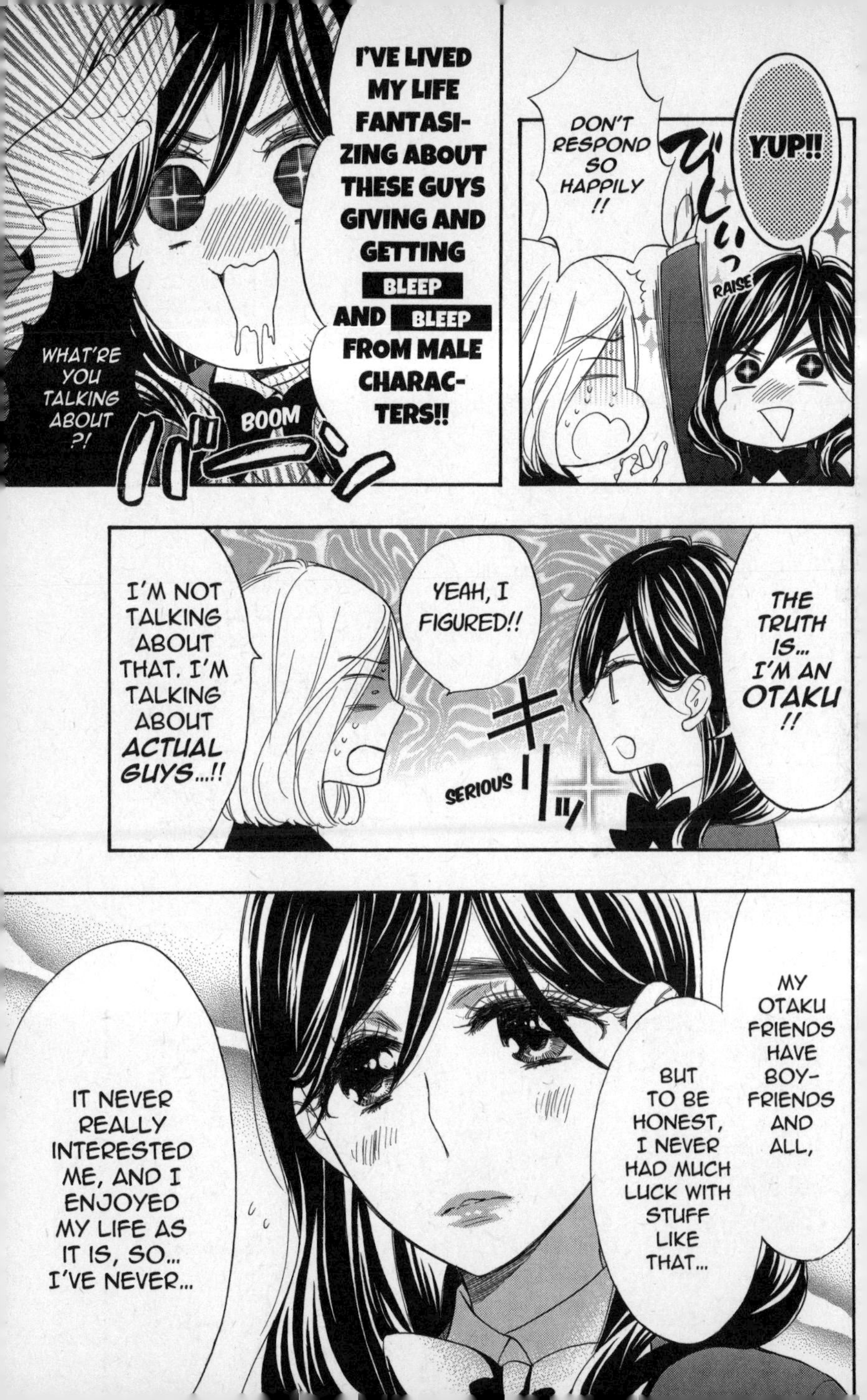
YUP!!
DON'T RESPOND SO HAPPILY!!
びしいっ
RAISE
I'VE LIVED MY LIFE FANTASIZING ABOUT THESE GUYS GIVING AND GETTING BLEEP AND BLEEP FROM MALE CHARACTERS!!
BOOM
WHAT'RE YOU TALKING ABOUT?!
THE TRUTH IS... I'M AN OTAKU!!
SERIOUS
YEAH, I FIGURED!!
I'M NOT TALKING ABOUT THAT. I'M TALKING ABOUT ACTUAL GUYS...!!
MY OTAKU FRIENDS HAVE BOYFRIENDS AND ALL,
BUT TO BE HONEST, I NEVER HAD MUCH LUCK WITH STUFF LIKE THAT...
IT NEVER REALLY INTERESTED ME, AND I ENJOYED MY LIFE AS IT IS, SO... I'VE NEVER...

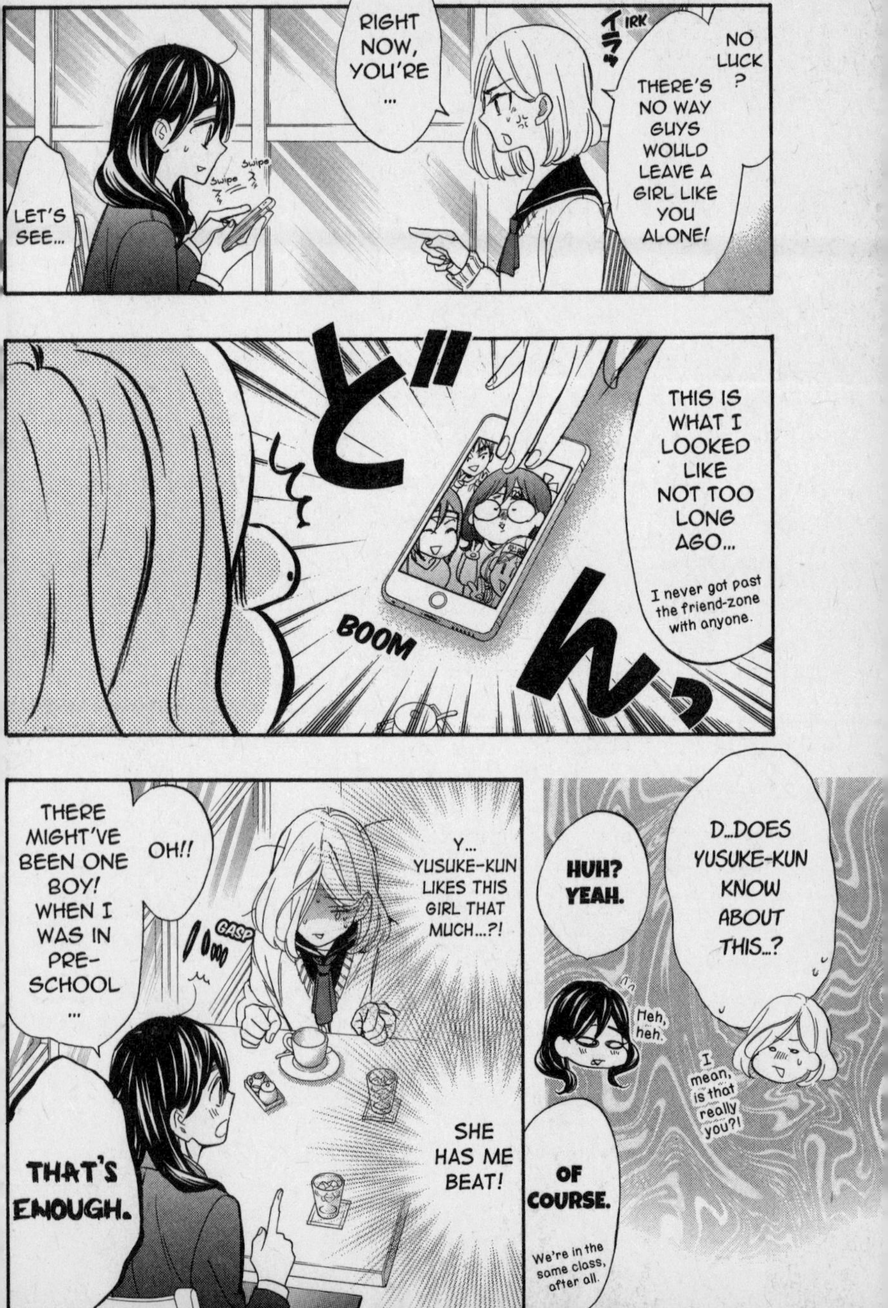
イラッ
IRK
NO LUCK?
THERE'S NO WAY GUYS WOULD LEAVE A GIRL LIKE YOU ALONE!
RIGHT NOW, YOU'RE ...
Swipe
Swipe
LET'S SEE...
THIS IS WHAT I LOOKED LIKE NOT TOO LONG AGO...
I never got past the friend-zone with anyone.
どん
BOOM
D...DOES YUSUKE-KUN KNOW ABOUT THIS..?
HUH? YEAH.
I mean, is that really you?!
Heh, heh.
OF COURSE.
We're in the same class, after all.
Y... YUSUKE-KUN LIKES THIS GIRL THAT MUCH...?!
OH!!
THERE MIGHT'VE BEEN ONE BOY! WHEN I WAS IN PRE-SCHOOL ...
GASP
SHE HAS ME BEAT!
THAT'S ENOUGH.

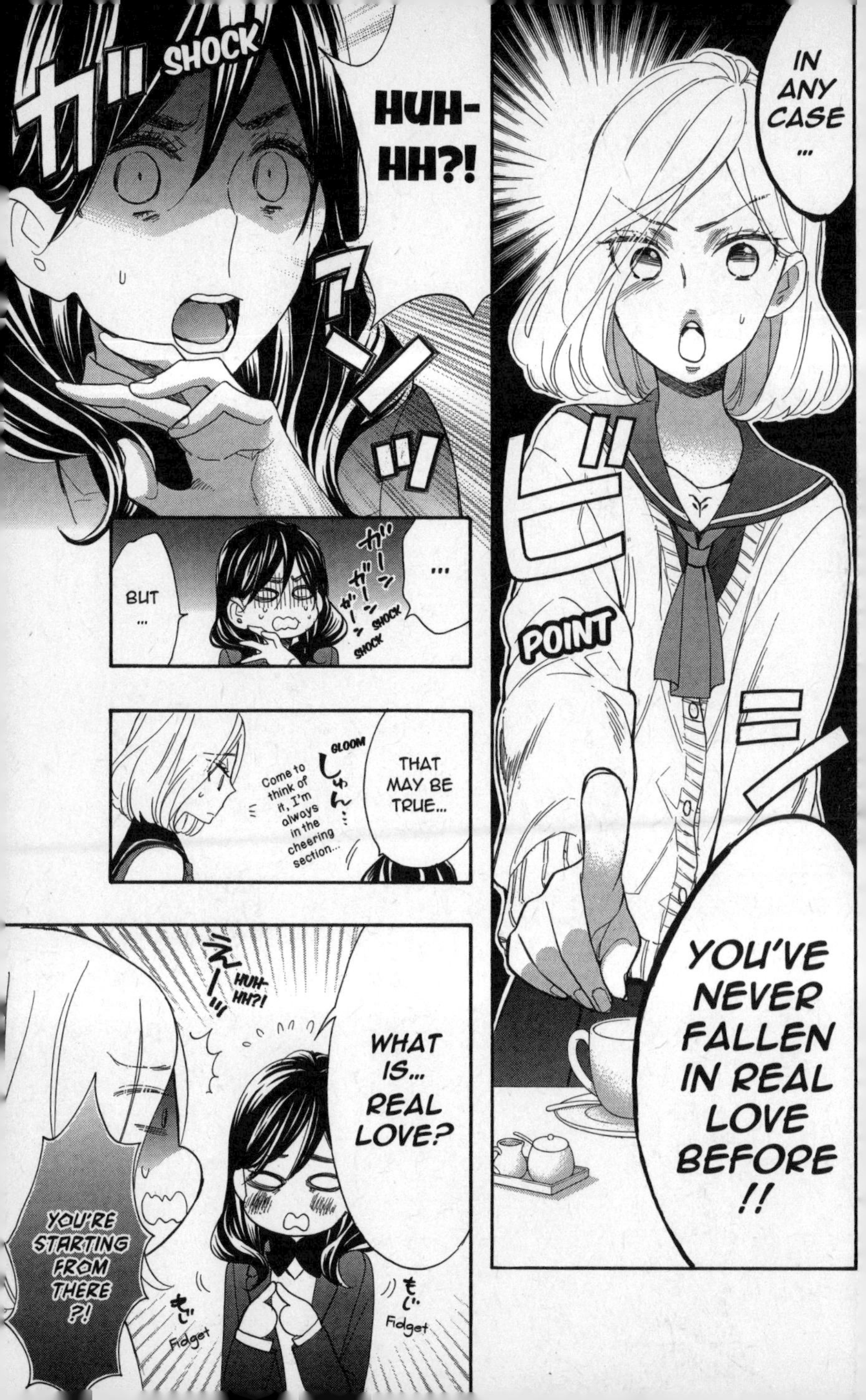
IN ANY CASE ...
POINT
YOU'VE NEVER FALLEN IN REAL LOVE BEFORE !!
SHOCK
HUH-HH?!
...
SHOCK
SHOCK
BUT ...
THAT MAY BE TRUE...
GLOOM
Come to think of it, I'm always in the cheering section...
WHAT IS... REAL LOVE?
HUH-HH?!
Fidget
Fidget
YOU'RE STARTING FROM THERE ?!

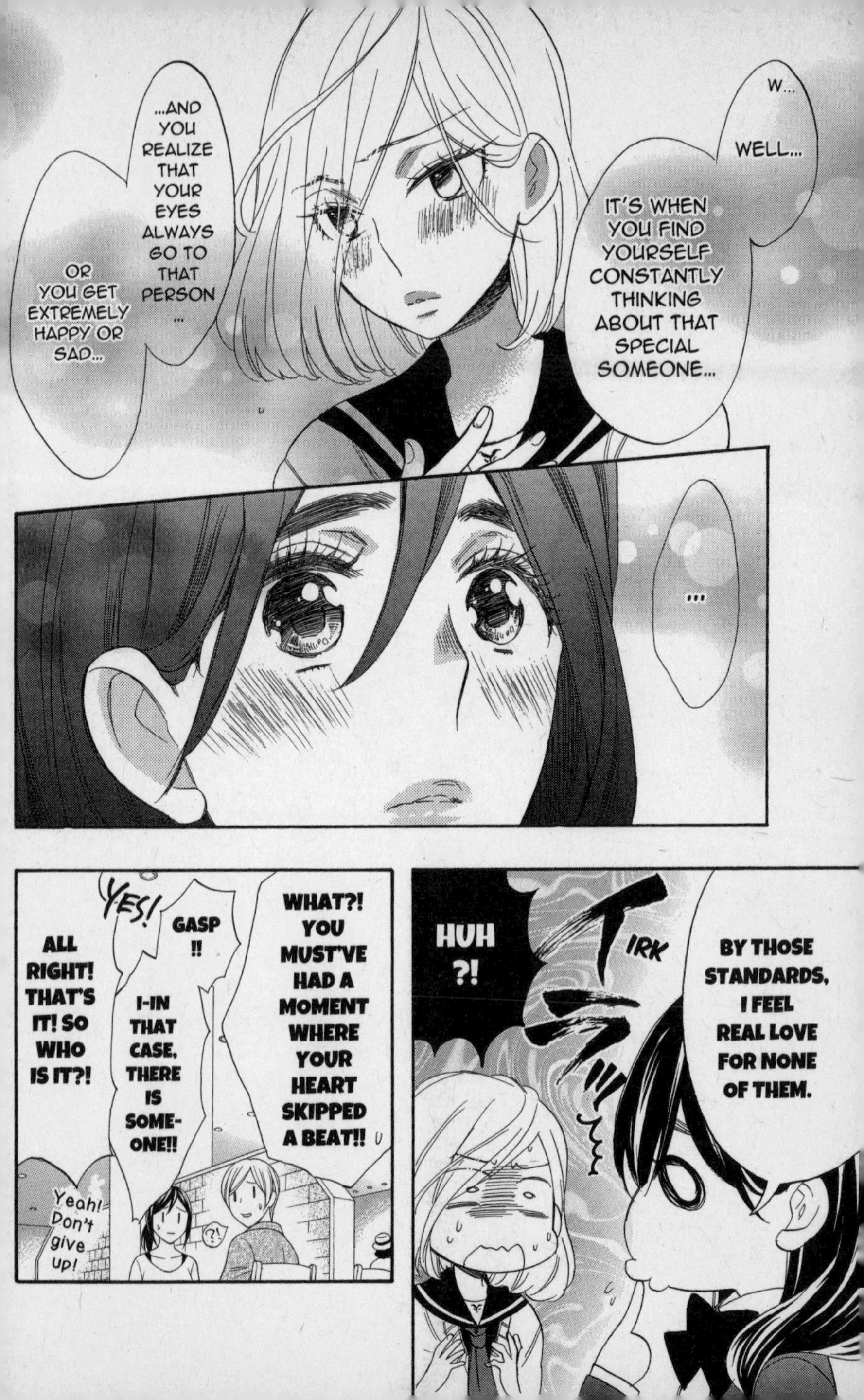

W... WELL...
IT'S WHEN YOU FIND YOURSELF CONSTANTLY THINKING ABOUT THAT SPECIAL SOMEONE...
...AND YOU REALIZE THAT YOUR EYES ALWAYS GO TO THAT PERSON ...
OR YOU GET EXTREMELY HAPPY OR SAD...
...
BY THOSE STANDARDS, I FEEL REAL LOVE FOR NONE OF THEM.
IRK
HUH ?!
WHAT?! YOU MUST'VE HAD A MOMENT WHERE YOUR HEART SKIPPED A BEAT!!
GASP !!
I-IN THAT CASE, THERE IS SOME-ONE!!
YES!
ALL RIGHT! THAT'S IT! SO WHO IS IT?!
?!
Yeah! Don't give up!

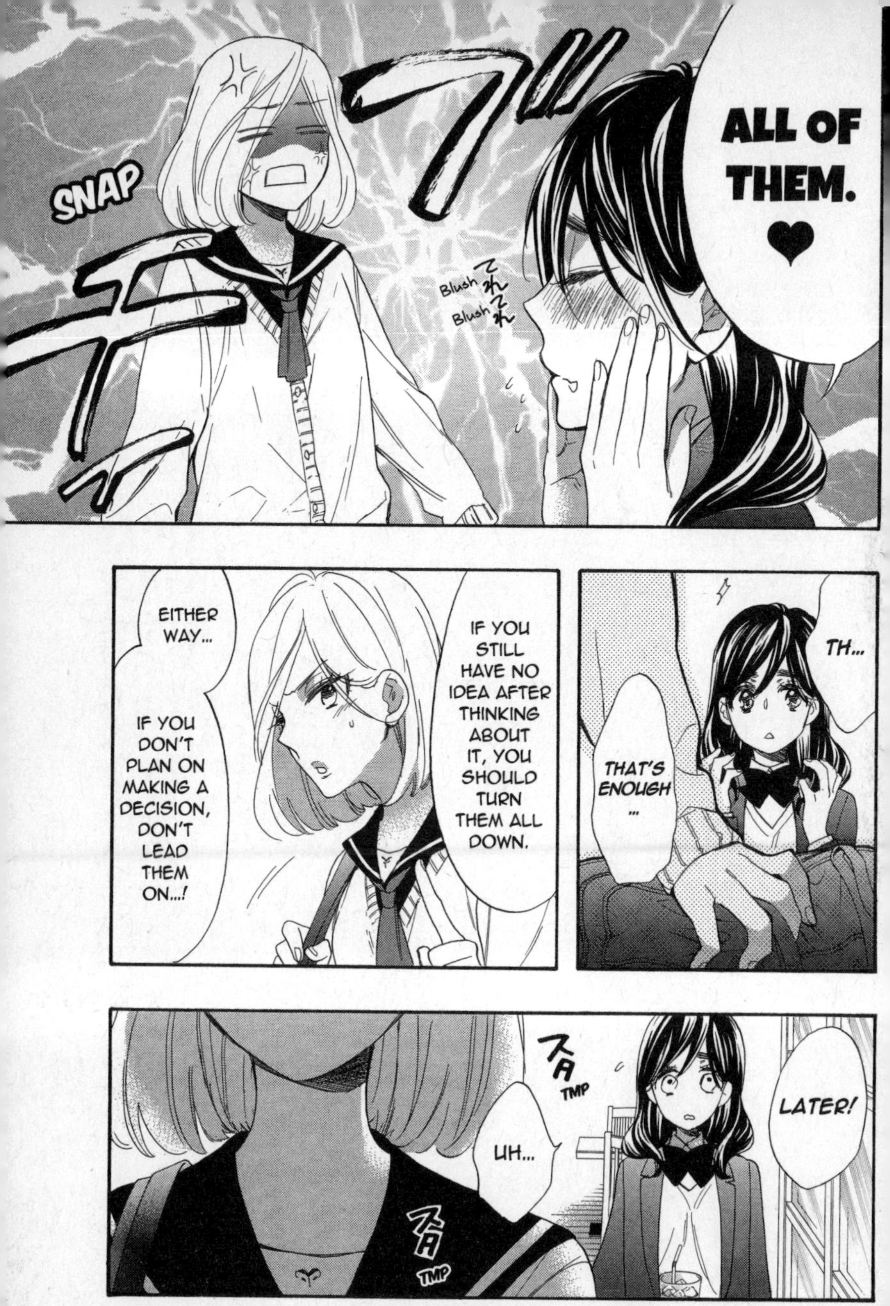
ALL OF THEM. ♥
Blush てれ
Blush てれ
SNAP
TH...
THAT'S ENOUGH ...
IF YOU STILL HAVE NO IDEA AFTER THINKING ABOUT IT, YOU SHOULD TURN THEM ALL DOWN.
EITHER WAY...
IF YOU DON'T PLAN ON MAKING A DECISION, DON'T LEAD THEM ON...!
LATER!
TMP
UH...
TMP

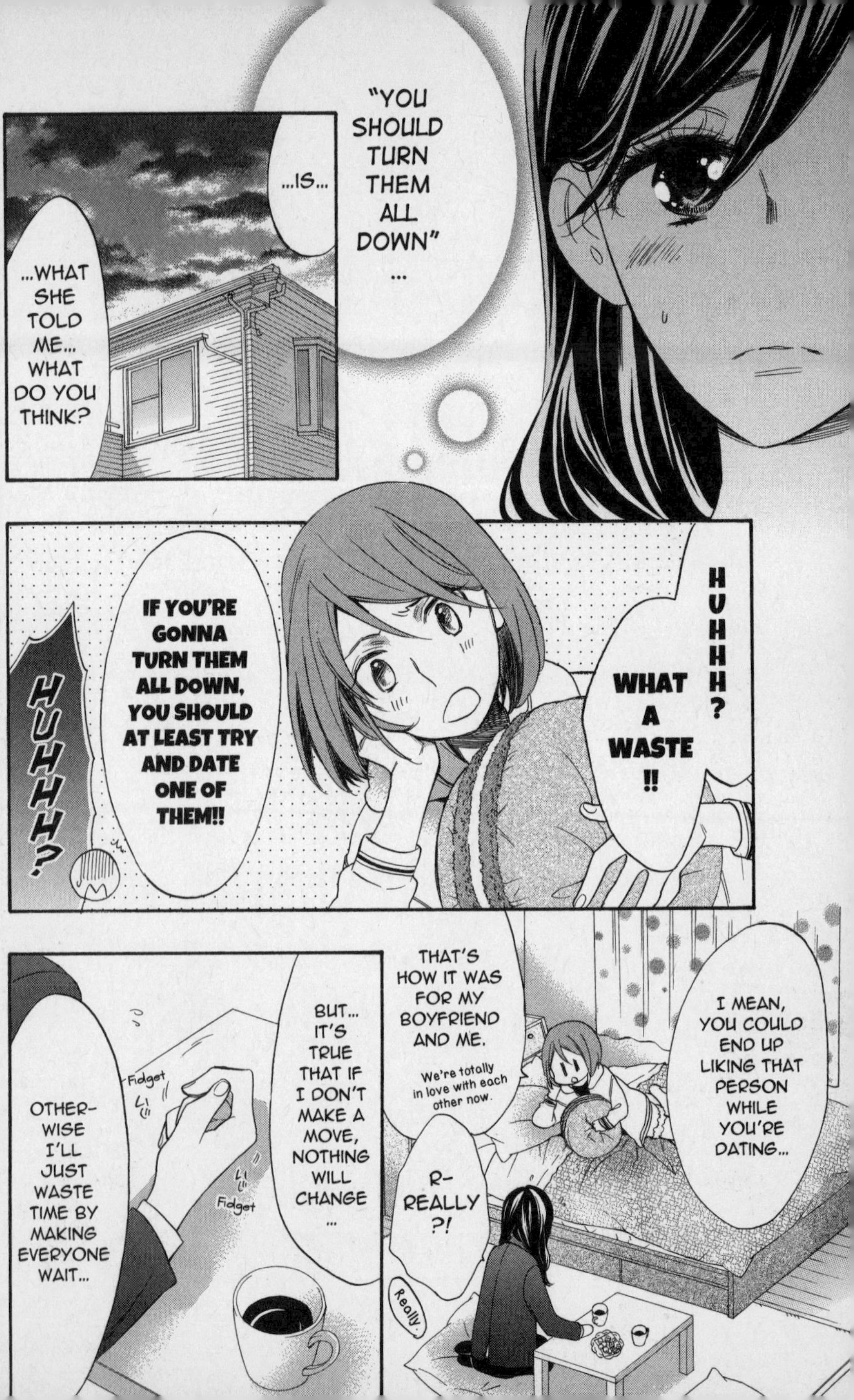
"YOU SHOULD TURN THEM ALL DOWN" ...
...IS...
...WHAT SHE TOLD ME... WHAT DO YOU THINK?
HUHHH?
WHAT A WASTE!!
IF YOU'RE GONNA TURN THEM ALL DOWN, YOU SHOULD AT LEAST TRY AND DATE ONE OF THEM!!
HUHHHH?
I MEAN, YOU COULD END UP LIKING THAT PERSON WHILE YOU'RE DATING...
THAT'S HOW IT WAS FOR MY BOYFRIEND AND ME.
We're totally in love with each other now.
R-REALLY?!
Really.
BUT... IT'S TRUE THAT IF I DON'T MAKE A MOVE, NOTHING WILL CHANGE...
Fidget
Fidget
OTHER-WISE I'LL JUST WASTE TIME BY MAKING EVERYONE WAIT...

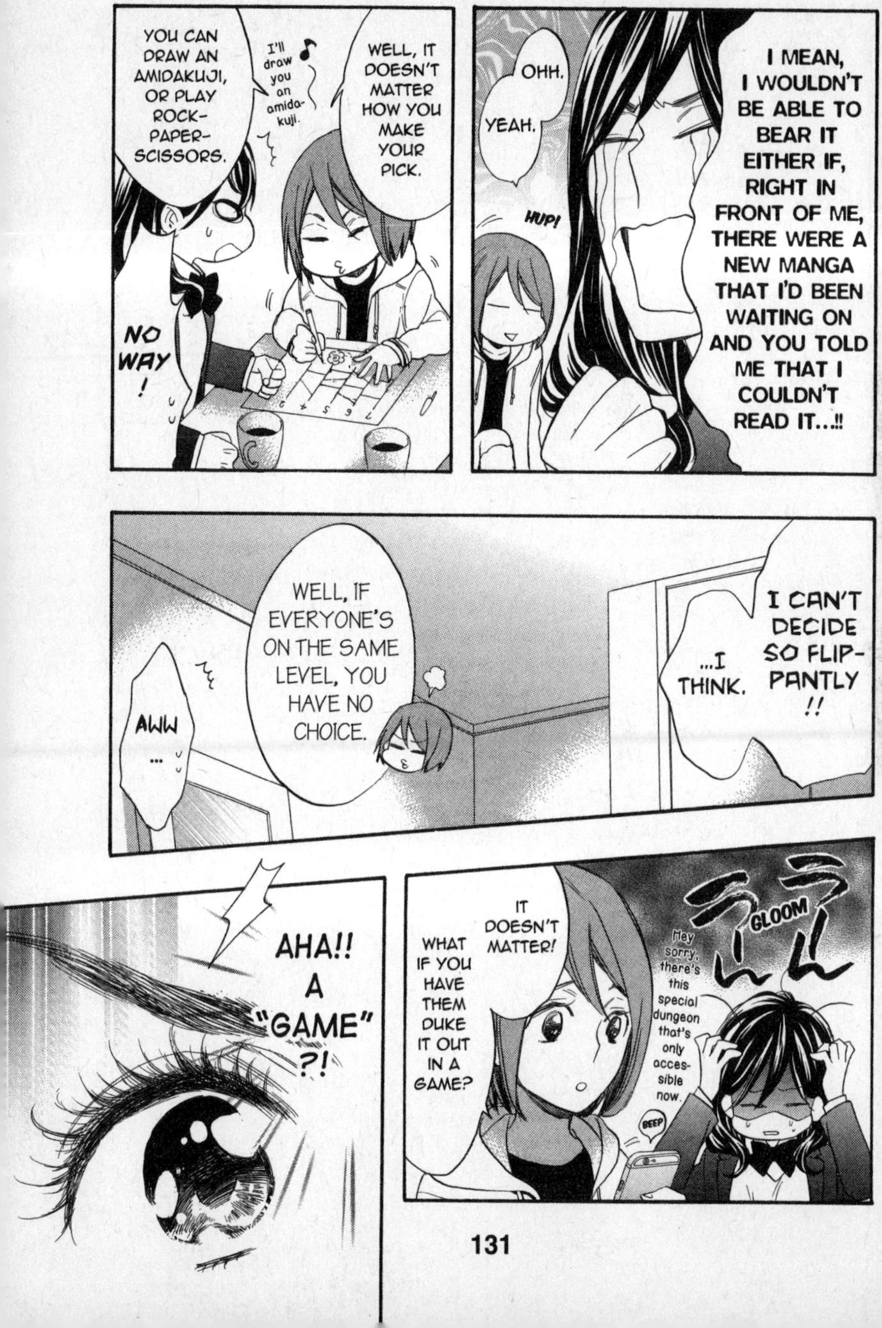
I MEAN, I WOULDN'T BE ABLE TO BEAR IT EITHER IF, RIGHT IN FRONT OF ME, THERE WERE A NEW MANGA THAT I'D BEEN WAITING ON AND YOU TOLD ME THAT I COULDN'T READ IT...!!
OHH.
YEAH.
HUP!
WELL, IT DOESN'T MATTER HOW YOU MAKE YOUR PICK.
I'll draw you an amidakuji.
YOU CAN DRAW AN AMIDAKUJI, OR PLAY ROCK-PAPER-SCISSORS.
NO WAY!
I CAN'T DECIDE SO FLIPPANTLY!!
...I THINK.
WELL, IF EVERYONE'S ON THE SAME LEVEL, YOU HAVE NO CHOICE.
AWW...
GLOOM
Hey sorry, there's this special dungeon that's only acces-sible now.
BEEP
IT DOESN'T MATTER!
WHAT IF YOU HAVE THEM DUKE IT OUT IN A GAME?
AHA!! A "GAME"?!

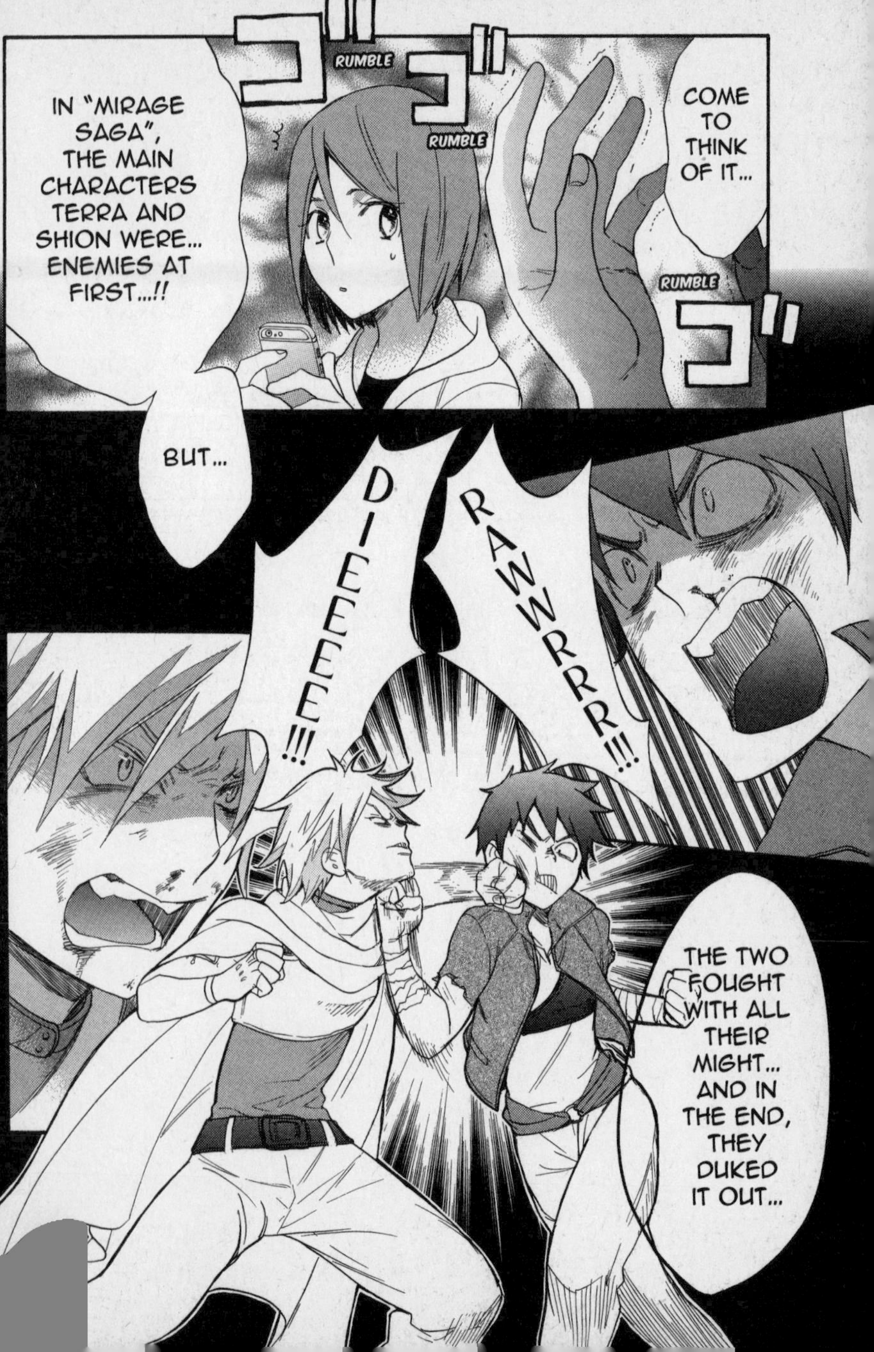
COME TO THINK OF IT...
RUMBLE
RUMBLE
RUMBLE
IN "MIRAGE SAGA", THE MAIN CHARACTERS TERRA AND SHION WERE... ENEMIES AT FIRST...!!
BUT...
RAWWRRR!!!
DIEEEEE!!!
THE TWO FOUGHT WITH ALL THEIR MIGHT... AND IN THE END, THEY DUKED IT OUT...

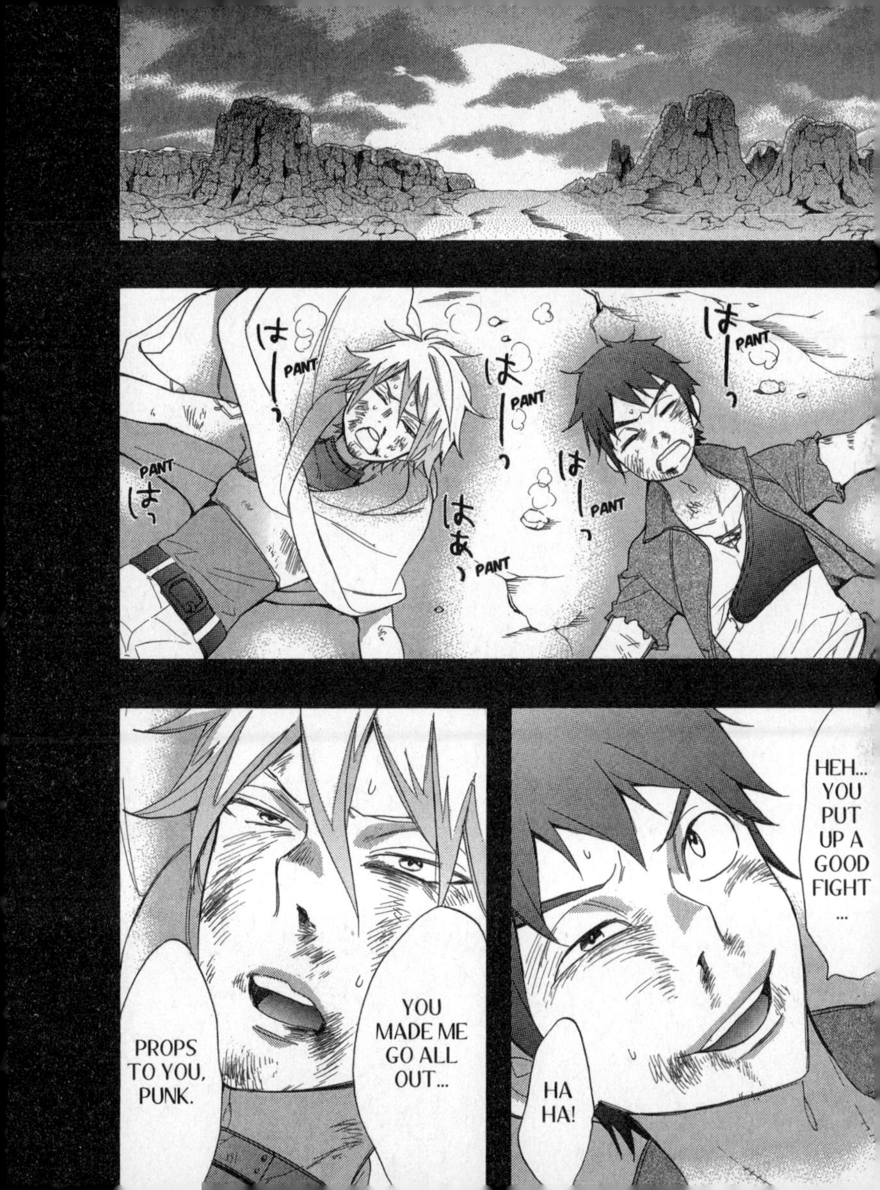

はーっ PANT
はーっ PANT
はーっ PANT
はぁっ PANT
はっ PANT
HEH... YOU PUT UP A GOOD FIGHT ...
HA HA!
YOU MADE ME GO ALL OUT...
PROPS TO YOU, PUNK.

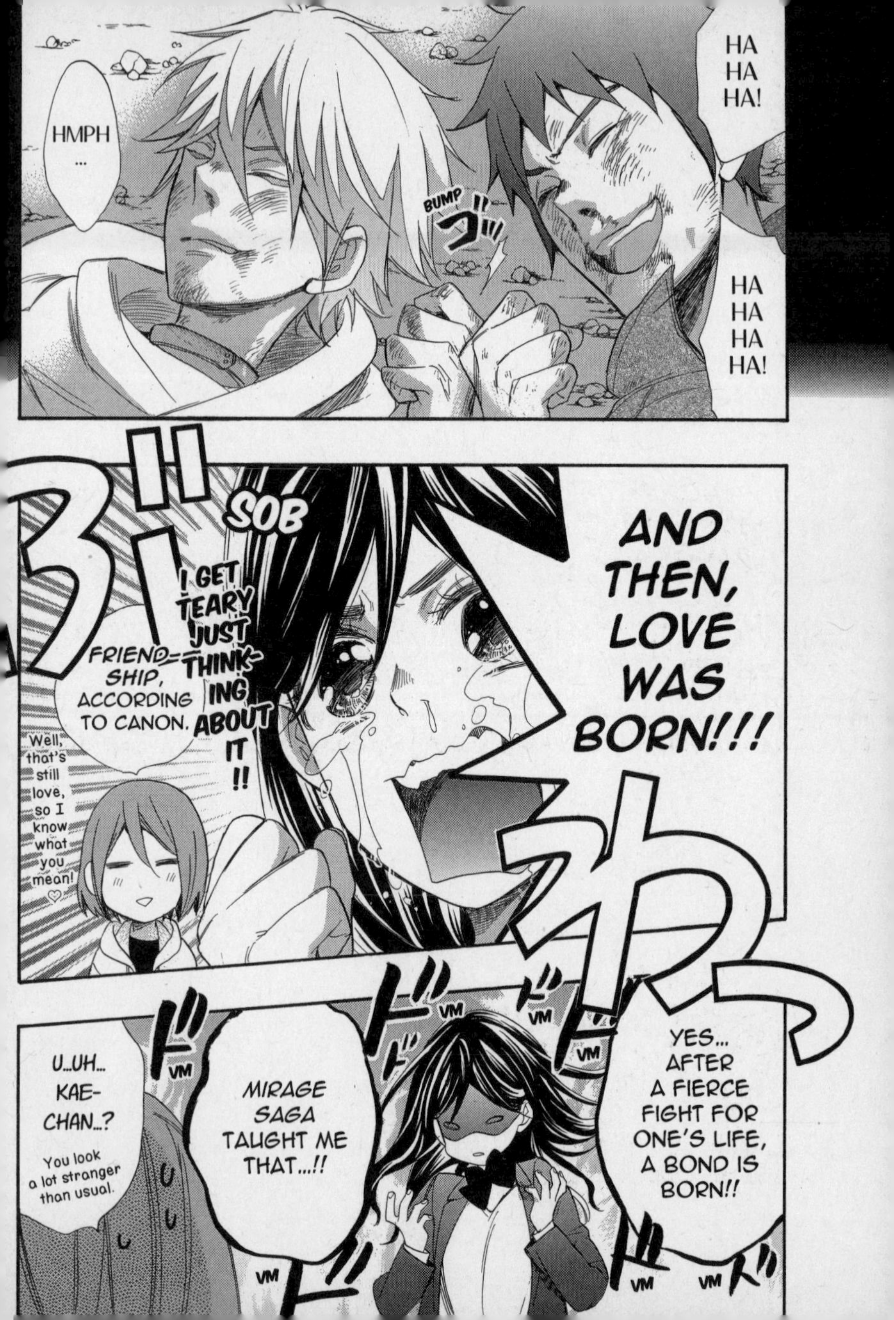
HA HA HA!
HA HA HA HA!
BUMP
HMPH ...
AND THEN, LOVE WAS BORN!!!
SOB
I GET TEARY JUST THINKING ABOUT IT !!
FRIENDSHIP, ACCORDING TO CANON.
Well, that's still love, so I know what you mean! ♡
VM
YES... AFTER A FIERCE FIGHT FOR ONE'S LIFE, A BOND IS BORN!!
MIRAGE SAGA TAUGHT ME THAT...!!
U...UH... KAE-CHAN...?
You look a lot stranger than usual.

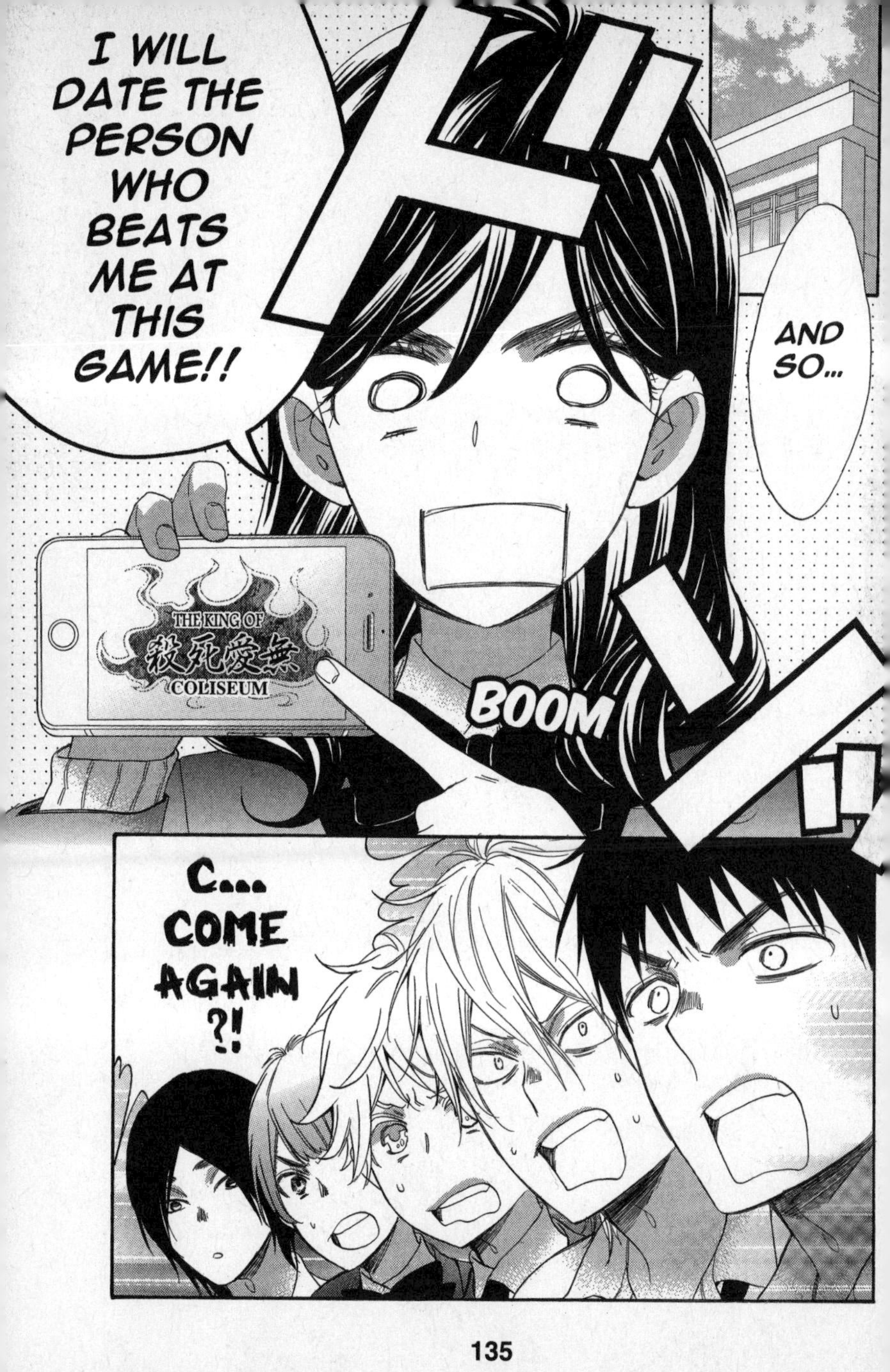
AND SO...
I WILL DATE THE PERSON WHO BEATS ME AT THIS GAME!!
THE KING OF 殺死愛無 COLISEUM
BOOM
C... COME AGAIN ?!

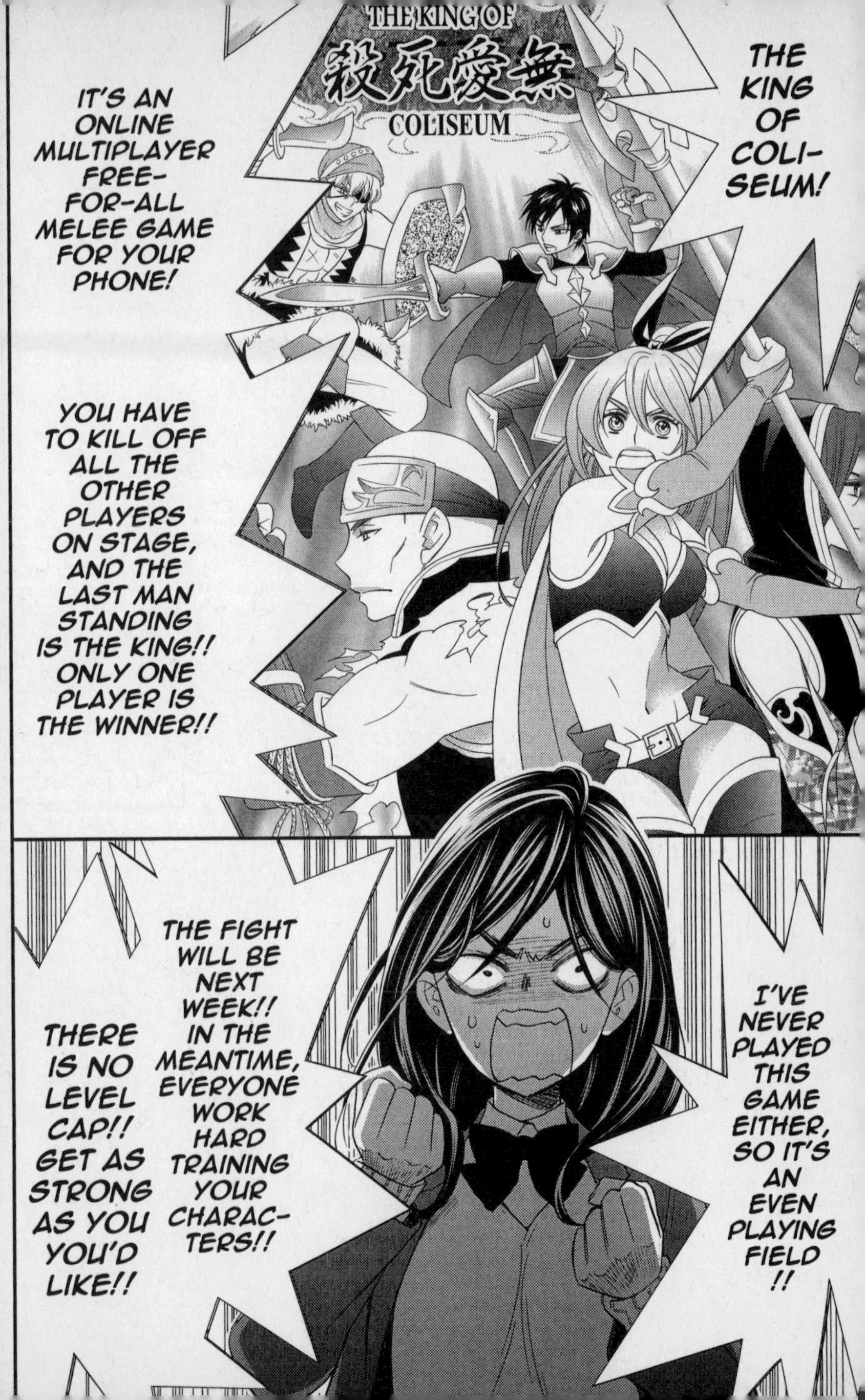
THE KING OF COLI-SEUM!
THE KING OF 殺死愛無 COLISEUM
IT'S AN ONLINE MULTIPLAYER FREE-FOR-ALL MELEE GAME FOR YOUR PHONE!
YOU HAVE TO KILL OFF ALL THE OTHER PLAYERS ON STAGE, AND THE LAST MAN STANDING IS THE KING!! ONLY ONE PLAYER IS THE WINNER!!
I'VE NEVER PLAYED THIS GAME EITHER, SO IT'S AN EVEN PLAYING FIELD!!
THE FIGHT WILL BE NEXT WEEK!! IN THE MEANTIME, EVERYONE WORK HARD TRAINING YOUR CHARAC-TERS!!
THERE IS NO LEVEL CAP!! GET AS STRONG AS YOU YOU'D LIKE!!

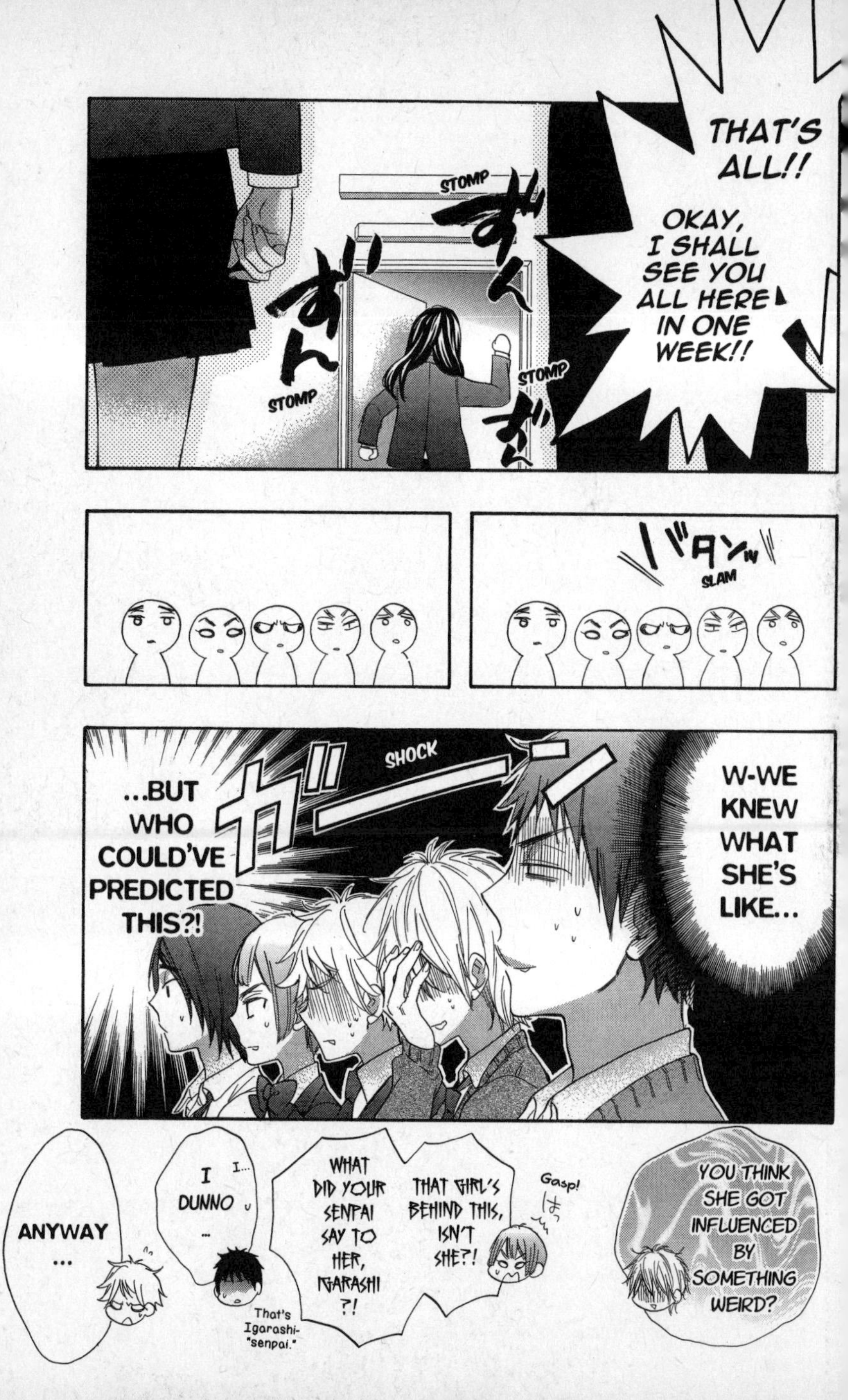
THAT'S ALL!!
OKAY, I SHALL SEE YOU ALL HERE IN ONE WEEK!!
ずん
STOMP
ずん
STOMP
ずん
STOMP
バタン
SLAM
W-WE KNEW WHAT SHE'S LIKE...
ガーン
SHOCK
...BUT WHO COULD'VE PREDICTED THIS?!
YOU THINK SHE GOT INFLUENCED BY SOMETHING WEIRD?
Gasp!
はっ
THAT GIRL'S BEHIND THIS, ISN'T SHE?!
WHAT DID YOUR SENPAI SAY TO HER, IGARASHI?!
That's Igarashi-"senpai."
I... I DUNNO...
ANYWAY...

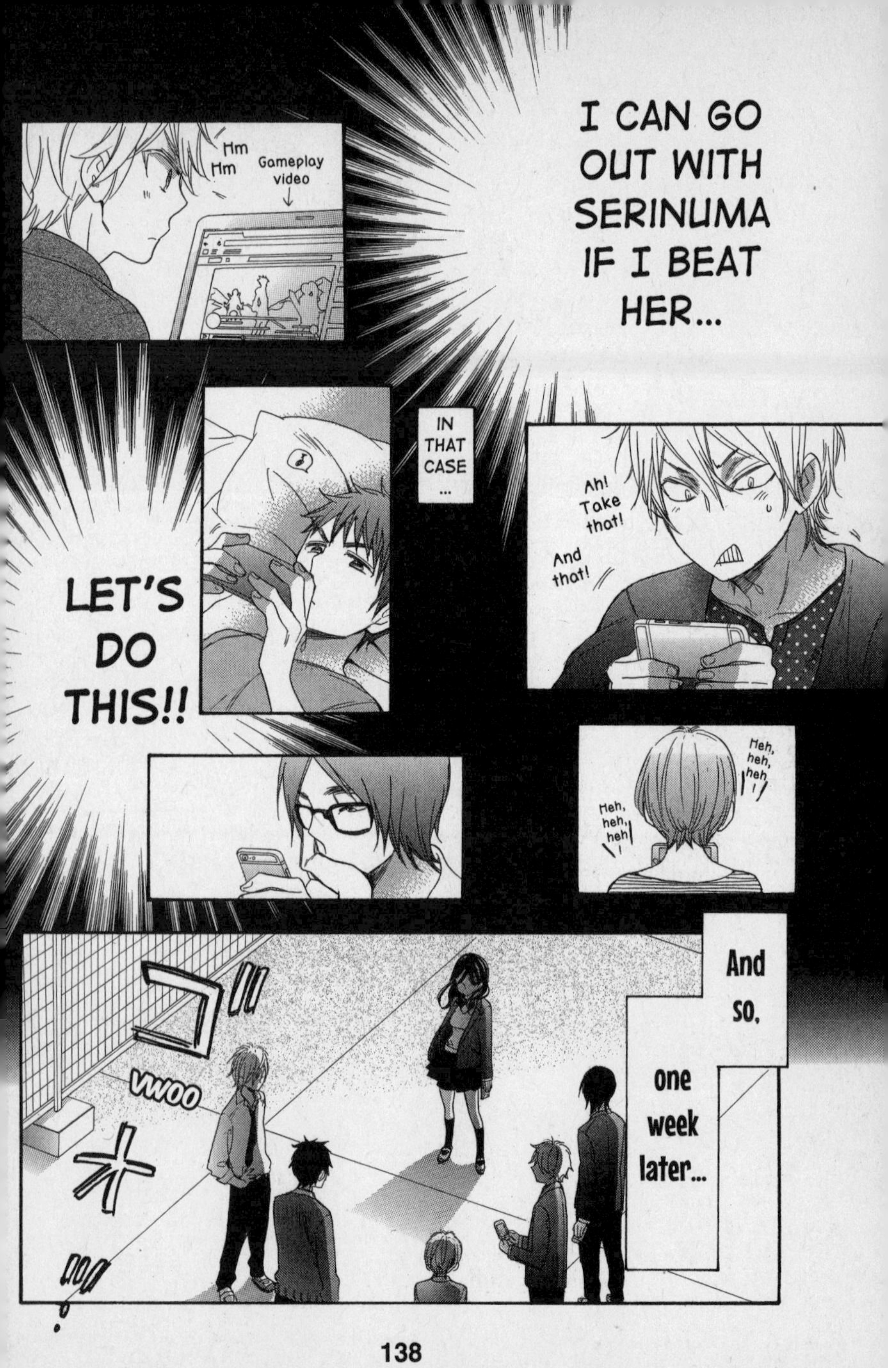
I CAN GO OUT WITH SERINUMA IF I BEAT HER...
Hm Hm
Gameplay video
Ah! Take that!
And that!
IN THAT CASE...
LET'S DO THIS!!
Heh, heh, heh
Heh, heh, heh
And so, one week later...
vwoo

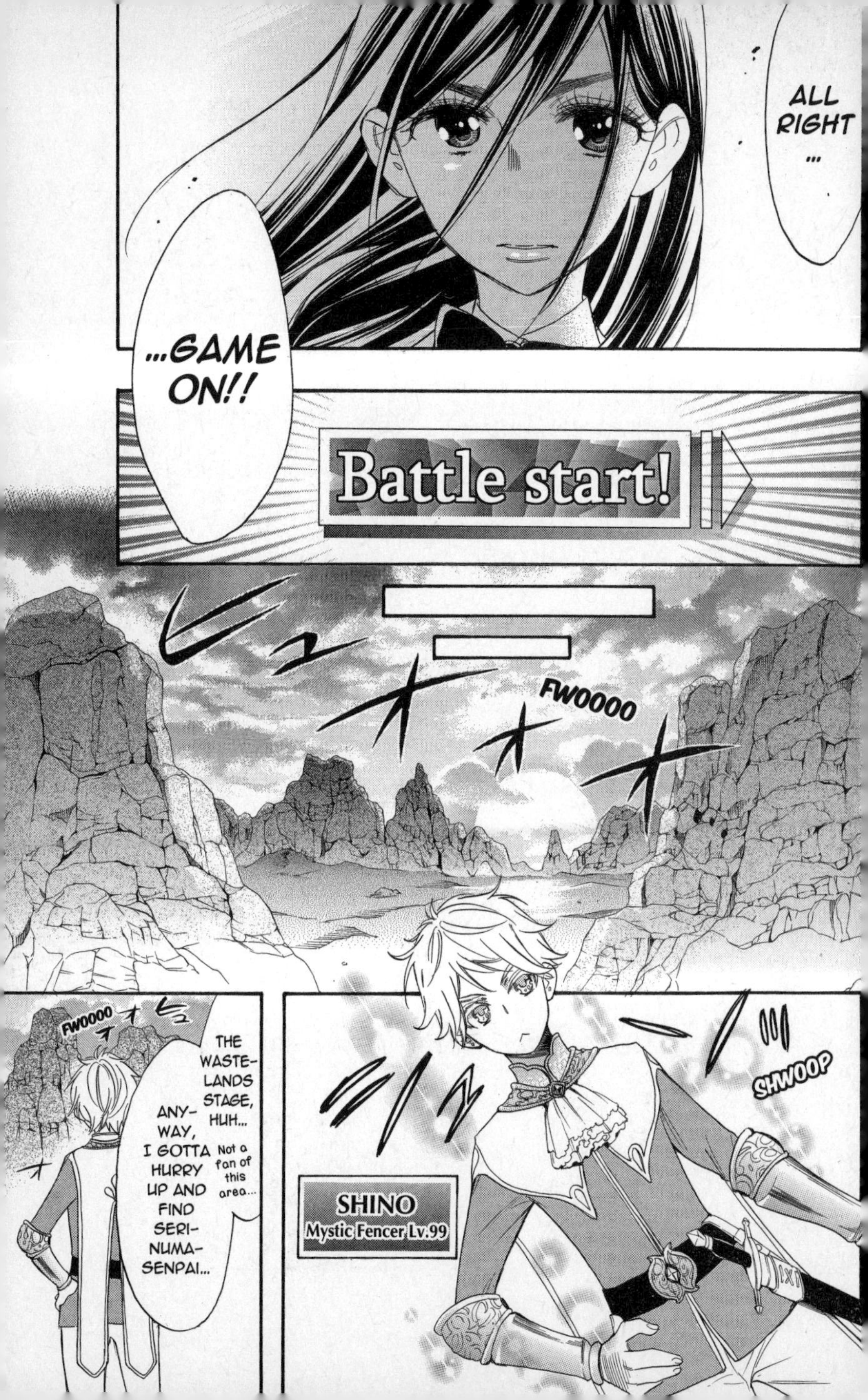
ALL RIGHT ...
...GAME ON!!
Battle start!
FWOOOO
SHWOOP
SHINO
Mystic Fencer Lv.99
FWOOOO
THE WASTE-LANDS STAGE, HUH...
Not a fan of this area...
ANY-WAY, I GOTTA HURRY UP AND FIND SERI-NUMA-SENPAI...

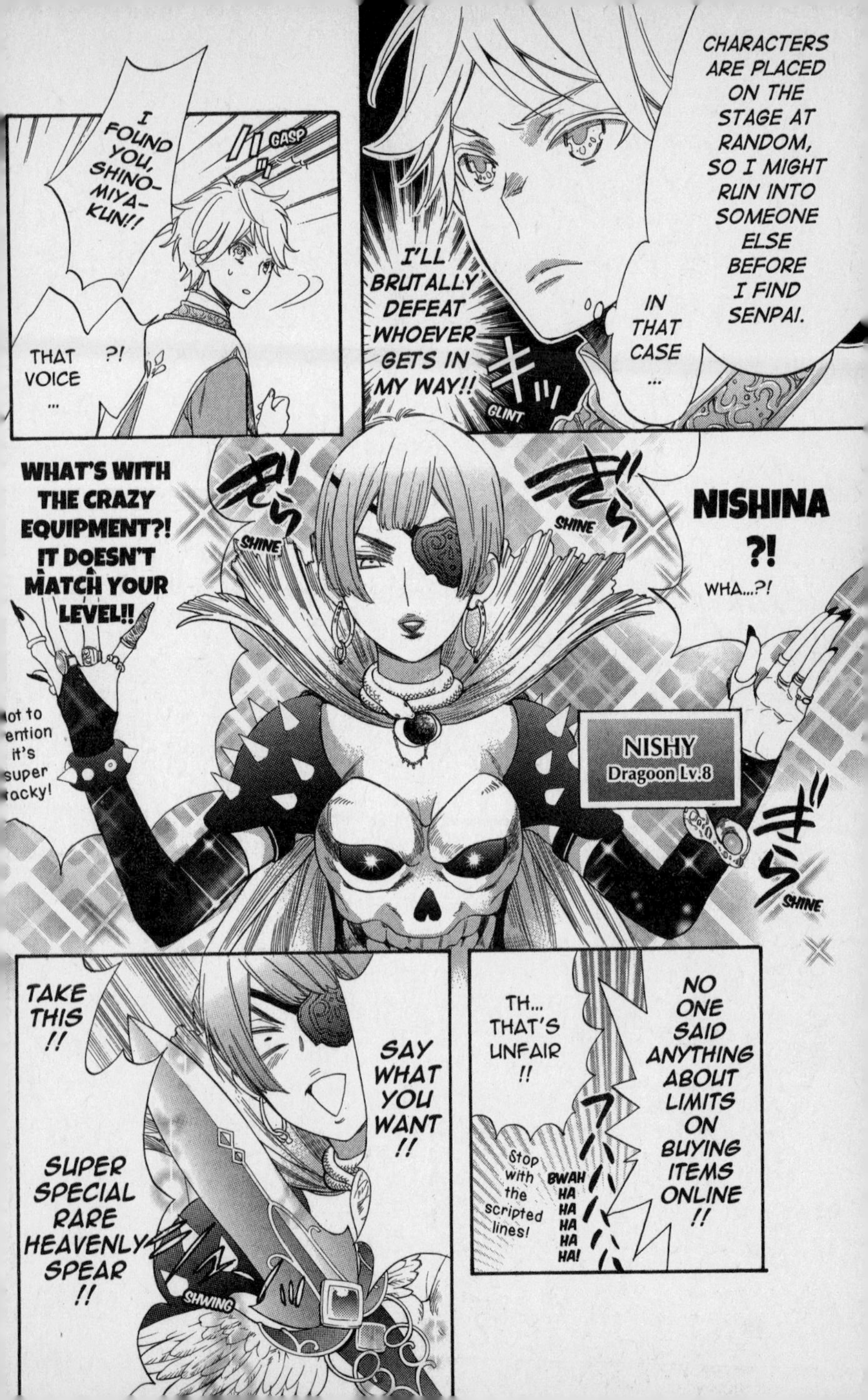
CHARACTERS ARE PLACED ON THE STAGE AT RANDOM, SO I MIGHT RUN INTO SOMEONE ELSE BEFORE I FIND SENPAI.
IN THAT CASE ...
I'LL BRUTALLY DEFEAT WHOEVER GETS IN MY WAY!!
GLINT
I FOUND YOU, SHINOMIYA-KUN!!
GASP
?!
THAT VOICE ...
NISHINA ?!
WHA...?!
SHINE
SHINE
NISHY
Dragoon Lv.8
SHINE
WHAT'S WITH THE CRAZY EQUIPMENT?! IT DOESN'T MATCH YOUR LEVEL!!
ot to ention it's super acky!
NO ONE SAID ANYTHING ABOUT LIMITS ON BUYING ITEMS ONLINE !!
TH... THAT'S UNFAIR !!
BWAH HA HA HA HA HA!
Stop with the scripted lines!
SAY WHAT YOU WANT !!
TAKE THIS !!
SUPER SPECIAL RARE HEAVENLY SPEAR !!
SHWING

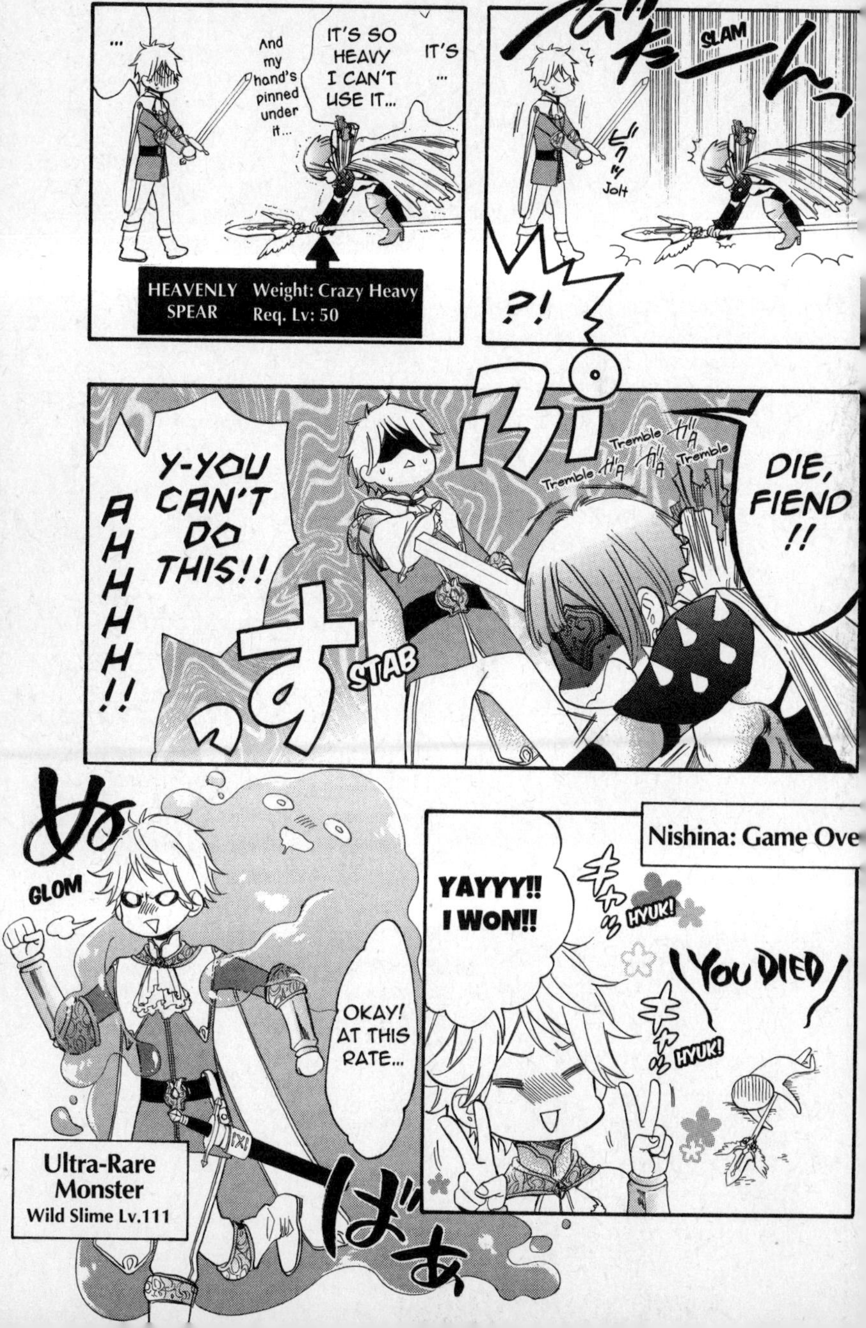

SLAM
Jolt
?!
IT'S ...
IT'S SO HEAVY I CAN'T USE IT...
And my hand's pinned under it...
...
HEAVENLY SPEAR
Weight: Crazy Heavy
Req. Lv: 50
ぷ
DIE, FIEND!!
Tremble
Tremble
Tremble
Y-YOU CAN'T DO THIS!!
AHHHHH!!
す
STAB
Nishina: Game Ove
YAYYY!! I WON!!
HYUK!
YOU DIED
HYUK!
ぬ
GLOM
OKAY! AT THIS RATE...
ばぁ
Ultra-Rare Monster
Wild Slime Lv.111

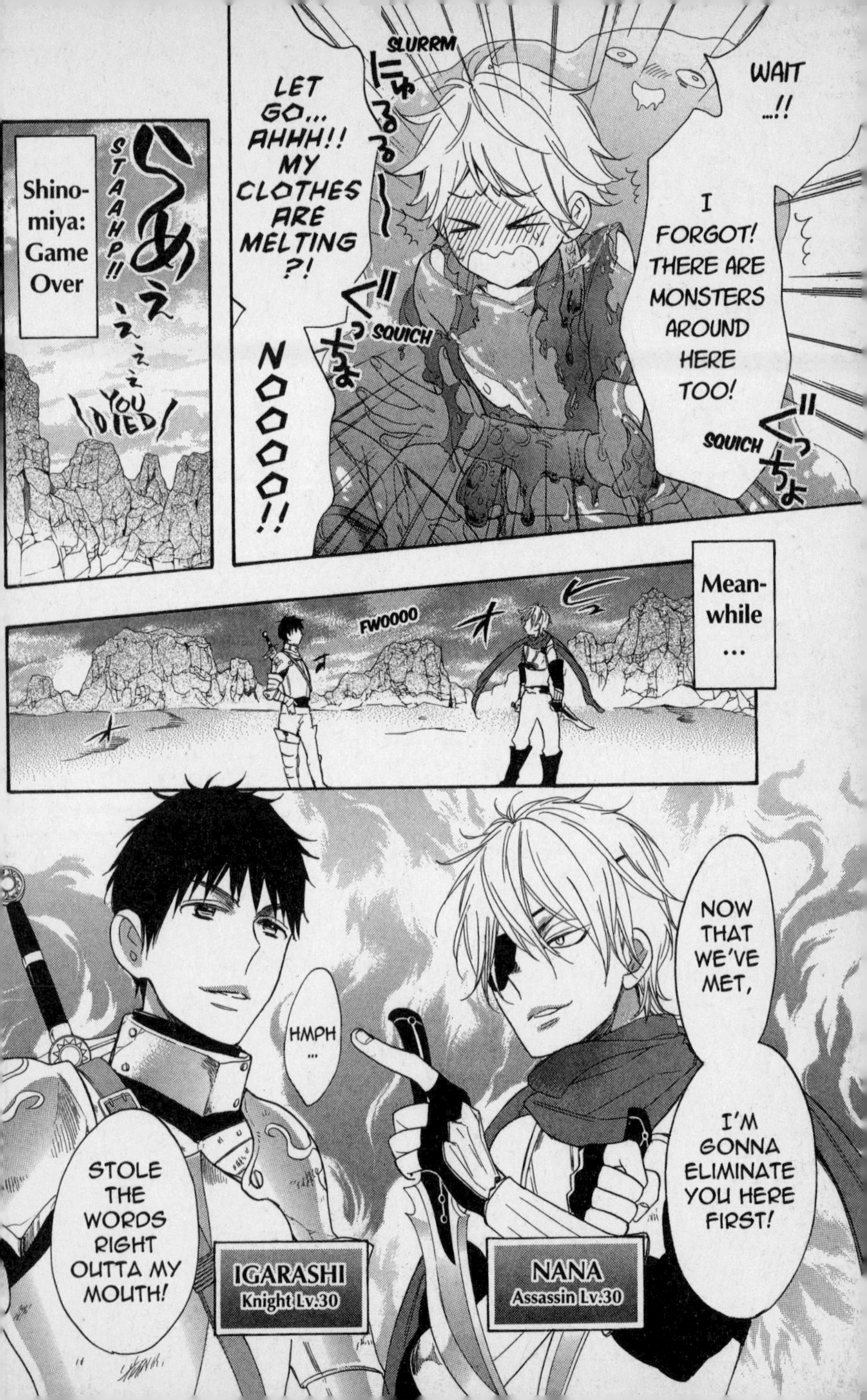
WAIT ...!!
SLURRM
にゅるる~
LET GO... AHHH!! MY CLOTHES ARE MELTING?!
I FORGOT! THERE ARE MONSTERS AROUND HERE TOO!
SQUICH
ぐっちょ
SQUICH
ぐっちょ
NOOOOO!!
Shino-miya: Game Over
らめぇぇぇぇ
STAAAHP!!
YOU DIED
Meanwhile...
FWOOOO
NOW THAT WE'VE MET,
I'M GONNA ELIMINATE YOU HERE FIRST!
NANA
Assassin Lv.30
HMPH...
STOLE THE WORDS RIGHT OUTTA MY MOUTH!
IGARASHI
Knight Lv.30

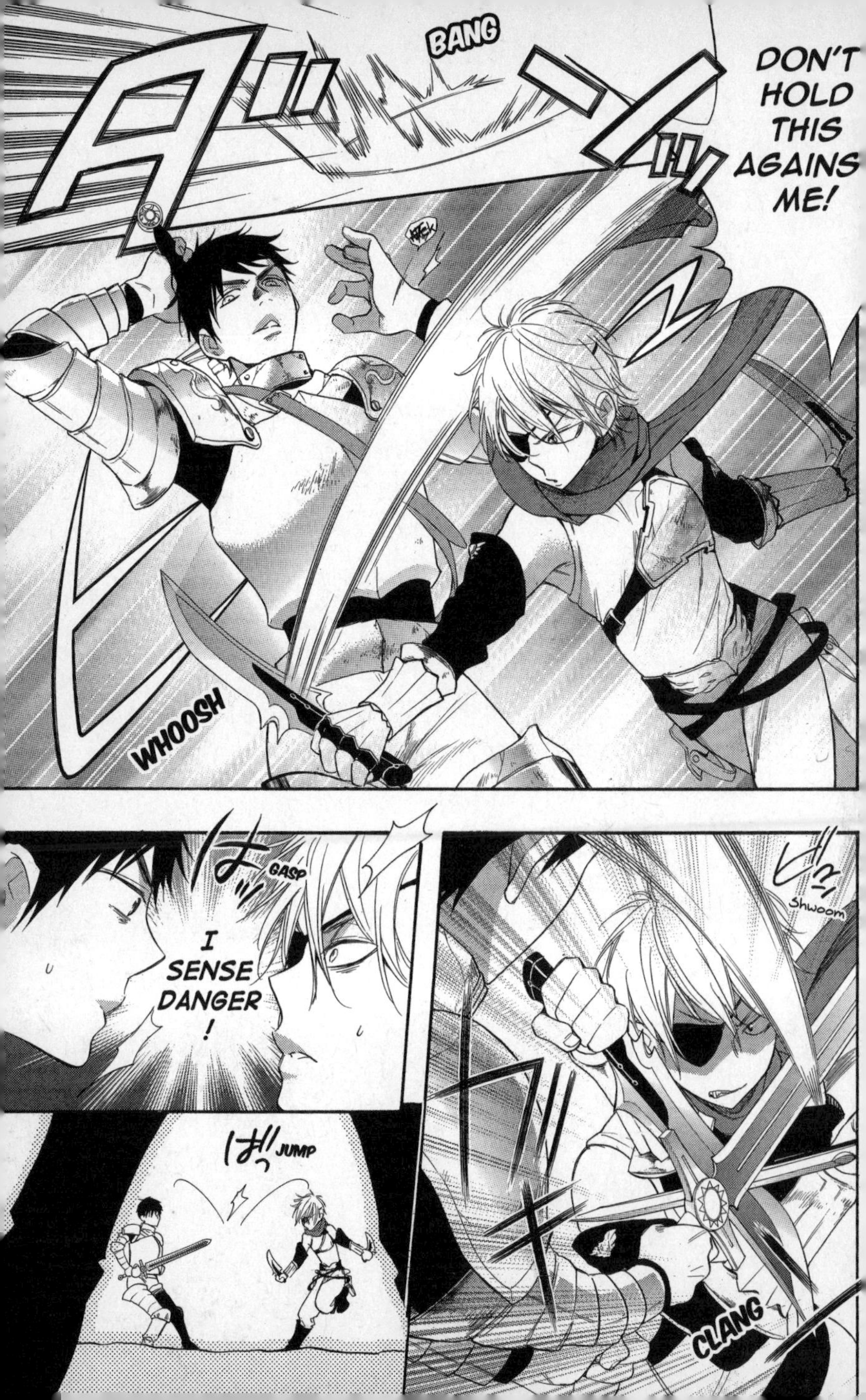
DON'T HOLD THIS AGAINS ME!
BANG
WHOOSH
Shwoom
CLANG
GASP
I SENSE DANGER!
JUMP

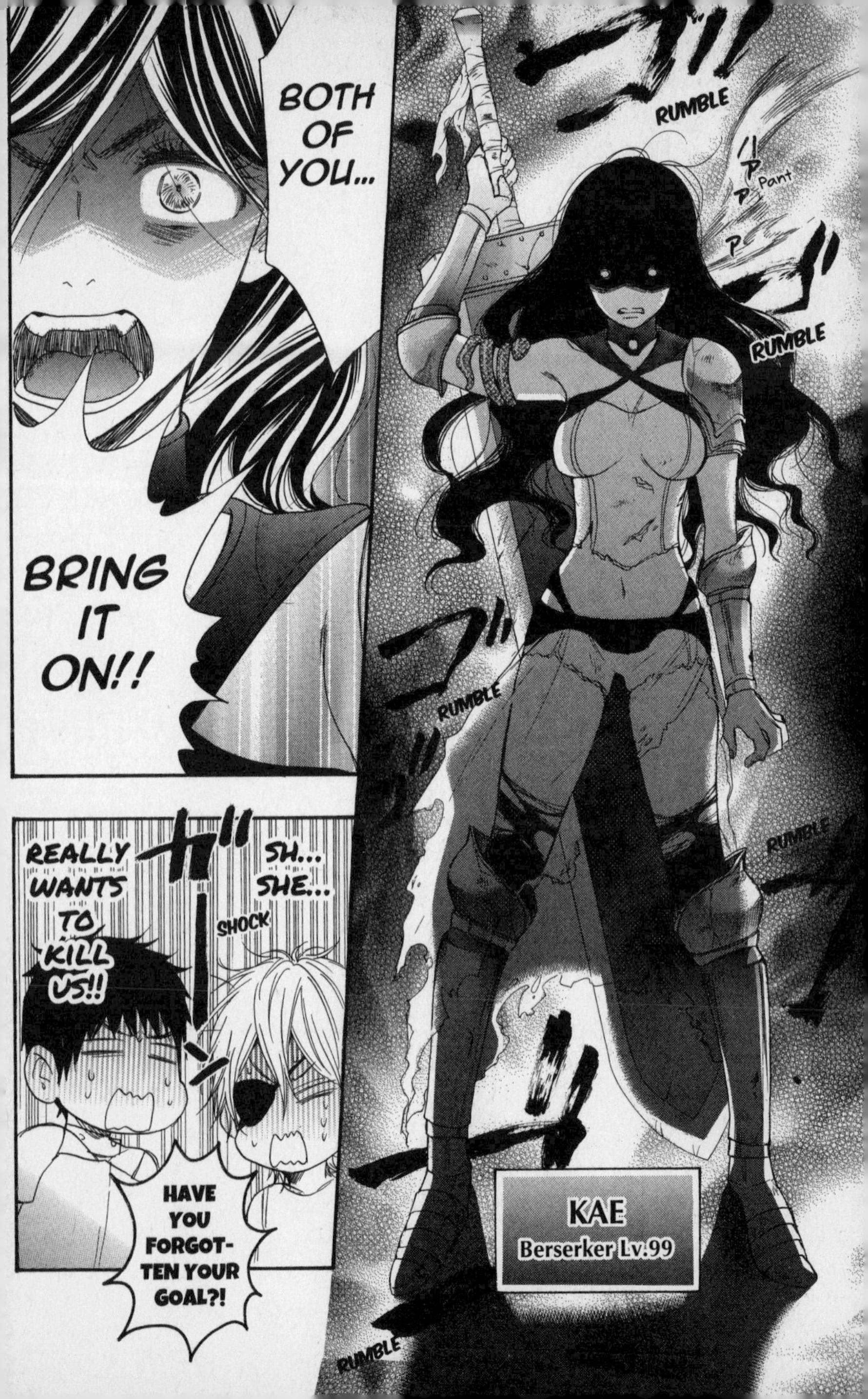
RUMBLE
Pant
RUMBLE
RUMBLE
RUMBLE
KAE
Berserker Lv.99
RUMBLE
BOTH OF YOU...
BRING IT ON!!
SH... SHE...
SHOCK
REALLY WANTS TO KILL US!!
HAVE YOU FORGOT-TEN YOUR GOAL?!

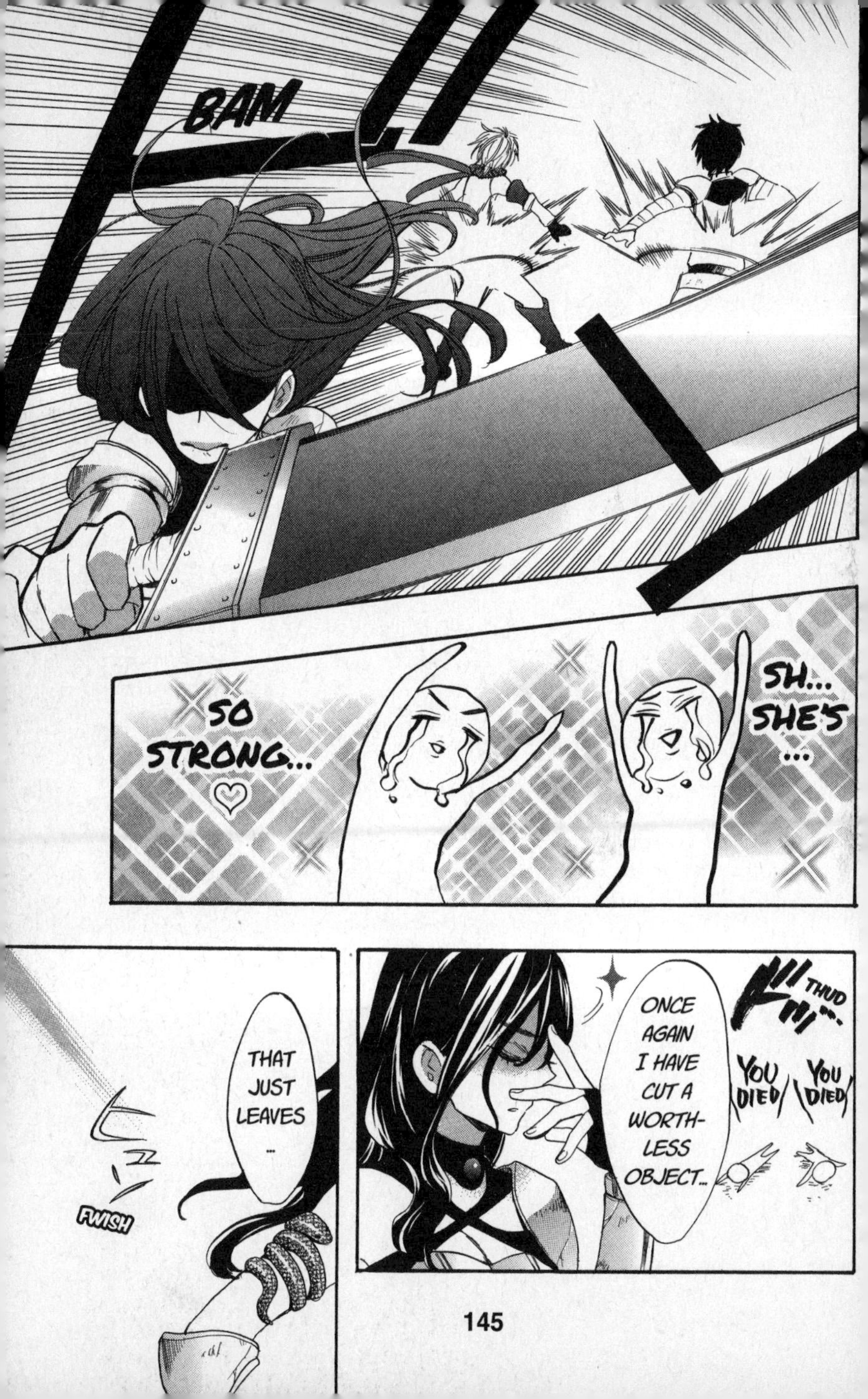
BAM
SH... SHE'S ...
SO STRONG... ♡
ONCE AGAIN I HAVE CUT A WORTHLESS OBJECT...
THUD...
YOU DIED
YOU DIED
THAT JUST LEAVES ...
FWISH

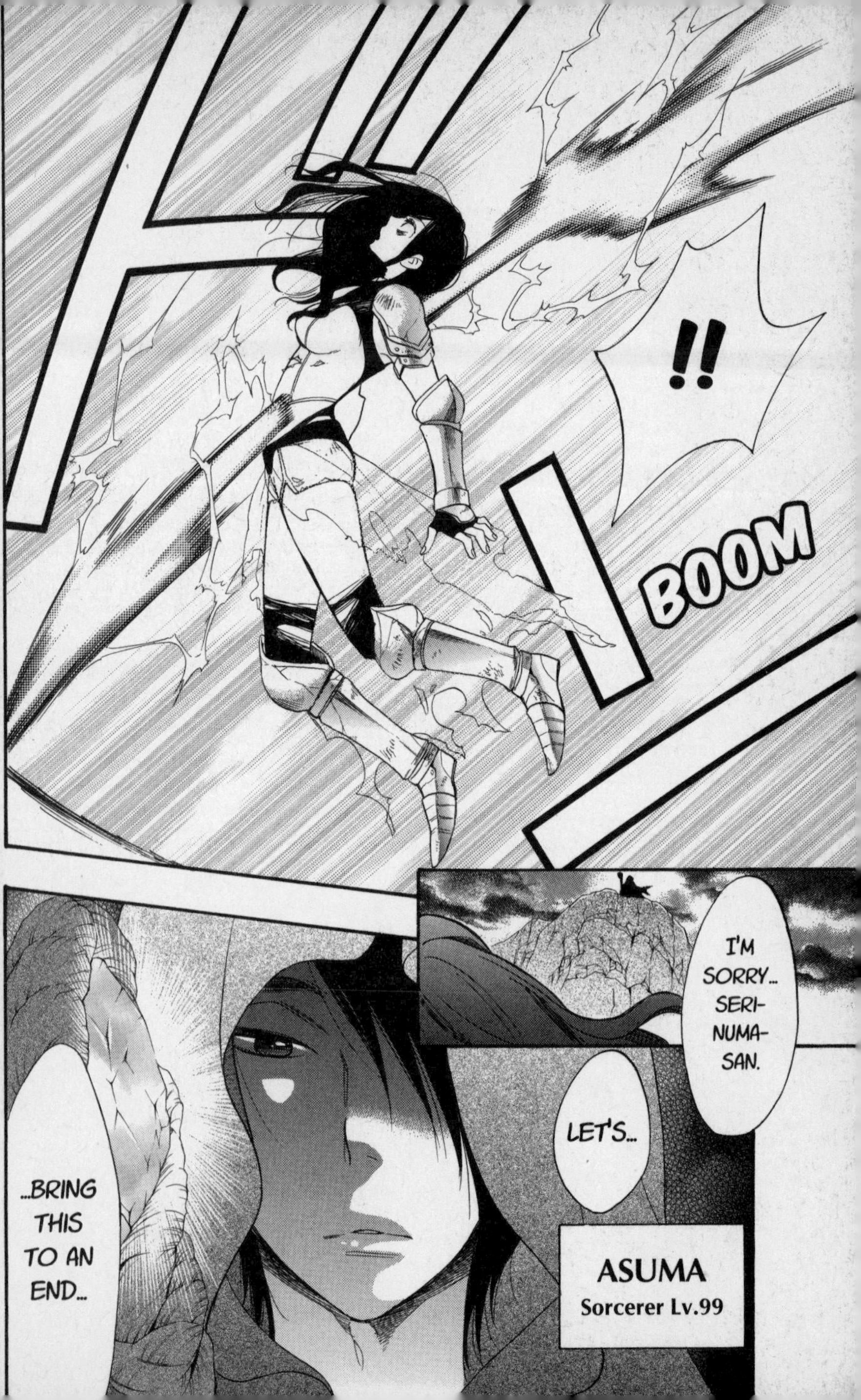
!!
BOOM
I'M SORRY... SERI-NUMA-SAN.
LET'S...
ASUMA
Sorcerer Lv.99
...BRING THIS TO AN END...

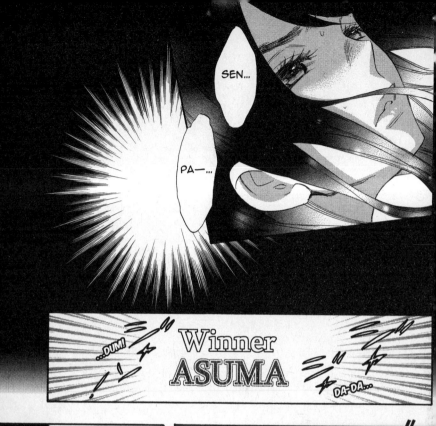

SEN...

PA—...

...DUM!

Winner
ASUMA

DA-DA...

...SET-TLED...

ゴクッ
GULP

...

SO IT'S...

WHOOSH

...

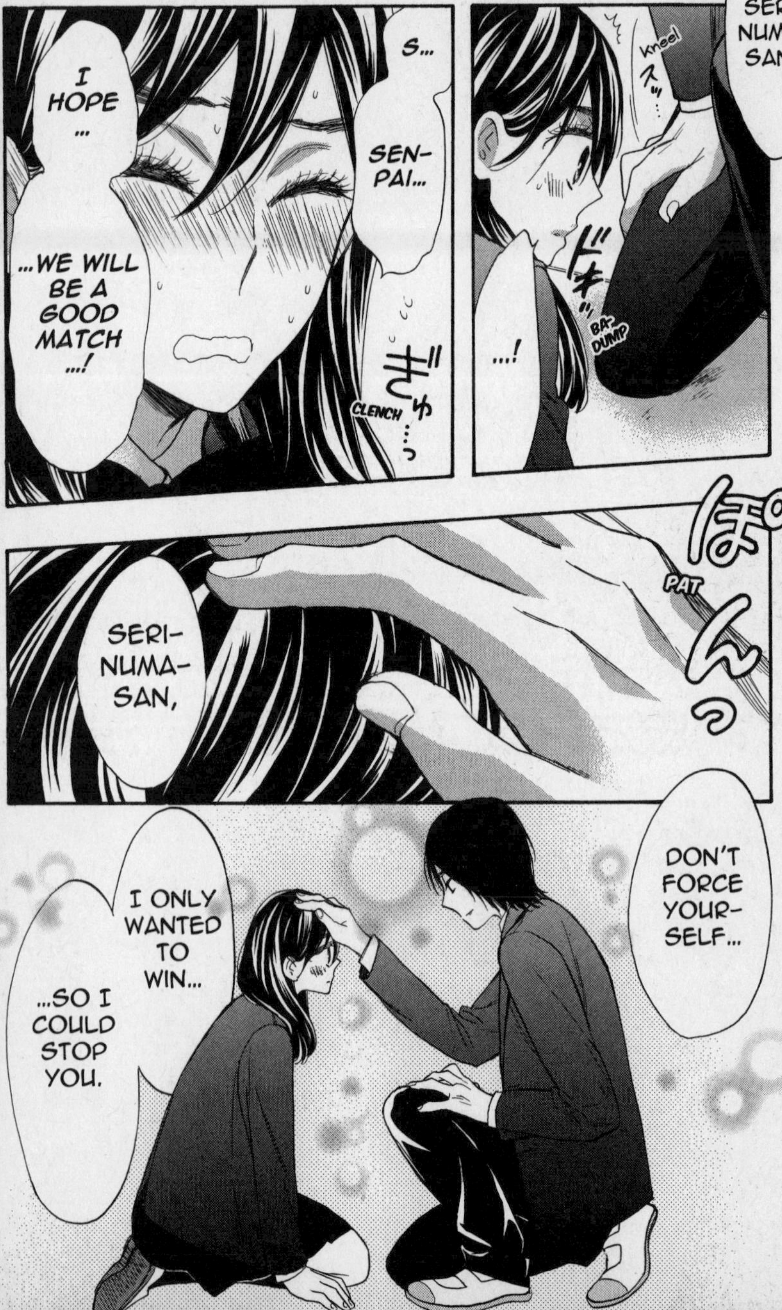
SERI-NUMA-SAN...
kneel
スッ…
ドキッ
BA-DUMP
...!
S... SEN-PAI...
I HOPE ...
...WE WILL BE A GOOD MATCH ...!
ぎゅ…っ
CLENCH
ぽんっ
PAT
SERI-NUMA-SAN,
DON'T FORCE YOUR-SELF...
I ONLY WANTED TO WIN...
...SO I COULD STOP YOU.

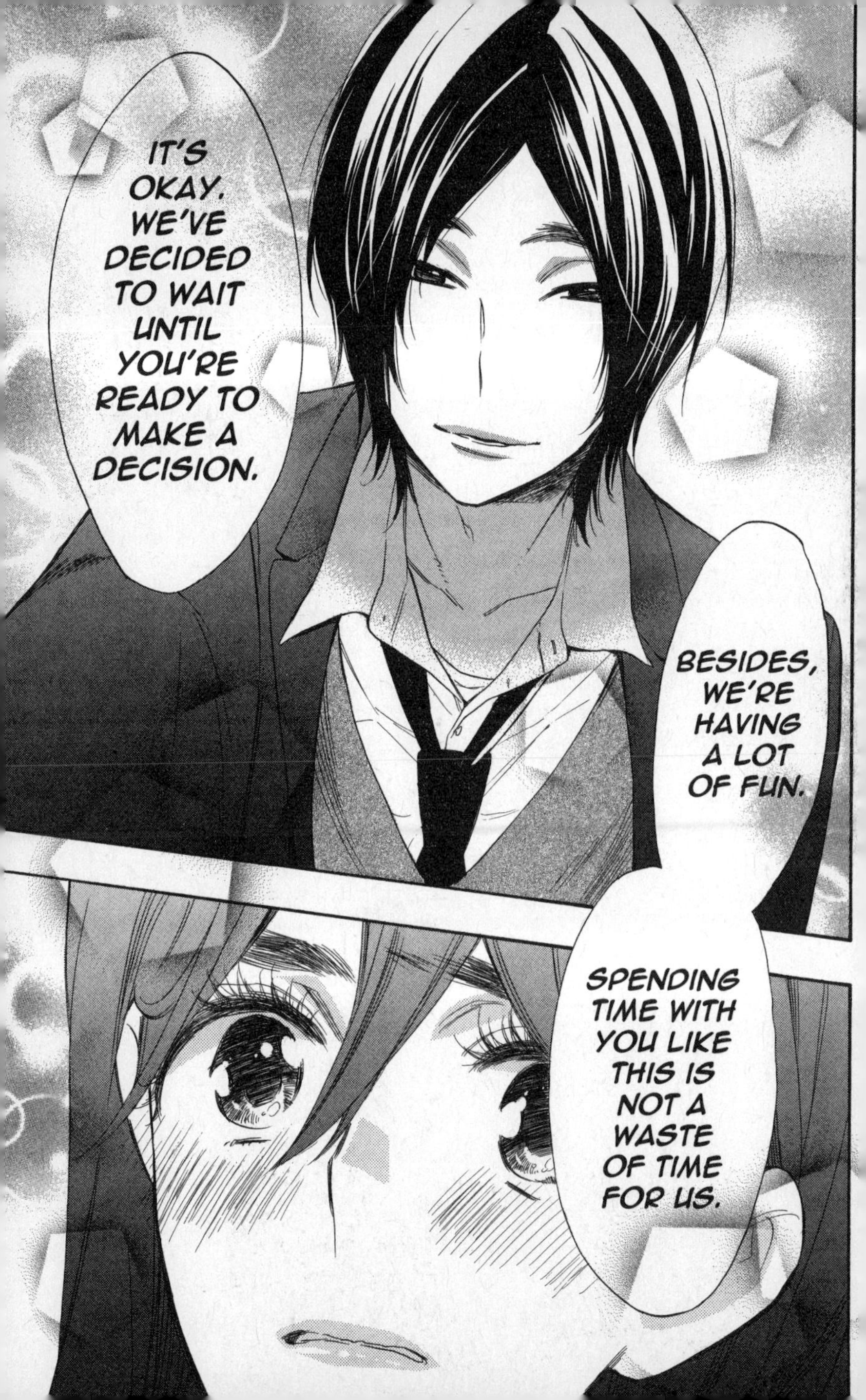
IT'S OKAY. WE'VE DECIDED TO WAIT UNTIL YOU'RE READY TO MAKE A DECISION.
BESIDES, WE'RE HAVING A LOT OF FUN.
SPENDING TIME WITH YOU LIKE THIS IS NOT A WASTE OF TIME FOR US.

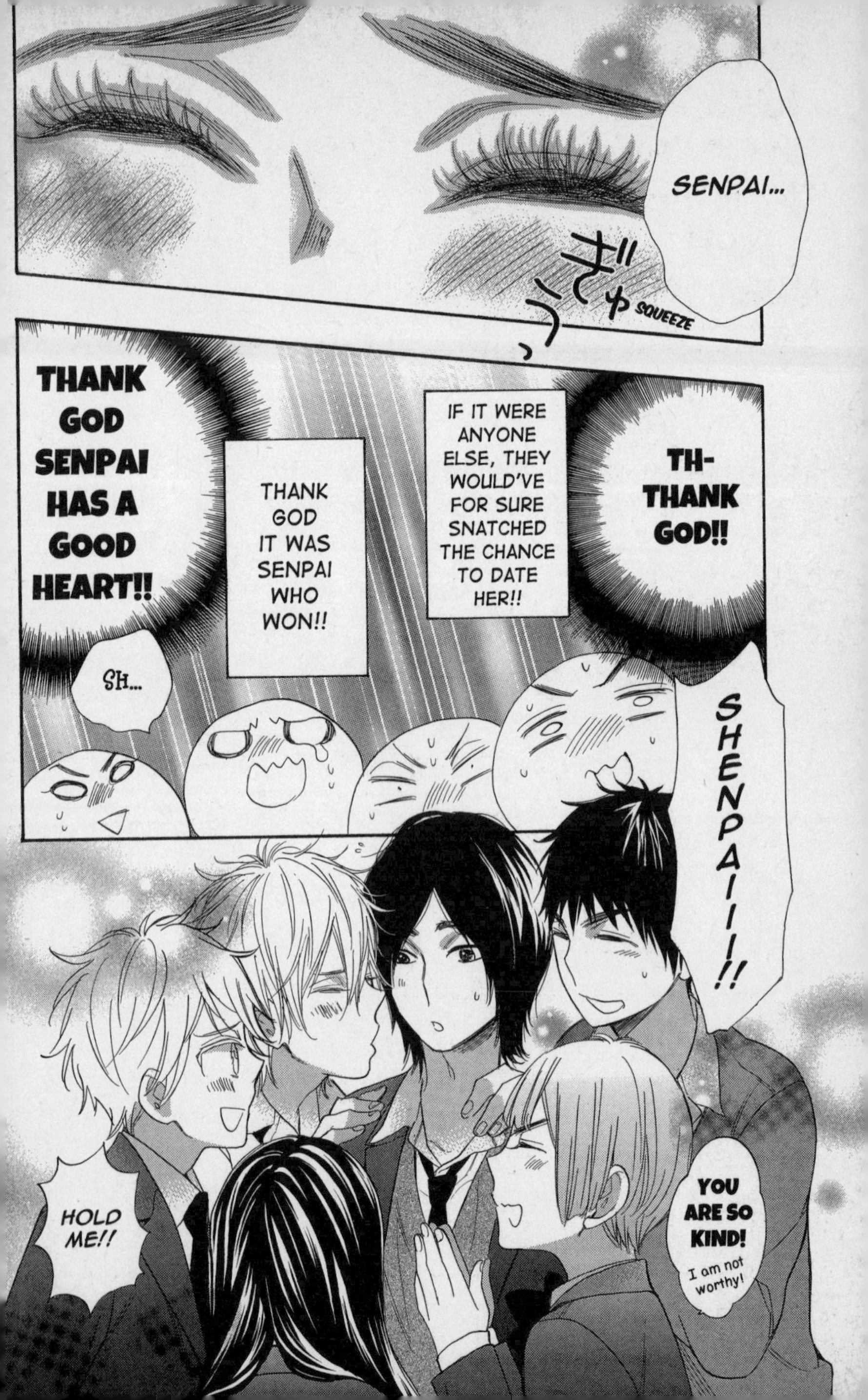

SENPAI...
ぎゅう
SQUEEZE
TH-THANK GOD!!
IF IT WERE ANYONE ELSE, THEY WOULD'VE FOR SURE SNATCHED THE CHANCE TO DATE HER!!
THANK GOD IT WAS SENPAI WHO WON!!
THANK GOD SENPAI HAS A GOOD HEART!!
SH...
SHENPAIIII!!
YOU ARE SO KIND!
I am not worthy!
HOLD ME!!

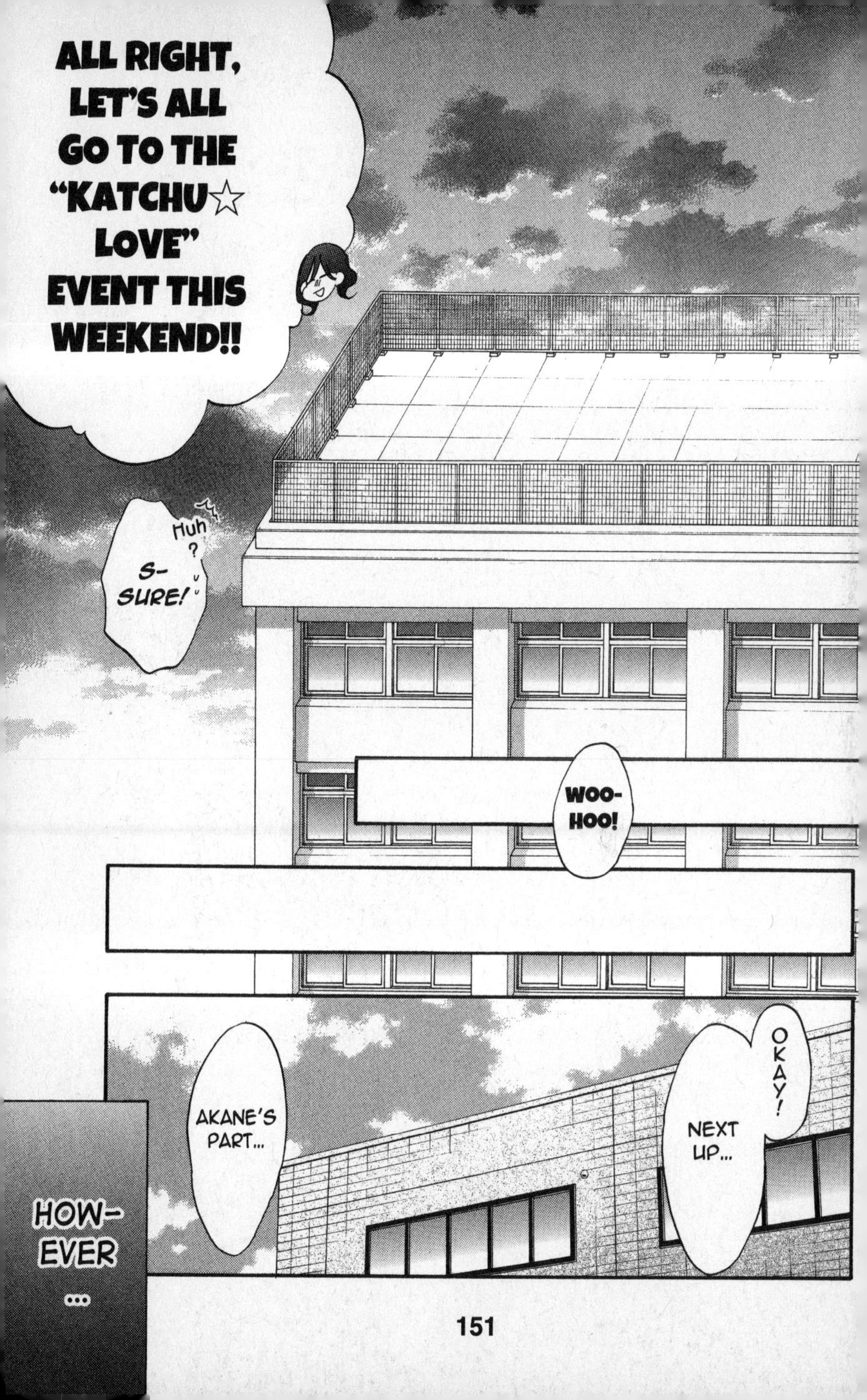
ALL RIGHT, LET'S ALL GO TO THE "KATCHU☆ LOVE" EVENT THIS WEEKEND!!
Huh? S-SURE!
WOO-HOO!
OKAY! NEXT UP...
AKANE'S PART...
HOW-EVER...

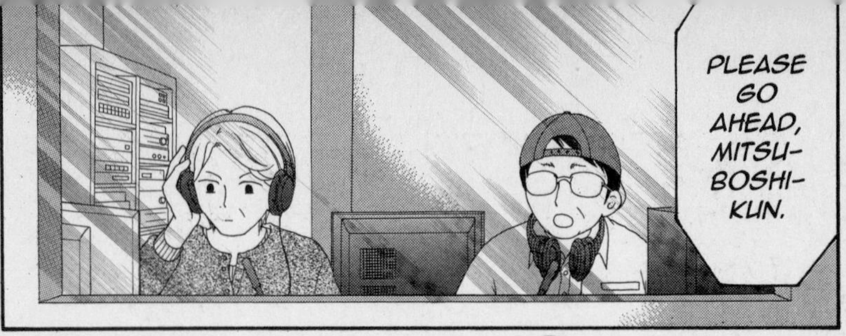
PLEASE GO AHEAD, MITSU-BOSHI-KUN.
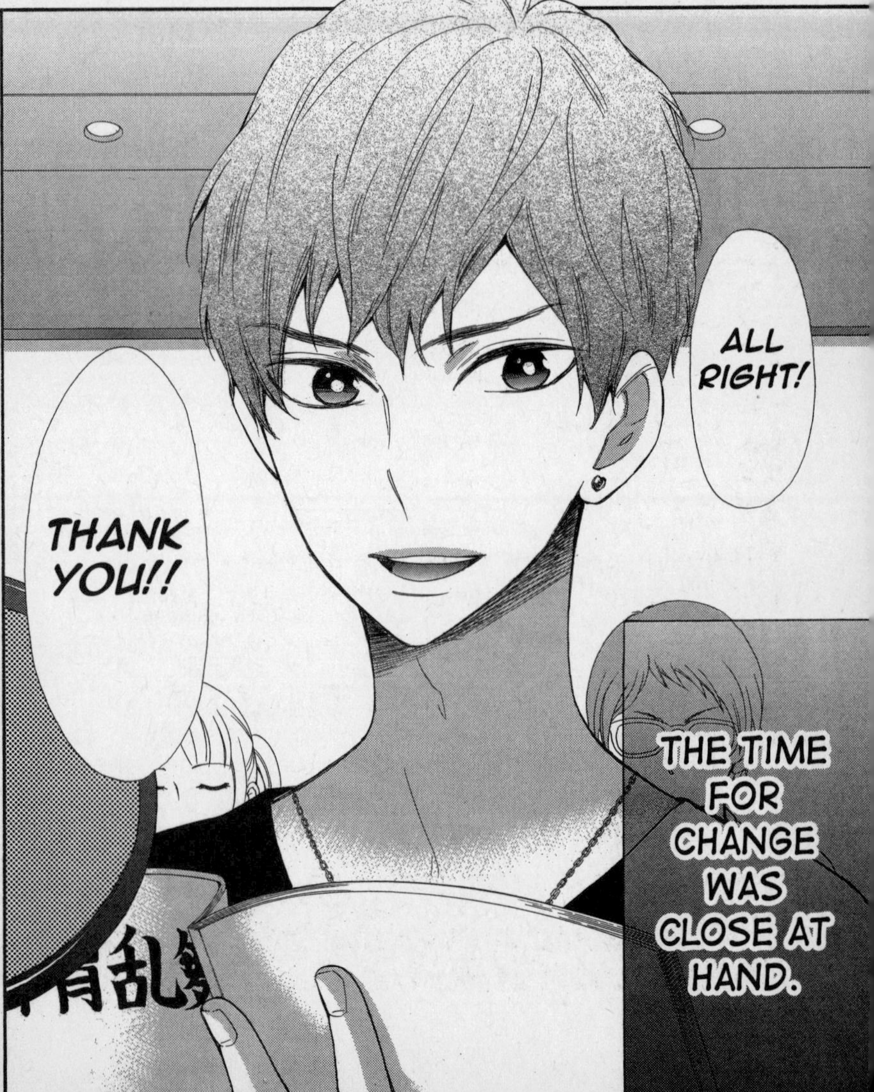
ALL RIGHT!
THANK YOU!!
THE TIME FOR CHANGE WAS CLOSE AT HAND.
Booklet: Katchu Love

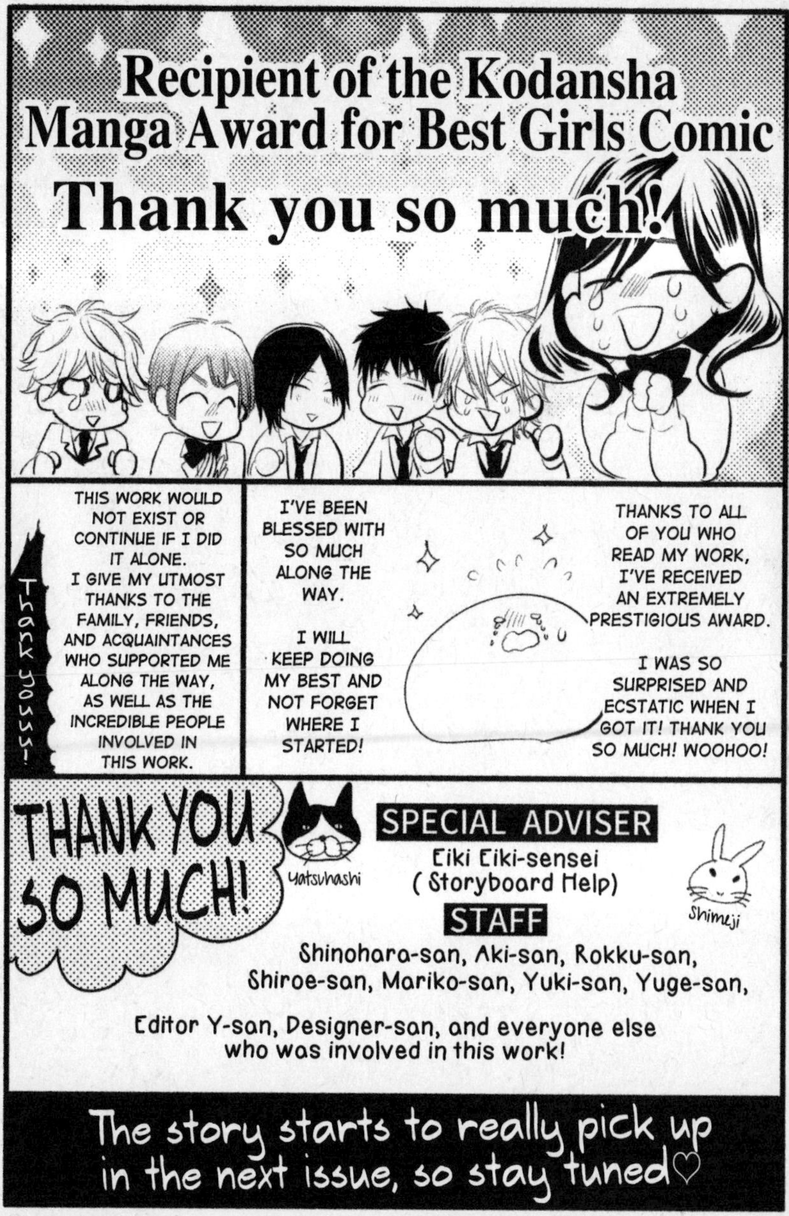
Recipient of the Kodansha Manga Award for Best Girls Comic
Thank you so much!
THANKS TO ALL OF YOU WHO READ MY WORK, I'VE RECEIVED AN EXTREMELY PRESTIGIOUS AWARD.
I WAS SO SURPRISED AND ECSTATIC WHEN I GOT IT! THANK YOU SO MUCH! WOOHOO!
I'VE BEEN BLESSED WITH SO MUCH ALONG THE WAY.
I WILL KEEP DOING MY BEST AND NOT FORGET WHERE I STARTED!
THIS WORK WOULD NOT EXIST OR CONTINUE IF I DID IT ALONE.
I GIVE MY UTMOST THANKS TO THE FAMILY, FRIENDS, AND ACQUAINTANCES WHO SUPPORTED ME ALONG THE WAY, AS WELL AS THE INCREDIBLE PEOPLE INVOLVED IN THIS WORK.
Thank youuu!
SPECIAL ADVISER
Eiki Eiki-sensei
(Storyboard Help)
Shimeji
Yatsuhashi
THANK YOU SO MUCH!
STAFF
Shinohara-san, Aki-san, Rokku-san, Shiroe-san, Mariko-san, Yuki-san, Yuge-san,
Editor Y-san, Designer-san, and everyone else who was involved in this work!
The story starts to really pick up in the next issue, so stay tuned♡

AUTHOR'S NOTE

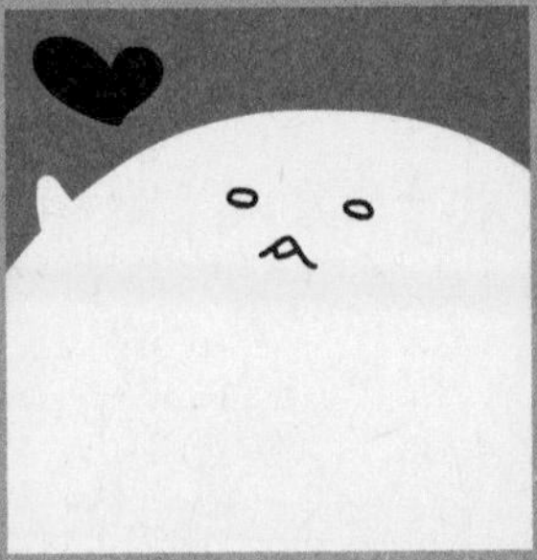

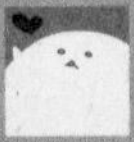

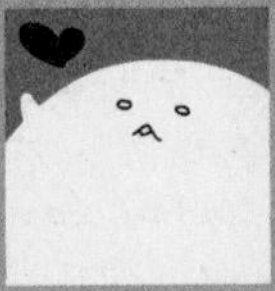

WHEN I ADJUST THE
AIR FOR MY CAT, WHO'S
SENSITIVE TO HEAT, ME
AND MY RABBIT GET COLD.
WHEN I ADJUST IT FOR
ME AND MY RABBIT, AS
EXPECTED, MY CAT GETS
HOT AND WILL OFTEN
SPLAY ITSELF OUT.
IT'S HARD...
-JUNKO

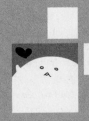

I ♥ BL

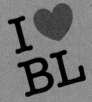

Translation Notes

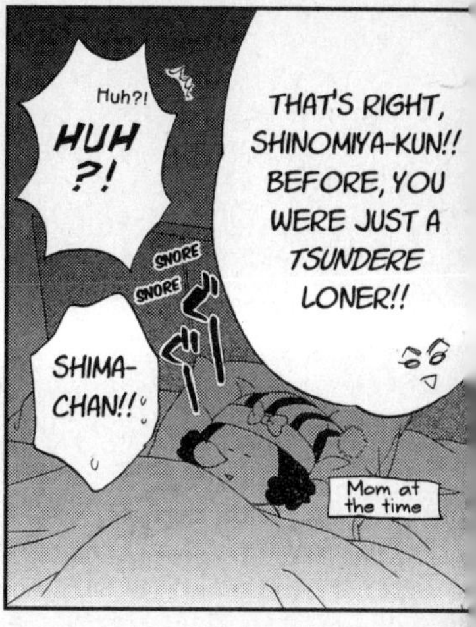
THAT'S RIGHT, SHINOMIYA-KUN!! BEFORE, YOU WERE JUST A TSUNDERE LONER!!
Huh?!
HUH ?!
SNORE
SNORE
SHIMA-CHAN!!
Mom at the time

***Tsundere*, page 21**

Though it may be obvious to most readers of *Kiss Him, Not Me*, the term *tsundere* is used to describe someone who has a "hot and cold" personality. In most cases, this refers to a romantic interest whose personality has them mostly acting cold (*tsun*) to the main character, but over time they become progressively warmer (*dere*).

***Fumie*, page 60**

In the 16th century, Japan had its first contact with the Western world when the infamous "Black Ships" arrived on Japanese shores. Along with these Westerners came Christianity, and while it was first embraced, the leaders of the Tokugawa shogunate eventually saw it as a threat and banned Christianity throughout Japan. To discover Japanese citizens who were practicing this forbidden religion, the authorities would have the suspected person step on an image of Jesus Christ or the Virgin Mary. If they could not do so, then they were found to be practitioners of Christianity, and in most cases, they were tortured or executed.

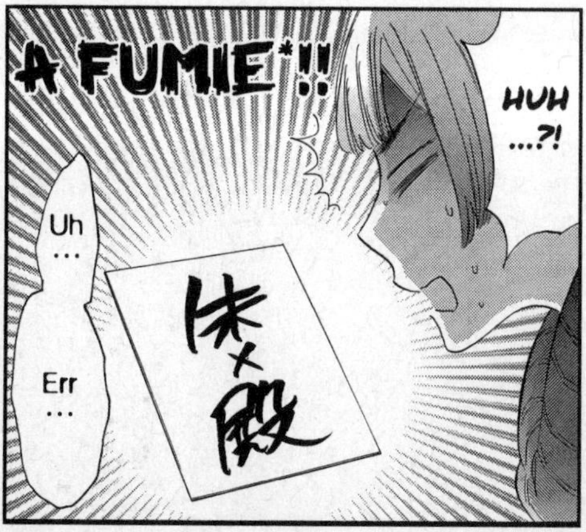
A FUMIE*!!
HUH ...?!
Uh ...
Err ...

Dolls' day, page 91

Hinamatsuri (translated as Doll's Day or Girls' Day) is a Japanese festival that is held on March 3rd. On this day, families will pray for the happiness and health of young girls. To do so, families usually set up a display of Japanese dolls (*hina*) that mimic the arrangement of the imperial court and make an offering of rice crackers and other foods.

Kae's misunderstandings, page 123

In the Japanese version, Kae's misunderstandings were two language-based jokes that couldn't really be replicated in English. The first has to do with Kotoha asking if anyone made Kae's heart beat faster (*tokimeku*). Kae then associated that with a famous 80s manga/anime called *Tokimeki Tonight*. In brief, the series was a shojo manga where the main character was an ordinary girl whose parents were a vampire (dad) and a werewolf (mom). The second joke is a pun with the word *koi*. *Koi* is a homonym in Japanese that can mean both "love" and "carp." Oblivious to the romantic sentiment of the word, Kae, imagines a "carp" when Kotoha mentions "love."

Kae's anime hubbies, page 124

Because of the lack of fair-use exclusions in Japanese copyright law, the use of names from other properties may not protect the user from a lawsuit, so most of the names were censored. The second panel is the name of a famous, love-sick cook with a killer kick and the third panel is the name of perhaps the most famous rival from the most famous supernatural ninja series in existence. In the last panel, Kae mentions Gazelle from *Inazuma Eleven*, Akashi from *Kuroko's Basketball*, Captain Levi from *Attack on Titan*, and Miyuki from *Ace of Diamond*.

MY FIRST LOVE WAS SA*JI-KUN...
UH-HUH... HUH?
AND AFTER THAT WAS SA**KE-KUN!
HUH..?
BESIDES THEM... GA*ELLE, AND AKA***-SAMA, AND THE CAPTAIN, AND MIYUKI-SENPAI, AND SHION...
AND NOW, AKANE-CHAN! ♡
H-H-HOLD ON!!
AREN'T THOSE ALL ANIME CHARACTERS?!
MY HUBBIES! ♡

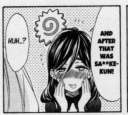

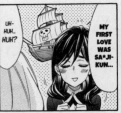

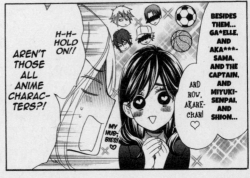

***Amidakuji*, page 131**

First mentioned in volume 3, *amidakuji* is a form of lottery that is typically used to make a decision when presented with multiple options. A number of vertical lines matching the number of participants or options are first drawn, followed by assorted horizontal lines in between the vertical lines to form ladder-like constructs. At the bottom of each vertical line is a prize or whatever else is relevant to the participants. Each participant selects a number and draws a line from that number, following a zig-zag pattern to the bottom where their fate awaits.

Coliseum, page 135

The kanji that's presented here literally means "kill," "death," "love," and "nothing," but actually sounds out to KORO-SHI-A-MU which is a phonetic match to how "coliseum" is pronounced in Japanese. This is one of many ways to play with words in Japanese and this method is probably mostly seen emblazened on the backs of motorcycle gang jackets. Perhaps the most famous of these word constructs, called *ateji*, is 夜露死苦 . This literally means, "night-dew-death-suffering," but sounds out to "*yoroshiku*" which can be interpreted as "nice to meet you."

"Once again I have cut a worthless object," page 145

This is one of a few well-known phrases from the *Lupin III* series. It is often said by Goemon Ishikawa, one of Lupin's cohorts, after he has cut someone down with his sword.

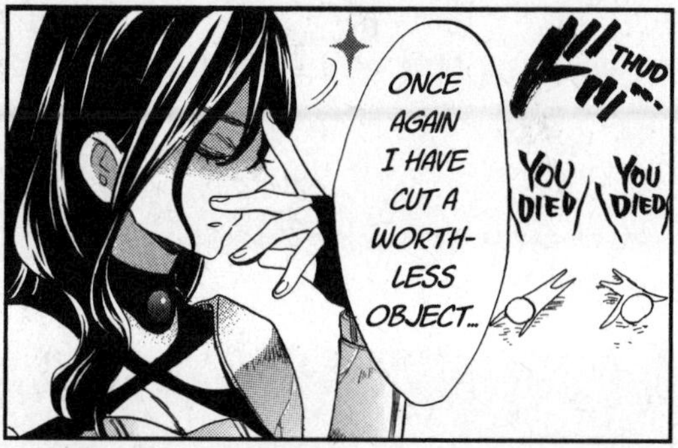
THUD
YOU DIED
YOU DIED
ONCE AGAIN I HAVE CUT A WORTH-LESS OBJECT...